Starting A Business Blueprint

The New Way to Plan, Launch, and Run Your Dream Business While Avoiding Costly Mistakes (2-in-1)

The Business Plan Shortcut

Starting a Business Roadmap

Russel Grant

Contents

The Business Plan Shortcut

Supercharge Your Game Plan With ChatGPT
for Smarter Moves Even If You Are a Beginner

Russel Grant

GET YOUR FREE
PROMPT ENGINEERING
CHEAT SHEET!

THE PROMPT ENGINEERING
— FOR CHATGPT —
CHEAT SHEET

SCAN ME

Go to the address below,
or scan the code.

https://cheatsheet.tips

Introduction

O n a chilly afternoon, my phone rang—it was my friend Sarah. I could hear the mix of excitement and nerves in her voice. We'd been through a lot together over the years, always supporting each other through life's highs and lows. But this call was different. Sarah was about to embark on something big—she was starting her own business.

Sarah had always loved woodworking but had a new idea she was passionate about. She wanted to create furniture that combined wood with resin art. She wanted to create pieces that weren't just functional but also beautiful. But turning that idea into a real business was harder than she expected.

"I have this amazing idea," she said as we met at our usual coffee spot, "but I'm overwhelmed by everything it takes to start a business." Her table was covered in notebooks filled with sketches and plans, but her business plan was a mess. She didn't know where to start.

Sarah confided that she didn't have any business experience. Like many first-time entrepreneurs, she was lost. Market research, financial planning, marketing—it was all new to her. And the big question in her mind was, how could she make the right decisions to avoid failure?

That's when I told her about my struggles. "Remember when I told you about Chat-GPT?" I asked. It's not just for writing or marketing—it's also been a game-changer for my business planning."

I explained how, while I loved spending time creating beautiful, handmade furniture in my workshop, I had a hard time figuring out how to effectively market my products online and scale my business digitally. That's when I turned to AI. ChatGPT didn't just help me get by—it allowed me to transform my business. It guided me in crafting a compelling online presence, reaching new customers, and integrating my newfound digital skills into my business plan.

Sarah listened closely as I explained how AI had guided me through the complexities of market analysis, customer insights, and financial planning. "Imagine having someone experienced to guide you and help you figure out what steps to take," I said.

Sarah decided to give it a try. We sat down together, and she typed her first prompt into ChatGPT: "Help me create a business plan for a woodworking studio that specializes in resin-infused furniture." The results were amazing. AI didn't just give her ideas; it gave her direction. AI offered insights into her target market, suggested strategies that appealed to modern design lovers and traditional woodworking fans, and helped her uncover potential challenges she hadn't considered.

Over the next few weeks, I saw Sarah grow more confident. With AI's help, she organized her thoughts, set realistic goals, and created a marketing strategy that made sense. What had seemed impossible started to feel within reach.

As Sarah prepared to open her woodworking studio, I couldn't have been prouder. She had faced her fears and used AI to help build her dream. A few months later, her studio opened, and people were immediately drawn to her beautiful, unique pieces.

Sarah's story shows how powerful AI can be in business planning. If you're new to starting a business, like Sarah was, this book will show you how to use AI to find clarity and make decisions that lead to success. It's about turning your dreams into reality, one step at a time.

In *The Business Plan Shortcut*, you'll learn how to use AI to cut through the confusion and build a business that stands out. Whether you're just starting or curious about what AI can do, this book is here to help you succeed.

Are you ready to start your journey? Are you ready to use AI to find the clarity and confidence you need? Let *The Business Plan Shortcut* be your guide to turning your business dreams into reality.

Chapter One

What is Business Development and Entrepreneurship Anyway?

I recently stumbled upon a study that resonated with me, and I believe many business owners can relate to it. This study examined companies and uncovered something remarkable: 71% of fast-growing companies were backed up by a business plan (Parsons, 2024, para. 11).

Another study also piqued my interest, revealing that businesses with solid planning strategies experienced a staggering 30% faster growth rate than those without (Akiko Design, 2023).

Planning appears to be a fundamental element of success, yet many of us fail to give it the attention it deserves. Consider this: Things tend to go more smoothly when you plan your day. The same principle applies to businesses. Beyond just staying organized, planning is about laying a strong foundation for your business to thrive.

This chapter is all about business planning. Before we dive deeper and learn to write a business plan, let's first establish a clear understanding of business development and entrepreneurship. We can then explore how business planning has evolved over time, becoming a critical component of success in today's dynamic market.

Defining Business Development and Entrepreneurship

Business has a rich history, dating back to when people traded goods and services. However, the concept of business as we know it today began to take shape when entrepreneurs started using their skills to make significant advancements in trade.

The establishment of trade routes like the Silk Route changed the game for business and entrepreneurship, turning them into pathways to success and opportunity.

The United States of America, often called the land of opportunity, has always been a hotspot for entrepreneurs. Entrepreneurs played a crucial role in building the nation by seizing its opportunities and creating more opportunities for others.

Entrepreneurship has evolved significantly over time, from expanding businesses through trade routes to using computers and the internet for growth. However, businesses continue to flourish, showing no signs of slowing down.

Entrepreneurship is Far From a Modern Concept

The term "entrepreneur" stems from the French word *entrepreneur*, which means "initiating something, an inception of something, or starting something new"—a perfect description of what an entrepreneur does. While businesses have existed throughout history and across cultures, entrepreneurs possess a unique ability to identify opportunities and create new ventures.

A prime example of entrepreneurial ingenuity leading to a significant paradigm shift is the rise of Silicon Valley giants such as Apple, Microsoft, and Facebook. These companies revolutionized the tech industry and changed how we live and work.

Not too long ago, computers were massive machines that occupied entire rooms and required large fans for cooling. Today, in just 50 to 75 years, we have smartwatches that offer performance comparable to those early computers. This remarkable progress exemplifies the transformative power of well-executed entrepreneurship.

Impact of the Digital Era on Business

The digital era has completely transformed how businesses operate, especially with the introduction of computers and automation. Once mere human calculators, computers now perform tasks at lightning speed, revolutionizing mundane processes into streamlined operations.

Artificial Intelligence (AI) has emerged as a game-changer, taking over tasks that computers now handle. In today's business world, AI is crucial in easing an entrepreneur's workload by efficiently managing repetitive tasks. It has taken automation to new heights, tackling tasks that typically require human intelligence and time.

A prime example of AI's impact is its ability to revolutionize the automation process. Previously, automating tasks required extensive research and decision-making. With AI, it's as simple as a button press. Data Science and Data Analytics further enhance this, providing businesses with invaluable insights to predict customer responses and tailor products accordingly.

The integration of AI, Machine Learning, Data Science, and Data Analytics offers businesses unparalleled flexibility. Data Analytics helps comprehend market dynamics, while Data Science introduces innovative data study methods. Conversely, AI provides practical solutions to intricate business challenges, empowering entrepreneurs to strategize and execute their plans effectively.

This digital evolution has significantly shifted business paradigms. The rise of online presence allows businesses to network and connect with potential customers. The internet has transformed from a passive marketing tool to an active engagement platform, fostering employee collaboration and enhancing overall business performance.

Entrepreneurship today is like riding a wave—you're constantly navigating the dynamic waters of technology, consumer behavior, and market trends. In this fast-paced environment, business development has taken a customer-centric and innovation-driven turn.

It's all about understanding your customers intimately and crafting offerings that speak to their needs and desires. Innovation is the key here, pushing you to think outside the box and differentiate yourself in the market. This dynamic nature of entrepreneurship demands agility and adaptability, traits that are crucial for thriving in today's competitive landscape. Here is how entrepreneurs are redefining the dynamics.

Data Security and Privacy

In today's digital world, the internet has become a vital tool for businesses, enabling growth and success. However, this digital reliance has also raised data security and privacy concerns. Phishing scams and cyber attacks pose serious threats to businesses' sensitive information. Despite efforts to protect data, many businesses still have genuine privacy concerns. Entrepreneurs are deploying AI to boost data security and privacy as it can provide solutions humans often struggle to find, potentially easing these worries.

Customer Centricity

Customer satisfaction is now at the forefront of business strategies. How happy customers are reflects directly on a business's performance. Understanding and meeting customer needs has become paramount, and successful businesses prioritize customer satisfaction, shaping their strategies around this principle. This approach ensures the development of high-quality products and services that resonate with the market.

Innovation

Innovation is also key to business success. It demonstrates how well an idea is implemented within a business. Companies that embrace innovation tend to progress more in the competitive business world. With technology and ideas evolving rapidly, innovation has become essential. Companies like Microsoft, McDonald's, and Amazon have used innovation to maintain market leadership.

Bringing Customer Centricity and Innovation Together

When customer focus and innovation come together, the impact on a business can be profound. Customer needs drive the demand for innovative products, fueling further innovation. This relationship enhances both aspects, aligning innovation with customer expectations. By integrating customer-centric practices with innovation, businesses can create products that meet and exceed customer expectations, paving the way for long-term success.

However, beyond innovation and ideas, long-term success is also dependent on a certain set of traits that most successful entrepreneurs exhibit.

Key Traits of Successful Entrepreneurs and Business Developers

Seasoned business leaders will agree that success in entrepreneurship and business development is not just a matter of luck or chance. It results from deliberate actions, cultivated habits, and a mindset geared toward growth and innovation.

Here are some of the key traits of successful entrepreneurs and business developers that I witnessed. I personally try to incorporate them into my life and motivate others to do the same.

Curiosity

It's funny that curiosity is many times frowned upon. You've probably heard the saying—"curiosity killed the cat."

But in entrepreneurship and business development, curiosity is an asset. Successful entrepreneurs and business developers possess a deep-seated curiosity that drives them to explore new ideas, challenge the status quo, and seek innovative solutions to complex problems. This curiosity fuels their passion for learning and growth, propelling them to new heights of success.

Take, for example, the story of Sara Blakely, the founder of Spanx (Wikipedia contributors, 2024).

Back in 1998, Blakely, a door-to-door fax machine salesperson, was getting ready for a party when she realized she didn't have the right undergarment to wear under white pants without highlighting the linings. This sparked a simple curiosity in her—is there a better solution?

That spark of curiosity led to a chain of events in which she searched for fitting products. She saw that there were no such undergarments in the market, and that gave her the idea that turned her into a pioneer in the shapewear industry. Today, her company, Spanx, is a multi-million-dollar empire, all because Sara Blakely dared to ask a simple question and followed her curiosity to its conclusion.

Experimentation

Success in entrepreneurship and business development often hinges on experimenting with new ideas. Curiosity raises many questions, and experimentation helps answer those questions. Successful entrepreneurs and business developers are not afraid to step out of their comfort zones and try new approaches, even if it means facing failure along the way.

James Dyson, the inventor of the bagless vacuum cleaner, spent years experimenting with different designs and prototypes, facing numerous failures and setbacks along the way (Wikipedia contributors, 2024d). However, his willingness to experiment and learn from his mistakes eventually led to creating a revolutionary product that transformed the vacuum cleaner industry.

In business, as in life, the willingness to experiment and try new things is often the key to unlocking new opportunities and achieving greater success. By embracing experimentation, entrepreneurs can discover new ways of doing things, uncover hidden opportunities, and, ultimately, drive innovation in their industries.

Self-Awareness

Amidst all the curious questions and insightful experiments, entrepreneurs must not lose their self-awareness. This crucial trait involves a profound understanding of one's strengths and weaknesses, emotional states, and the impact of one's actions on others and on the business at large.

Consider the journey of Howard Schultz, the visionary behind Starbucks (Wikipedia contributors, 2024c). Schultz's deep self-awareness allowed him to recognize the importance of coffee and the experience surrounding coffee. He understood his passion for community and connection, which he translated into the Starbucks ethos of creating a "third place" between work and home. His self-awareness helped him cultivate a brand that resonates deeply with consumers on an emotional level.

Self-aware leaders are also better equipped to handle the stress and high stakes of entrepreneurship. They can step back and assess situations objectively, identify their emotional responses, and adjust their approach to maintain effective leadership and decision-making processes.

Decisiveness

Decisiveness is another hallmark of successful entrepreneurs and business developers. Making timely and informed decisions is crucial in a fast-paced and competitive business environment. Successful leaders understand that indecision can lead to missed opportunities and stagnation, so they are decisive.

One notable example of decisiveness is the story of Reed Hastings, the co-founder and CEO of Netflix (Suster, 2022). In the early 2000s, Hastings boldly decided to pivot Netflix from a DVD rental service to a streaming platform despite investors' and industry experts' skepticism. This decisive move transformed Netflix into a global powerhouse in the entertainment industry, disrupting traditional media and changing how people consume content.

Decisiveness is about being confident in your judgment and willing to take calculated risks.

Adaptability

Adaptability is crucial for success in the ever-evolving world of entrepreneurship and business development. Successful entrepreneurs and business developers understand that change is inevitable, and they are willing to adapt their strategies, plans, and approaches to meet new challenges and opportunities.

One shining example of adaptability is Nokia's transformation. Once a giant in the mobile phone industry, Nokia struggled to keep up with the rapid pace of technological change in the smartphone era. However, instead of clinging to outdated models, Nokia adapted by shifting its focus to other areas, such as telecommunications infrastructure and digital health, demonstrating a willingness to evolve and embrace change.

Successful entrepreneurs and business developers constantly scan the horizon for new opportunities and threats and are quick to pivot when necessary.

Risk Tolerance

Risk tolerance is the capacity to endure uncertainty and potential setbacks while pursuing innovative and potentially lucrative opportunities. A high tolerance for risk allows business leaders to venture where others might hesitate, breaking new ground and setting trends within their industries.

Elon Musk's entrepreneurial journey epitomizes high-risk tolerance (Blystone, 2024). From founding X.com, which later became PayPal, to spearheading ambitious projects like SpaceX and Tesla, Musk has consistently pushed the boundaries of what's possible despite facing substantial financial and technological risks. His success across these ventures is a testament to his ability to embrace risk as an integral part of innovation and leadership.

Entrepreneurs with high-risk tolerance are calculated. They understand the importance of balancing potential rewards with risks. They prepare extensively, gather as much information as possible, and make informed decisions considering both best- and worst-case scenarios.

Strategic Thinking

Strategic thinking is key for anyone looking to succeed in business. It helps you see beyond today's tasks and understand how your decisions impact your future. Understanding the bigger picture and how your decisions affect your future sets successful entrepreneurs apart.

In my experience, being strategic means always asking, "What's next?" It's about preparing for changes and making decisions that keep you ahead of the game. It means not just reacting to the market but shaping it. Every choice, from hiring to new product lines, is a part of your strategy.

Just look at Indra Nooyi's journey at PepsiCo (Wikipedia contributors, 2024b). She repositioned PepsiCo well beyond its soda roots, focusing on healthier alternatives and global expansion. Her strategic vision was clear: adapt to changing consumer tastes and expand market reach. Instead of just responding to trends, she set a course to keep PepsiCo relevant and competitive in a fast-evolving market.

Strategic thinking is all about being proactive, not reactive, and making choices that solve today's challenges and pave the way for future opportunities.

Resilience

Resilience in business is about thriving amidst difficulties. Whether navigating financial strains or adapting to market changes, staying the course and innovating through adversity is the key to longevity and success in new business ventures.

A compelling example of this is Brian Chesky, CEO of Airbnb (Wikipedia contributors, 2024f). During the global financial crisis of 2008, Chesky and his co-founders launched Airbnb, a concept many viewed as risky and unconventional. The idea of strangers renting out their homes to other strangers was met with skepticism.

However, they pressed on, even when faced with the immense challenge of gaining users and trust. Their resilience paid off during the COVID-19 pandemic when travel was severely disrupted. Chesky quickly pivoted the company's strategy to focus on local and long-term stays, allowing Airbnb to survive and thrive when global travel resumed.

It's essential to see every setback as a learning opportunity and to keep striving toward your goals, no matter the difficulties. This attitude helps in overcoming immediate challenges and building a business that lasts.

Networking

Networking is a powerful tool in business, essential for gaining new opportunities and surviving and thriving in today's competitive environment.

A prime example of effective networking is Lei Jun, the founder of Xiaomi (Wikipedia contributors, 2024e). Jun leveraged his extensive network to secure initial funding and strategic partnerships, which were crucial for Xiaomi's rapid growth. His ability to connect with like-minded entrepreneurs and tech enthusiasts helped catapult Xiaomi into becoming one of the world's leading smartphone manufacturers. Jun's networking skills were key in understanding market needs and navigating the tech ecosystem.

Effective networking also means being a valuable resource to others. It's about offering help and support when possible, often leading to reciprocal gestures. This give-and-take is at the heart of building a strong, supportive business network.

Empathy

Entrepreneurship requires making tough choices and decisions, and it's never an easy journey. That is why traits like willingness to experiment, quick decision-making, resilience, risk tolerance, and strategic thinking are the foundations of successful entrepreneurs. But amidst all that, empathy is the glue holding everything together. It's the ability to understand and share the feelings of others, and it's critical for building meaningful relationships and fostering a supportive workplace environment.

A notable figure who exemplified empathy in his leadership was Danny Meyer, the renowned restaurateur behind Union Square Hospitality Group. Meyer's approach to hospitality is grounded in empathy; he focuses intensely on the customer experience and employee satisfaction, believing that caring for people leads to business success (Roth, 2021). This philosophy has made his restaurants popular and created a loyal customer base and a positive workplace culture.

As entrepreneurs, while we strive to be strategic, resilient, and well-connected, we must also remain empathetic. Empathy will ensure our decisions are smart but also humane and considerate of the broader impact on our community and employees.

Entrepreneurship is a complex and demanding journey, so it is crucial to possess or develop these essential traits, which we have witnessed in many successful entrepreneurs. As you develop these traits, you'll grow your business and contribute positively to the lives of those around you, building a legacy that goes beyond profits.

But not everyone is born with all these qualities; for most people, it's a matter of consciously building them up. So how do you achieve that?

Tips and Actionable Strategies to Develop Entrepreneurship Qualities

Building strong entrepreneurship qualities requires conscious effort and gradual practice. You may not develop new traits in a day or two, but here are some actionable items you can practice regularly to slowly (but surely) incorporate the above traits into your mindset and personality.

Cultivate Curiosity

- Engage in continuous learning by reading widely across genres and industries.

- Always ask "Why?" and "What if?" to challenge the status quo and encourage innovation.

- Experiment with new hobbies or skills outside your comfort zone to stimulate different ways of thinking.

Encourage Experimentation

- Implement a trial-and-error approach where small-scale tests are encouraged before full rollouts.

- Develop a safe-to-fail environment to support learning from mistakes.

- Establish rapid feedback loops to iterate on ideas based on real-time data.

Enhance Self-Awareness

- Schedule regular self-reflection sessions to assess personal strengths, weaknesses, and motivations.

- Actively seek and welcome constructive feedback from colleagues and mentors.

- Practice mindfulness exercises, such as meditation, to better manage emotions and stress.

Be Decisive

- Use decision-making frameworks like pros-and-cons lists or SWOT analysis (more on this in the next chapter) to clarify choices.

- Set specific deadlines for decisions to avoid delays and drive progress.

- Review and analyze the outcomes of past decisions to refine future decision-making processes.

Adapt to Change

- Stay updated with industry trends to anticipate shifts and prepare adaptive strategies.

- Engage in scenario planning exercises to envision potential future scenarios and appropriate responses.

- Embrace flexibility in both thought and practice to respond effectively to unexpected changes.

Build Risk Tolerance

- Clearly define your risk boundaries and gradually extend them with small, calculated risks.

- Educate yourself on fundamental risk management principles to better understand and mitigate risks.

- Reflect on past risk-taking experiences to identify lessons learned and apply them in future situations.

Develop Strategic Thinking

- Set long-term goals and reverse-engineer strategies to achieve them.

- Analyze how different elements of your business interconnect to anticipate the impacts of your decisions.

- Seek advice and insights from experienced mentors and industry leaders to sharpen your strategic skills.

Foster Resilience

- Cultivate a positive mindset that views challenges as opportunities for growth.

- Build a solid support network of colleagues, friends, and mentors who can provide guidance and encouragement.

- Commit to your goals and persist through setbacks, focusing on long-term achievements.

Enhance Networking Skills

- Regularly attend industry networking events, workshops, and seminars.

- Offer your skills and expertise in volunteer capacities to build connections and give back to the community.

- Leverage social media platforms to establish and maintain professional relationships effectively.

Practice Empathy

- Develop active listening skills to understand and respond to the needs of others.

- Engage in role reversal exercises to appreciate different perspectives, especially in conflict situations.

- Foster a culture of compassion within your team, emphasizing the importance of considering the human element in business decisions.

By integrating these practices into your daily life and business operations, you can build and strengthen the essential traits that characterize successful entrepreneurs. These strategies promote personal growth and enhance your ability to lead effectively and adaptively in an ever-changing business landscape.

The Evolution of Business Planning

Now, let's talk about how business planning has changed over time, especially with the help of modern technology. It used to be as simple as jotting down ideas on paper, but now it's all about complex, data-driven strategies.

In ancient times, people like the Sumerians carved their business decisions into clay tablets. Other ancient civilizations took similar approaches. Moving forward in time, the roots of modern business planning can be traced back to the DuPont company in the 18th century. Pierre Samuel du Pont de Nemours' detailed letters to investors for a gunpowder mill in Delaware are considered some of the earliest examples of what we now call business plans.

By the 19th century, business planning became a cornerstone of success. Competitions encouraged creative ideas, which fueled business growth. By the 20th century, a solid business plan was necessary for any successful business.

Business Planning in the Digital Age

Fast-forward to today's digital age, business planning has become even more sophisticated. Thanks to modern technology and tools, planning is now dynamic and data-driven. What was once stacks of paper are now neatly organized and easily accessible through content management systems.

Being agile is super important in today's business world. It's all about making quick changes and responding to market trends on the fly, which is crucial in our fast-paced environment.

Data is a big player now. Businesses rely on data from various sources to understand the market, analyze customer needs, and craft strategies for success. Analytics give valuable insights into market trends, competitor performance, and customer preferences.

Agility and Adaptability in Today's Market

The market today demands agility and adaptability from businesses. Being agile means responding quickly to market changes, while adaptability is adjusting to new trends and customer preferences.

Netflix is a great example of agility and adaptability in action. Starting as a DVD mailing service, it quickly shifted to online streaming as the internet became more widespread. Its ability to adapt to new technologies and market demands made it the leader in online streaming.

Hence, business planning has evolved a lot over the years. What used to be simple ideas on clay tablets have transformed into complex, data-driven strategies in the digital age. Agility and adaptability are key in today's fast-paced market—just ask Netflix!

Role of AI in Modern Business Practices

AI, like ChatGPT, has become a game-changer in modern businesses, offering many benefits. Its ability to automate tasks with just a little guidance has transformed fields such as Automated Market Research, Data Analytics (especially Predictive Analytics), and Customer Experience. It speeds up tasks efficiently, ensuring they're done in the best possible way.

Automated Market Research with AI

AI's knack for analyzing huge amounts of data makes Automated Market Research much more efficient. By digesting diverse data sets, AI can come up with theories and models that improve business strategies, giving valuable insights to cater to customer needs and market trends.

Predictive Analytics

Predictive Analytics uses past data to predict future outcomes. AI plays a crucial role here, helping companies plan based on historical data, performance metrics, and competitor analysis.

Operational Efficiency and Strategic Agility

AI's efficiency and agility are unparalleled. It handles repetitive tasks quickly and efficiently. AI also plans tasks in the best order, ensuring everything is completed as quickly as possible. This efficiency and strategic thinking are key to business success.

Key Benefits of AI Integration Into Business

Integrating AI into business strategies offers numerous advantages:

- **Better Decisions**: AI makes smart decisions based on data analysis, spotting potential issues and optimizing business plans.

- **Improved Speed**: AI speeds up business processes, completing tasks swiftly and highlighting potential problems or shortcuts.

- **New Capabilities and Business Expansion**: AI helps businesses grow efficiently by suggesting suitable business models and identifying new growth areas.

- **Personalized Customer Services**: AI analyzes data to understand customer preferences, enabling businesses to tailor services to individual needs.

- **Better Quality and Reduced Errors**: AI boosts overall business performance and reduces human errors, ensuring higher quality work across various business functions.

Overall, AI is a powerful tool that enhances business efficiency, agility, and decision-making, driving growth and success in the modern business landscape.

Key Takeaways

- Business plans drive success, with 71% of fast-growing companies having a business plan and businesses with solid planning strategies growing 30% faster than those without (Parsons, 2024b).

- Planning provides a strong foundation for business success and is essential for organization and long-term growth.

- Business development and entrepreneurship have evolved from ancient trade routes like the Silk Route to modern digital innovation, with notable impacts in the USA.

- The digital era, marked by the introduction of computers and AI, has revolutionized business operations by enhancing automation, data analysis, and business strategy.

- Modern entrepreneurship focuses on understanding customer needs and driving innovation, integrating customer feedback and market trends to stay competitive and relevant.

Having explored the modern landscape of business development and the transformative power of AI, you're now ready to examine it more deeply. Let's explore how these insights and tools can be applied to the foundation of any successful business: crafting a compelling, comprehensive business plan. In the next chapter, we'll uncover the secrets to turning your plan into action.

Chapter Two

Creating a Blueprint for Success

In entrepreneurship, a well-crafted business plan is the cornerstone of success. It's a roadmap that guides every decision and action, ensuring that your venture stays on course amidst the uncertainties of the business world. But despite its importance, I've seen many aspiring entrepreneurs overlook the effort and details that go into creating a comprehensive business plan. It can ultimately lead to pitfalls and setbacks that could have been avoided.

In fact, recent statistics have shown that almost 80% of businesses fail due to poor planning and a lack of accurate cash flow forecasting (ForwardAI, 2023).

That's why, in this chapter, I'll walk you through the basics of writing a business plan, equipping you with the essential tools and knowledge to create a solid plan that sets your business up for success. From understanding your market to setting achievable goals, we'll go through all the steps necessary to develop a business plan that attracts investors and serves as a strategic blueprint.

So, I hope that by the end of this chapter, you'll gain much-needed clarity on writing a detailed, convincing business plan.

Key Components of a Successful Business Plan

To create a strong business plan, you must first understand every component that goes into it. And so, I've broken down all the key elements of a business plan for you to follow.

Executive Summary

The executive summary is like a sneak peek of your business plan, giving a quick snapshot of your business. It's the place to hook your readers (venture capitalists, bankers, angel investors, partners, customers, suppliers) and get them excited about your idea without diving into all the nitty-gritty details just yet.

Here's what you should include:

- **Business Description:** A brief intro to your business, what you do, and who you do it for. For example, "We're XYZ Tech, and we develop user-friendly software that helps small businesses manage their inventory and sales more efficiently."

- **Mission Statement:** A short and snappy statement about why your business exists and what it aims to achieve. For instance, "Our mission is to empower small business owners with the tools they need to succeed in a competitive market, without breaking the bank."

- **Product or Service Description:** A quick overview of your main product or service, highlighting what makes it special. For example, "Our flagship product, ABC Inventory Manager, is a cloud-based solution that simplifies inventory tracking, ordering, and sales analysis for retail stores."

- **Market Analysis:** A brief look at the market you're in, including who your competitors are and why your business stands out. For instance, "We've done our homework and found a big need for simple inventory solutions among small retailers, with no one offering quite what we do."

- **Financial Highlights:** A quick peek into your financial future, including your sales forecasts and how much funding you need to get there. For example, "We're aiming to hit $1 million in sales by year three, and we're looking for partners to help us get there."

- **Growth Projections:** A glimpse into where you see your business going in the future and how you plan to get there. For instance, "We're planning to grow by expanding our product line and reaching new customers, with a yearly goal of 20% growth."

Remember, the key to a great executive summary is to keep it short, sweet, and to the point. You want to excite your readers about your business but leave them wanting more.

Business Description

The business description section of your business plan is like giving a quick tour of your company. It's where you introduce your business idea, what makes it special, and who you serve. This section helps investors and stakeholders understand the basics of your business and its potential.

A solid description should include the following details:

1. Company name and legal structure

2. Mission statement

3. Business model

4. Target market

5. Unique selling proposition (USP)

6. Location(s)

7. Team/Partners

Here's a quick example:

[Company Name] Inc., a leader in innovative inventory management solutions, offers a comprehensive software suite designed to optimize inventory processes for businesses worldwide.

Our mission is to empower businesses with intuitive and efficient inventory management tools that drive growth, enhance productivity, and exceed customer expectations.

We operate on a subscription-based model, providing businesses with flexible pricing plans tailored to their needs. Our software-as-a-service (SaaS) model ensures customers receive continuous updates and support.

We serve diverse industries, including retail, manufacturing, wholesale, and e-commerce. Our scalable and adaptable software makes it ideal for businesses of all sizes. It stands out for its user-friendly interface, robust features, and seamless integration capabilities.

[Company Name] is based in [Location], with additional offices in [Location] and [Location]. Our local presence allows us to serve our community effectively. We have a team of dedicated professionals focused on delivering exceptional service and support. Our partnerships with leading technology providers ensure that our solutions are tailored to meet the specific needs of small businesses, enhancing functionality and integration capabilities.

Market Analysis and Strategy

Any business plan is incomplete without in-depth market research. In this section of your business plan, here's what you need to cover:

Analysis

Provide an industry overview highlighting key trends, growth drivers, and challenges. Consider factors such as market size, growth rate, and regulatory environment. Next, identify and segment your target market based on factors such as demographics, psychographics, and behavior. This will help you tailor your marketing and sales strategies to specific customer segments.

Finally, move on to two essential areas: competitor analysis, which reveals your competitors' strengths, weaknesses, and strategies, and user behavior analysis, which helps you understand the requirements of your target audience and deliver the same.

Strategy

Highlight how your product or service differs from competitors and why customers should choose you. This could include features, quality, price, or customer service. Decide on the most appropriate digital marketing channels to gain visibility and attract leads. Describe how you will distribute your product or service to customers: direct sales, online sales, retail partnerships, or distribution agreements.

While not so important in the early stages of a business plan, you must still have some long-term strategies for customer retention and business expansion.

Marketing and Sales Plan

I briefly mentioned marketing in the previous section, but it's a central part of a business plan that deserves a more thorough discussion. Marketing and sales bring life to your business in the beginning, as it's the first step to market visibility and the last step until your customers convert. Of course, there's a long journey in between, which is what we call a "marketing/sales funnel."

But to help you quickly understand that journey and develop your marketing and sales plan, I like to think of it in just five simple steps:

Step 1: Visibility

It's ideal to have a website and search engine marketing (SEO) strategy, as that's the first step toward putting your business on the radar of search engines, especially Google. At the start, when your target audience is barely aware of your business, a good SEO strategy will be your lifesaver.

Step 2: Traffic

Appearing on search engines and gaining visibility is no good if you don't turn those viewers into visitors. To convert visibility into traffic, you must have a strategy for converting visitors into consumers.

Step 3: Engagement

Once your website has a steady flow of traffic, the next step is to engage them with valuable content and interactive ways to promote your product or service and its features and benefits. In this stage, having a strong value proposition is important so that people are interested in your offerings. A strong value proposition clearly communicates your product or service's unique benefits and advantages to potential customers, emphasizing what makes it stand out from the competition. It should be concise, compelling, and tailored to the needs and desires of the target audience.

Step 4: Conversion

Once your audience is engaged, the next step is to turn them into customers. You must lay out clear strategies in your business plan, including strong call-to-actions, personalized marketing messages based on your audience's pain points, limited-time discounts and offers, etc.

Step 5: Retention and Loyalty

After converting customers, the focus shifts to keeping them coming back and building loyalty. In this area, your business plan must focus on a strong customer support system, regular communication channels, upselling opportunities, feedback systems, and community-building activities.

Of course, I won't go into the details of each step as the focus is on learning the basics of a business plan. But, understanding these five pillars of marketing and sales strategy is fundamental for entrepreneurs and aspiring business developers.

Management and Organization Description

The management and organization section of your business plan outlines your company's organizational structure, the background of your leadership team, and the internal framework that supports your operations.

This section is crucial for demonstrating to investors and stakeholders that you have a competent and experienced team capable of executing your business strategy.

Here's what you should include:

- **Organizational Structure:** Describe your company's hierarchy, detailing key positions and their roles. A visual chart can help show the relationships between different team members.

- **Leadership Team:** Provide brief bios for each member of your leadership team. Highlight their relevant experience, skills, and contributions to your business. This should include the CEO, CFO, COO, and other key executives.

- **Advisors and Board Members:** If applicable, mention any advisors or board members who bring additional expertise and credibility to your business. Explain their role and how they contribute to your strategic direction.

- **Staffing Plan:** Outline your staffing needs, including current employees and future hiring plans. Describe the types of positions you plan to fill and the skills required for those roles.

- **Company Culture:** Briefly describe the company culture you aim to foster. This includes your core values, work environment, and initiatives to promote employee satisfaction and productivity.

- **HR Policies:** Summarize your human resources policies, including recruitment strategies, training programs, and performance evaluation processes. Highlight how these policies align with your overall business goals.

Products and Service Description

This section of your business plan provides a detailed overview of your business. It is vital for showcasing the value you bring to your customers and how you differentiate yourself from competitors.

There are five basic elements of a convincing product or service description:

Product/Service Overview

A straightforward description of your product or service, followed by a brief highlight of its features, what it does, and how customers benefit.

Unique Selling Proposition

What sets your product or service apart from others, whether it's a unique feature, superior quality, innovative technology, or exceptional customer service?

Pricing Model and Strategy

The pricing model is a key aspect of your business and one that requires considerable planning and analysis, especially seeing how there's such a variety of models that businesses implement these days, such as:

- Subscription models

- Tiered pricing

- Freemium pricing

- One-time purchase

- User-license-based pricing, and much more.

You decide which model suits your business best, but make sure to lay it out in your business plan, explaining how and why it will be ideal.

Production and Delivery

Detail the process for producing and delivering your product or service. For physical products, you might want to highlight your supply chain, ordering channel, and logistics, including inventory, warehouse, and shipping process. For digital products, mention the delivery channel, such as web-based applications, on-premise applications, etc. Similarly, for service-based businesses, explain how customers acquire these services, such as through online channels, in-person appointments, etc.

Customer Support

Lastly, most, if not all, businesses require some support system for their products and services. In this section, you must lay down the operational details such as support channels (phone, email, messaging, etc.), support timing, etc. But what's more important is to pinpoint key factors that will lead to high customer service standards, as well as a long-term vision to scale support if required.

Competitive Analysis

It's a no-brainer that your business plan must include competitive analysis, but this is also where many entrepreneurs struggle in their early stages. Especially when established competitors are already doing well in the market, it can seem challenging to study them and position your business idea as an equally good or perhaps a better alternative. Again, there's no limit to how deep you can go into analyzing your competitors, but for starters, I've broken down the fundamentals of a strong competitor analysis.

- **Industry Overview:** A broad-level overview of the industry where your business operates, including current trends, market value, growth potential, and major players.

- **Market Position:** Categorizing your direct competitors (those offering similar products or services) and indirect competitors (those offering alternate solutions to the same target audience).

- **SWOT Analysis:** A quick breakdown of the strengths and weakness of your competitors, potential opportunities where your business can successfully compete with them, and threats that could harm them, which could act to your advantage.

- **Market Share:** Analyze the market share of your main competitors. This involves determining the size of the market each competitor has captured and how many customers they have acquired.

Here is a sample prompt for you to seek help from ChatGPT on competitive analysis:

I need help with conducting a competitive analysis for my business in [Location]. Can you outline a structured approach for identifying competitors, the key data to gather, and provide relevant examples?

You can look into more factors, but the ones mentioned above are must-haves for a sound competitor analysis.

Operations Plan

The operations plan is integral to your business plan as it outlines the day-to-day activities necessary to run your business efficiently. This section provides a clear picture of how your business will function on a practical level, detailing the processes, resources, and infrastructure required to achieve your business goals.

Start with a basic outline of your operations: locations and facilities, production process, supply chain management, technology and equipment, and staffing. Then, move into more intricate details such as:

- Technology stack and IT infrastructure

- Daily operational costs

- Division of internal teams

- Project management methods such as an agile framework

- OKR frameworks to align the workforce with company goals. The OKR framework helps set and achieve goals by defining Objectives (what you want to achieve) and Key Results (how you measure success). Objectives are clear and inspiring targets, while Key Results are specific, measurable milestones. Together, they ensure focus, alignment, and measurable progress toward significant goals.

Feel free to customize and work around these details, as they will vary for every business. However, the idea is to make sure that this section of your business plan clarifies how your business operates every day and how those operations lead to growth and success.

Financial Projection and Needs

I already talked about mentioning financial and growth projections in the executive summary at the start of your business plan. But those will include just a brief highlight, and this section is where you elaborate. This is where you outline the company's financial future and demonstrate its potential for profitability and growth. This gives investors and stakeholders a clear understanding of your financial goals, funding requirements, and how you plan to manage your finances.

In this section, you must provide:

- Estimation of future revenue over the next three to five years, including projections for sales volume, pricing, and any other sources of revenue.

- Detailed breakdown of expected expenses, separating fixed and variable costs. Fixed costs might include rent, salaries, and insurance, while variable costs could include materials, production, and marketing expenses.

- Projected profit and loss (P&L) statement, summarizing revenues, costs, and expenses to show how your business will achieve profitability over time.

- Expected cash flow, including inflows and outflows, to ensure that your business can meet its financial obligations.

- A clear statement of funding requirements, what you need it for, and how you plan to use it. Break down your funding needs into specific categories, such as equipment, marketing, working capital, and expansion.

These factors will provide a clear overview of your company's financial outlook, outlining key projections and funding requirements for achieving your business goals and ensuring long-term success.

Here is a sample prompt to ask ChatGPT to help you with financial projections:

I'm seeking guidance on how to create financial projections for my business about [busines type] in [Location]. Can you explain how to estimate revenue and forecast expenses, recommend any tools for this process, and provide examples relevant to my area?

Exhibits and Appendices

Exhibits and appendices are additional materials that support and complement the information presented in your business plan. These materials provide detailed information, data, and documentation that may interest investors, lenders, or other stakeholders. This is the concluding section of the document.

These usually include legal documents, contracts and agreements, and supporting documents such as marketing materials, organizational charts, etc. There are no hard and fast rules here, so you can add supplementary information that strengthens your business plan and enhances your credibility with investors and stakeholders, like letters of support or financial statements showcasing impressive growth in past years.

As is evident by now, you need to understand your market well to write an effective business plan. So, how do you do that? I will discuss this in depth in the next section.

Understanding Your Market

Thorough market research can help products and services reach their desired goals and popularity. Market research is critical to keep your product ahead of the competition.

Conducting proactive market analysis gives you a major edge by helping you identify key players in the market. By offering high-quality products and competitive prices, you can stay ahead of the competition and establish yourself as a market leader. Regularly analyzing consumer trends helps you understand current demands and adjust your products or services to meet those needs, keeping you at the top of your game.

Analysis and Research

Unless you know the market you are dealing with, it is almost impossible to have a product that will shake up the existing players and make a stronghold on the target audience. This is why I recommend following these steps to conduct a market analysis and research:

- Research to create a strong brand. Your brand value will decide how you draw the target audience and how your product or services are placed in the market for customer loyalty.

- Testing your product before it hits the market can help you understand what needs to be improved before your customers start using it and give feedback.

- The previous step will ensure you understand your customers better and make the best of their choices. Understanding customers can be the key to building better and more efficient products.

- Review your marketing campaign. Getting insights from your click-through rates and the views of your online ads can help you understand consumer behavior. It will help you build better products or improve your present product to serve customers better.

- Understanding the market also refers to understanding the major players of the game. A thorough analysis of the major players and their strategies will help you build a product that can be equivalent to or better than the existing ones in the market, and you can compete with the existing players.

- Understand your consumers by dividing them into groups. By creating these segments, you can better identify your target audience and build effective marketing strategies.

- Develop the product and take a market view to see how sales are processing. If the sales seem to be dipping, there is a dire need to make product improvements and understand the market needs better. If you analyze how the consumers receive your product, you can launch a newer and improved version of your current product. For example, taking customer buying and usage behavior and taking into account the customer feedback, the mobile phone brands make improvements in the newer version of their products.

Conduct SWOT Analysis and Competitor Research

When you plan a new product rollout, a SWOT analysis is essential. I talked about SWOT in the previous sections, too. As the name indicates, a SWOT (Strengths, Weaknesses, Opportunities, Threats) analysis is a method to analyze your business or product as a whole or a segment of your business. You can get an account of the strengths of your organization or product to enhance it further. Understanding the weakness will help you learn from it and make process improvements. Opportunities in the market will help you understand where and how you should place your product for better reach. Whereas, the threat analysis will help you steer away from all danger and help you make wiser decisions.

There are some steps to follow when you are conducting a SWOT analysis:

- Begin with strengths. Determine the strength of your business. Understand the weakness. It might be a challenge to say that you are not good at something or there are some shortcomings in the product or your service. However, making this hard call can define how well you will be able to place your product in the future. Determine the weaknesses.

- Identify the opportunities. Marketing strategies could yield new outcomes, such as the availability of newer technology, new revenue streams, lower operational costs, etc. You should be aware of and utilize these opportunities to the fullest.

- Identify threats. Being well aware of market dynamics can help you identify the blockers that can hinder the usability and popularity of your product or service.

- Refine and redefine your understanding of each aspect and make the most out of the information available after analysis.

You can also ask ChatGPT to help you with SWOT analysis. Here is how:

Prompt:

Help me conduct SWOT analysis for my small business

Output:

Of course! Conducting a SWOT analysis for your small business can provide valuable insights into its current state and help in planning for the future. Here's how you can structure it:

1. Strengths:

- What advantages does your business have?

- What unique resources or capabilities do you possess?

- What do your customers see as your strengths?

2. Weaknesses:

- What areas need improvement?

- What challenges does your business face?

- Are there resources or capabilities you lack compared to competitors?

3. Opportunities:

- What trends or changes in the market could benefit your business?

- Are there new technologies or innovations you could leverage?

- Are there untapped customer needs or segments you could target?

4. Threats:

- What are the external factors that could negatively impact your business?

- Are there competitors or market trends that pose a threat?

- Are there regulatory changes or economic factors to consider?

To get started, think about these aspects in relation to your business. It might be helpful to involve key team members or stakeholders in the discussion to gain diverse perspectives. Once you've identified factors for each category, prioritize them based on their impact and likelihood, and use the insights to inform your business strategy and decision-making.

Steps to Conduct Effective Market Research

Conducting market research effectively is important to ensure that the results are usable and insightful. Some basic steps to conduct effective market research include the following:

- Understand your buyer behavior and create a buyer cohort. Once you have the buyer groups defined, try to understand the thought process of these groups of audiences when buying or opting for a certain product or a service. It will help you understand how to build or market your product better.

- It can also help you select a specific buyer cohort to sell your product or service to, and you can build your product or service accordingly to meet their needs.

- Prepare your research questionnaire in advance. Prepare for the market research. Without the right questions, the conversation can become baseless, with no takeaway points.

- List down your competitors and see how they are performing in the market. It might also be that a certain segment of a company competes with the whole of your product, making it a bigger challenge, so be vigilant when you list down your competitors. You can get insights on your competitors from market reports, social media analysis, and the like.

- In the end, you summarize the above four points to gain insight. Decide what you wish to do next and prepare a proper action plan for your team.

Tools and Strategies for Gathering Market Intelligence

You can use some of the common strategies to gather market intelligence. These include:

- **A Customer Feedback System**: The customer is king. Getting insights from the end users can help you better understand the market's needs, aiding you in building better products.

- **Analysis of Competitors and Market Trends**: Always know what your competitors are offering and the general market trends.

- **SEO**: You can gather insights from SEO research. You can use this strategy to build customer engagement, improve customer retention, and grow more effectively in the market.

- **Industry Analysis**: You need to have a clear vision of the industry's latest developments. Multiple market intelligence data sources are available online that you can use for this purpose.

- **Understanding the Target Market**: Understanding your target audience is the key to building sustainable products and reliable services. Understand the market to serve it better.

Market research is an essential aspect of any business. If market research is not done before launching a product or service, it can undermine your whole effort to make the product available. Hence, before you build a product, you should do thorough market research and hit the target.

Once you have conducted market research, the next step is to define clear objectives and goals for your business plan.

Setting Clear Objectives and Goals for Your Business Plan

Establishing SMART goals is a powerful method to define your business objectives with precision and clarity. SMART stands for Specific, Measurable, Achievable,

Relevant, and Time-bound. Using this framework ensures that your business pa-rameters and expectations are clearly outlined.

Understanding the Importance of SMART Goals

SMART goals significantly enhance the effectiveness of a business plan. Here's how each component contributes:

Specific

Setting specific goals clarifies your objectives, making it clear what you aim to achieve. For instance, a goal like "Sell 'x' number of units by the end of the next quarter" is straightforward and actionable. This clarity helps you focus on optimizing marketing strategies to meet this exact target, unlike a vague goal such as "become a successful business."

Measurable

Measurable goals allow you to track progress using clear metrics. For example, the "x" in your goal could represent selling 1,000 units. Knowing this exact number helps you design your strategies to meet this target efficiently.

Achievable

Setting realistic goals is key. Aiming to sell 1,000 units might be achievable, but setting a target of selling a billion units when past sales have never exceeded 1,500 in a quarter is unrealistic. Achievable goals turn your business vision into reality, ensuring your efforts are likely to succeed.

Relevant

Goals must be relevant to your business and industry. For example, a washing machine company aiming to sell 1,000 units of chocolates is irrelevant and won't contribute to the company's growth. Relevant goals ensure that your efforts align with your core business objectives.

Time-Bound

Goals should have a deadline. This component of the SMART framework ensures that you work within a specific timeframe, adding urgency and helping you pace your efforts to achieve the goal on time.

Utilizing the Past/Present/Future Model

The past/present/future model is another useful framework for achieving your goals. This model helps you understand your current situation and how long it may take to reach your goals. Ask questions like "How far along am I in reaching my goal?" and "Is my current progress sufficient to achieve my goal in the future?" These questions provide valuable insights and highlight any necessary adjustments.

Leveraging Marketing Software

Marketing software like HubSpot, Buffer, and Google Analytics can also be instrumental in achieving your goals. The data they provide act as a catalyst for creating and refining SMART goals. With a wealth of information at your fingertips, you can outline clear, achievable objectives tailored to your business needs.

By setting SMART goals and using the past/present/future model, you can create a robust business plan that guides you toward success. Leveraging marketing software further enhances your ability to track progress and make informed decisions, ensuring your business objectives are met efficiently.

Key Takeaways

- A business plan guides decisions and actions, ensuring your venture stays on course.

- Poor planning and inaccurate cash flow forecasting lead to the failure of almost 80% of businesses.

- Key components of a business plan include an executive summary, business description, market analysis, marketing and sales strategies, management and organization, product/service details, competitive analysis, operations plan, financial projections, and exhibits/appendices.

- The executive summary should hook readers, providing a snapshot of the business.

- Detailed market research is crucial for understanding the industry, target audience, and competitors.

- Financial projections and funding needs demonstrate the business's potential for profitability and growth.

- Clear strategies for marketing, sales, and operations are fundamental for success.

Now that you've learned the basics, it's time to move from planning to execution. You're not on this journey alone. In the next chapter, you'll meet your new business planning ally—ChatGPT. Discover how this powerful AI can streamline the process, enhance your strategies, and make creating a business plan more efficient and effective.

Chapter Three

ChatGPT: Your Business Architect

I magine you've hired the perfect business planner. Every presentation is delivered before the deadline, backed by impeccable research, analysis, and insights. Always on time, never taking days off. You can't imagine your business running without him.

Sounds too good to be true? Perhaps. Such employees are rare and often retained by top companies.

But guess what? With ChatGPT, you can have a similar level of support. You can ask it to create business plans and make informed decisions. But how do you harness its power effectively?

In this chapter, we'll explore how to leverage ChatGPT to create business plans and, more importantly, how to use it efficiently. Think of ChatGPT as a high-performance car that needs a skilled driver. This chapter will transform you into that competent driver, ready to control a BMW at 150 mph.

Business Plan: A Micro-Course

Before I dig deeper into creating a business plan, let's revisit the basics from the last chapter and understand what a business plan is.

Investopedia defines a business plan as "a document that details a company's goals and how it intends to achieve them" (Hayes, 2024). Think of a business plan as your business's roadmap. It lays out your goals, how you plan to achieve them, and why you believe you'll be successful. It's like the GPS you use on a road trip—it keeps you on track and helps you avoid getting lost.

Many go-getters believe such a document is used only by big companies, but even mom-and-pop shops can benefit from having a business plan.

The length and content of a business plan can vary, ranging from a single page to dozens of pages or more, depending on the industry and the stage of the business. But here are some technical terms you'll find in every business plan.

- **Target Market**: These are your ideal customers, the specific group of people you're trying to reach with your product or service.

- **Value Proposition**: The main value you're offering to your ideal customers. Lower cost, sustainable packaging, free delivery—you name it.

- **Mission Statement**: This is a brief but powerful statement that captures your business's core purpose and values.

- **Marketing Strategy**: The strategy you wish to pursue to reach your ideal customers. This tells how you'll market your business, either through direct mail, Facebook advertisement, or radio broadcast ads.

- **Financials**: This section of your plan shows how much money you'll need to get started, how much you expect to make, and where that money will come from. Basically, it's the money map for your business adventure.

- **Break-Even Point**: This informs when you expect to be profitable after starting your business.

- **Competition**: These are the other businesses offering products or services similar to yours. Knowing your competition is key to making sure your business stands out from the crowd.

Now, let's get into the practical side of things.

Imagine you're opening a bakery. Your business plan would outline:

- What kind of baked goods will you sell? (Cupcakes, sourdough bread, fancy pastries?)

- Who are your target customers? (Busy commuters, families, health-conscious folks?)

- How will you price your products to make a profit?

- Where will you set up shop? (A trendy neighborhood, a bustling shopping district?)

- How will you market your bakery? (Social media, local events, eye-catching window displays?)

For the rest of the chapter, we'll take the example of a fictional bakery startup (say, Tom's Bakery). We'll develop a business plan for Tom's Bakery using ChatGPT in real life. This practical exercise should give you a gist of both the business plan and ChatGPT.

Introduction to ChatGPT and Its Capabilities

It's safe to say that ChatGPT (and related tools) has taken the world by storm. Users were blown away by the chatbot's human-like response. Greg Meyers, a Member of the Executive Committee at Bristol Myers Squibb, was one of the early reviewers of ChatGPT. His was, "I was blown away in my first conversation with ChatGPT, and I don't use that phrase casually."

This revolutionary capability made ChatGPT the fastest app to a million users in just five days (before Threads broke the record by achieving the feat in an hour) (Buchholz, 2023).

AI wasn't a new concept when ChatGPT was released to the public. Various AI and ML systems, like recommendation systems (as seen in YouTube recommendations or Amazon recommendations), exist. So, what made ChatGPT so radical and nuanced?

ChatGPT isn't a typical AI system that analyzes vast amounts of information and recognizes patterns. It is a new breed of AI system known as "Generative AI." It can generate new information by taking in existing content, and this capability makes ChatGPT and related tools revolutionary.

What Is Generative AI? (And Why It's the Future of Everything)

It doesn't take a computer scientist to know that algorithms and models power software. Each time you use a software or app, the algorithms work behind the scenes to provide the desired functionality. That is the case with ChatGPT, too.

ChatGPT is an app, and the model that powers it is called the "Generative AI" or "Gen AI" model.

So, to understand how ChatGPT works and how you can use it for market research, you need to understand Generative AI.

Renowned futurist Bernard Marr writes on Gen AI, "The concept of Generative AI takes us on a journey beyond the realm of binary logic, where AI is no longer just an executor of tasks but also an inventor (Marr, 2023). AI can be a creative companion capable of producing original outputs that can inspire, assist, and even astonish us. This innovative branch of AI opens up a world where machines can reflect some level of human-like creativity, bringing us closer to the vision of truly intelligent systems."

ChatGPT leverages a specific type of Generative AI model known as a Generative Pre-trained Transformer (GPT). GPTs don't directly create new data from scratch. Instead, they excel at predicting the next element in a sequence, making them ideal for tasks involving language.

The core of GPT lies in its training. ChatGPT is built on OpenAI's GPT-3 and its successor, GPT-4, which are trained on staggering amounts of text data scraped from the internet, books, articles, code, and more. This data exposes the model to various writing styles, sentence structures, and factual knowledge.

Through this training, the GPT model grasps the statistical relationships between words and phrases. It learns how words typically follow each other, how grammar dictates sentence structure, and how different writing styles utilize language.

ChatGPT doesn't stop at the first prediction. It continues using the same process iteratively, predicting the next most likely word based on the sequence it has generated so far. This allows it to build coherent and grammatically correct text, responding to user prompts with seemingly human-like conversation or creative writing.

The Various Capabilities of ChatGPT

If you haven't used ChatGPT before, it's high time you do. But why not tease you a bit about what's in store? Here is a list of capabilities that ChatGPT is amazing at.

Natural Language Processing

ChatGPT's strength lies in its impressive natural language processing (NLP) capabilities. It can understand and contextualize human speech like no tool ever did.

Unlike simpler chatbots with pre-programmed responses, ChatGPT utilizes transformers, a powerful neural network architecture, to grasp the context of a conversation. It analyzes the sequence of words, their relationships, and the overall tone to understand the meaning behind a prompt or question. This allows for more nuanced and relevant responses than chatbots with limited context awareness.

So what does this mean? You get relevant responses to your queries instead of a generic response. The responses come from the vast array of data on which it is trained. The ChatGPT model can contextualize both sides of the information (your inputs and trained data) and generate responses.

Here is an example prompt for you to try:

Prompt: *I am a skilled baker and wish to open my own community-focused bakery in Central City, Phoenix, where I live. I need your help understanding this business's target market so I can plan properly.*

As you can see, we've given the AI some background context here, stating our skills, our objectives, and where we live and want to do business. Now, ChatGPT can generate a detailed description that considers local demographics, customer preferences, and market trends. This would save you time and provide a solid foundation for the marketing section of his business plan.

Data Analysis

AI was good at analyzing data even before ChatGPT. You can perform basic data analysis inside this tool, too.

ChatGPT's premium version, ChatGPT Plus, gives you access to the GPT-4 model, which is more powerful than the free version. It also lets you attach files with your inputs, which the AI can analyze and respond accordingly.

So, if you have an Excel sheet or file that includes all your sales data, you can simply upload it to ChatGPT. Then, you can ask it to derive specific information for you from the vast data, such as:

How many powdered doughnuts and chocolate doughnuts have I sold in the previous three months?

Which item has been sold the most this month?

How many orders were canceled last month/week?

And you'll get the exact data. This information is fundamental for inventory management and marketing strategies, both essential business plan components.

Besides that, ChatGPT Plus offers a "Code Interpreter" plugin. This allows users to upload and run Python code directly within ChatGPT. This can be helpful for advanced data analysis tasks that require more control or complex calculations. However, it requires some programming knowledge and doesn't replace the need for dedicated data analysis tools.

Trend Prediction

Tools that could predict the future are always highly valued. When one of the Google Trends researchers used ChatGPT to successfully predict the fashion and beauty industry trends, it opened up another chapter on what ChatGPT can do (McDowell, 2023).

ChatGPT is trained on vast datasets that contain historical trend information. Analyzing this data can identify patterns and relationships that might suggest future trends.

The owner of Tom's Bakery can ask ChatGPT, *Is the doughnut market in the US expected to grow in 2025-26?*

What factors will affect the bakery industry in the next three years?

ChatGPT should return with an expected "yes" or "no" along with the reasoning and sources it has used. While still limited in nature, it can provide the groundwork for you to get started.

Trend prediction improves when supplied with richer data sets. As already said, with Code Interpreter, you can upload data and analyze it with ChatGPT. Its underlying technology is competent enough to draw insights and trends from the data.

Brainstorming Creative Research

Sometimes, fresh eyes are all you need. ChatGPT can be prompted to imagine the research topic from different angles, like the perspective of a specific consumer segment or a historical viewpoint. This can help you uncover hidden biases or blind spots in your initial approach.

For example, you can prompt, *Give me creative sauce ideas for pretzels,* and you should get a few new sauce options to try. You can even use new sauce pairs as a value proposition.

Remember, ChatGPT is designed to be creative and generate new insights from existing information. This creativity is what makes the tool so special for researchers.

Besides the above capabilities, you can use ChatGPT for a wide range of purposes. These include image generation, translation, speech-to-text conversion, code generation, and creating presentations.

ChatGPT has demonstrated capabilities that were deemed beyond reach half a decade ago. It is only going to get better from here on. Thus, it's wise to start utilizing the tool rather than be in denial or living with the perception that it's hard to implement.

How ChatGPT Can Assist in Market Research and Analysis

Entrepreneurs are often required to wear multiple hats. You need to be the sales guy one day, handle the books the next day, and run ads the day after.

But time and time again, you'd have to don the "market researcher" hat. It is essential to understand your market to be successful, but it's not a one-time task—it's something you need to do regularly.

Dr. James Bowen, a business professor at the University of Canada West, says, "The market is in constant evolutionary change. Startups need to be able to speak about how their solution fits where the market is going over the coming years, particularly in conjunction with other solution possibilities" (University Canada West, 2021).

Thus, market research is something you'll have to do every quarter at a minimum. But as you may know, thorough market research is expensive. Many reports cost several thousands of dollars. And the information they provide may not be suitable to your case.

In such scenarios, you can turn to ChatGPT to conduct quick market research and get valuable insight.

Here's a brief overview of how ChatGPT can assist in market research and analysis:

Obtain Relevant Information

Understanding the market starts with having the right information. Market research companies spend years to compile this data into comprehensive reports. Some data is acquired from publicly available information, and the rest is generated through interviews and in-house research.

ChatGPT is good at finding publicly available information and preparing a preliminary report based on that. As already said, ChatGPT is trained on a massive dataset that likely includes public information like government reports and statistics, business magazines like Forbes, press releases, and thought leadership articles.

You can ask ChatGPT to gather and compile data on a specific domain. For example, you can ask, *Can you give me an overview of how the bakery industry has changed in the past decade, from 2014 to today? I want to know how consumers have evolved and how the major players in this industry have grown in this period.*

Again, you may notice that I'm using detailed prompts as examples. I always try to include additional context that will help ChatGPT better understand my requirements and give me an appropriate response.

Analyzing Competitors

Understanding your market also involves keeping an eye on your competitors. ChatGPT can help you with that, and you can do it in various ways.

If you're struggling to pinpoint your main rivals, craft a prompt like: *Who are the top three competitors in the bakery market in Seattle?*

ChatGPT can analyze data to identify relevant companies. Based on publicly available information, it can also gather data points such as each company's market share, revenue, profit, number of employees, etc.

Likewise, if you want to understand how your competitors market themselves, use a prompt like *Analyze the marketing messages used by our top competitors in the Seattle bakery market. What features do they emphasize? What target audience do they focus on?*

While not comprehensive, you'll get enough information about your competitors.

Role Playing

Traditionally, market research often relies on surveys and focus groups. While valuable, these methods can sometimes feel artificial and are time-consuming. That's when you can use ChatGPT for role play.

You can simulate certain roles and get insights into how something may play out. Imagine practicing your sales pitch or gauging customer reactions to a new product prototype. ChatGPT can act as a stand-in customer, responding to your prompts and questions in a way that mimics real-life customer interactions.

A prompt for this can be, *Roleplay a conversation with a millennial customer who is interested in our new plant-based cookie but is concerned about allergies.*

ChatGPT can then respond with questions, concerns, and buying signals, helping you refine your pitch and anticipate customer objections.

You can also roleplay when developing briefs or questionnaires. You can ask ChatGPT to act as Rory Sutherland or Steve Jobs and generate text based on their personalities. ChatGPT is trained on these personalities and can mimic their way of conversation.

Creating Survey Questionnaire

Developing engaging and informative surveys is crucial for market research. It's often a manual process that requires the expertise of a market researcher. But ChatGPT is here to replace many professionals.

If you're designing a survey and staring at a blank page, you can turn to ChatGPT for quick ideas. Provide it with keywords related to your research topic and target audience. It will then generate different question formats like multiple choice, open-ended, or Likert scale questions to explore various aspects of your research.

Prompt ChatGPT with *Here is what I know about my customers: [Insert facts here]. Develop survey questions to understand customer satisfaction with our sauce for pretzels.*

ChatGPT might generate questions like: *How satisfied are you with the new sauce we offer?* or *On a scale of 1 to 5, how likely are you to recommend this sauce-pretzel combination to a friend?*

This will give you ideas to work on and refine further.

Analyzing Responses

After receiving responses from real-world customers, you can use ChatGPT to analyze the responses quickly. Its NLP capabilities allow researchers to get summaries and insights and prepare a quick report.

The premium version of ChatGPT, ChatGPT Plus, allows data files to be uploaded. You can upload your survey responses (ensure anonymization) and use prompts to guide the analysis.

You can enter a prompt like *Analyze the open-ended responses from our survey question, "What are the biggest challenges you face when trying to locate our bakery?" Identify the most common themes and provide a brief summary.*

You can also perform a quick sentiment analysis. ChatGPT can gauge the overall sentiment of your responses. This can help identify positive or negative trends in customer satisfaction, brand perception, or product experience.

An example prompt is: *Analyze the sentiment of all responses to our survey question: "How satisfied are you with our customer service?" Categorize responses as positive, negative, or neutral.*

Generating Business Plan Drafts With ChatGPT

You've done all the heavy lifting, gathered the information, and understood your target market. The next step is to put it all together into a business plan. A business plan serves as a document for every stakeholder to learn more about what you intend to do and how.

You can take the help of ChatGPT to draft your business plans. And guess what? It could save you hours of work. Let's go over the process of doing so.

But before that, it's wise to know how to structure a business plan. There's no one-size-fits-all plan. Instead, the plan varies from industry to industry. But there's a common theme. Harvard Business Review recommends you highlight four constituencies in your business plan, which are:

- The people (the founders, key employees, and other stakeholders)

- The opportunity (what you intend to sell and to whom)

- The context (the factors that cannot be controlled, like inflation and demographic trends)

- Risk and reward (the financial side of things) (Sahlman, 2023)

Here's a step-by-step guide on how to leverage ChatGPT's strengths throughout the process.

Define Your Business and Target Market

You should start with the target market. If you intend to get a loan or raise money, investors usually look at who you're targeting. So, create a prompt based on that.

Prompt: *Based on my market research findings (briefly summarize key findings), describe Tom's Bakery's core business concept. Who is our ideal target audience, and what specific needs or problems do we solve for them?*

Example Output:

Based on your research indicating a growing demand for animal-free, plant-based bakery products among eco-conscious millennials, your business concept focuses on developing and selling plant-based cookies, pastries, and shakes. Your target audience comprises environmentally responsible individuals aged 22-38 who prioritize healthy living and ethical consumption.

Craft a Compelling Value Proposition

Next comes a value proposition. This encapsulates what unique offerings your business brings to the table for customers.

Prompt: *Considering our competition and customer needs from the market research, help me create a unique value proposition that makes our bakery products stand out from other brands.*

You could get a response like:

Your brand offers a unique value proposition of plant-based bakery products, catering to the growing demand for animal-free food products that don't compromise on environmental responsibility.

Develop a Market Analysis

Here, you can provide ChatGPT with specific data points from your research to integrate into the analysis.

Prompt: *Using my market research, help me write a short market analysis for the business plan. Include details on market size, growth potential, main competitors, and important trends in the (your location) bakery industry.*

Example output (based on your provided data): *The local bakery market is healthy and growing, indicating constant demand for bakery products. There are a total of 15 bakery shops in the city, five of which are located nearby. The market also shows a trend toward plant-based ingredients and sustainable packaging.*

Outline Your Marketing and Sales Strategy

You need a marketing strategy to reach your customers, and investors would want to know how you'll do so. Thus, this section of your business plan should convey the same.

Prompt: *Based on our target audience from the market research, suggest marketing and sales strategies to reach and convert customers for our plant-based bakery products.*

Example output: *Based on your target audience of eco-conscious millennials, consider leveraging social media marketing platforms like Instagram and TikTok to showcase the effectiveness and sustainability of your products. Partnering with eco-friendly influencers or online retailers specializing in the sustainability niche can also be an effective strategy.*

Develop a Financial Plan

A business plan should also cover the financial side of things. While ChatGPT can't perform complex financial calculations (as of this writing), it can help with structuring the financial plan and suggesting relevant data points to include based on your market research.

Prompt: *Give me a simple outline for a financial plan for Tom's Bakery. What financial projections and cost estimates should be included?*

Example output: *A financial plan for your business should include projected revenue based on market research data on consumer spending habits and pricing strategies. Additionally, consider including cost estimates for product development, manufacturing, marketing, and operational expenses.*

While ChatGPT will do the heavy lifting of generating a business plan, it's not a substitute for human intelligence. ChatGPT and related tools have been known to provide factually incorrect outputs, known as hallucinations.

Therefore, when using ChatGPT for market research and business plan creation, you should take note of the following:

- **Human Expertise Remains Crucial**: While ChatGPT provides prompts and suggestions, critical thinking and business insight are essential for crafting a strong business plan. After all, you know more about your business than ChatGPT ever will.

- **Accuracy and Fact-Checking**: Double-check all information generated by ChatGPT, especially market data and financial projections. Ensure they align with your research findings and reliable sources. This applies to all of the data generated by ChatGPT.

- **Focus on Clarity and Conciseness**: Refine ChatGPT's outputs to ensure your business plan is clear, concise, and persuasive for potential investors or partners.

Key Takeaways

- ChatGPT is a powerful tool for market research. You can generate information and questionnaires and analyze responses.

- The technology behind ChatGPT's revolutionary capability is Gen AI, which generates new data from existing information.

- Gen AI models are trained on vast amounts of data. Because of the training, they understand the contextual relationship between words and sentences better than previous AI systems.

- ChatGPT is capable of data analysis, natural language processing, trend prediction, and brainstorming creative ideas.

- ChatGPT can assist you in market research in various ways, such as obtaining relevant information, generating questionnaires, analyzing responses, and preparing business plans based on the research.

- To get the best results, you need to provide good, specific prompts and fine-tune the responses until they're perfect.

- But ChatGPT isn't an accurate tool. At times, it provides irrelevant or non-factual information. Therefore, human expertise is needed to finalize a market research report or business plan.

We're done with market research. You're now one step closer to succeeding with your entrepreneurial dreams. In the next chapter, we'll explore how to further develop your plan into a detailed, actionable strategy that outlines what your business is about and how it will succeed, grow, and navigate the competitive landscape.

Chapter Four

Building a Smart Business Blueprint

S tarting a business without a solid plan is like setting sail without a map—you might get somewhere, but it's likely to be nowhere good. A business plan is perhaps the most vital element that can make or break your venture.

According to Investopedia, poor business planning is one of the top reasons businesses fail (Deane, 2024). It's not just about having a plan but a detailed and well-thought-out one from the beginning. Your plan needs to account for multiple scenarios—both good and bad—so that you can stick to it for the long haul. Constantly changing a poorly constructed plan will only lead to chaos and potential failure.

Many entrepreneurs understand the importance of a hearty business plan, but creating one is where they stumble. It's not for a lack of effort; it's often because they don't know how to develop a comprehensive plan. People may have the skills, expertise, or brilliant ideas for products, but they might not be versed in business studies or naturally savvy in business. Crafting a detailed business plan requires a learning curve and a lot of effort.

That's exactly what I'm going to cover in this chapter. Let's dive in and explore how you can leverage AI to create a business plan that sets you up for success.

Creating Powerful Product Descriptions With ChatGPT

In the previous chapter, we discussed the fundamentals of developing a business plan, touching on essential elements such as product descriptions. Now, it's time to probe deeper into the art of crafting compelling product descriptions with the help of ChatGPT.

I've broken things down into simple and clear steps to make it easy for you to follow along and create amazing descriptions for your products or services. By the end of this chapter, you'll have the tools and knowledge to make your offerings stand out and resonate with your target audience. Let's start turning your product descriptions into powerful marketing tools with some help from AI.

Step 1: The Three Foundations of a Compelling Description

Creating a compelling product description involves focusing on three key elements:

Identifying Pain Points

Understanding the pain points or needs of your audience is crucial. This knowledge allows you to tailor your business solutions to address these issues directly. ChatGPT can assist in brainstorming and identifying these pain points. For example, if you run a small bakery, you can engage ChatGPT in a conversation to uncover potential customer pain points.

Example prompt: *I own a small bakery that specializes in artisan bread and pastries. My target audience includes local residents, office workers, and families. Can you help me identify their pain points or needs related to baked goods and bakery services?*

Offering Relevance and Value

Once you've identified the pain points, the next step is to explain how your product or service addresses them. While ChatGPT can't define the relevance and value of your specific business, it can help you articulate it effectively once you provide the necessary details.

Example prompt: *Based on the pain points you mentioned, my bakery offers fresh, organic ingredients, quick service for busy office workers, and a cozy atmosphere for families to enjoy. Can you help me phrase this in a compelling way that highlights the relevance and value of my bakery?*

Unique Selling Proposition (USP)

Knowing your audience's pain points and how your business can solve them is essential, but it's not enough to stand out. You need a Unique Selling Proposition (USP) that differentiates you from the competition. While ChatGPT can't create your USP, it can help you express it clearly once you define what makes your product unique.

Example prompt: *What sets my bakery apart from competitors is our commitment to using only locally sourced ingredients and offering a special weekly menu of unique, seasonal pastries. Can you help me craft a description that highlights this unique selling proposition?*

Based on ChatGPT's response to these prompts, you can put together the pain points, value and relevance, and your USP to build the first draft of your product description. Now, we still have some more work to do!

Step 2: Refining ChatGPT's Responses

Using the tips and prompts from the previous section, you'll get some great advice, insights, and content from ChatGPT. But in today's competitive business landscape, near-perfection is required in many aspects, especially in your product descriptions. Let's dive into how you can further refine ChatGPT's responses using ChatGPT itself!

Clarity in Your Message

Lack of clarity can confuse potential customers and lead to missed opportunities. For example, suppose you own a small bakery, and your product description says, "We make bread and pastries." While true, it's vague and doesn't highlight what makes your bakery special.

Compare that to, "We create artisan bread and pastries using locally sourced, organic ingredients, ensuring fresh and delicious baked goods every day."

The latter is clear, specific, and conveys the unique value of your bakery. Clarity in your message helps potential customers understand exactly what you offer and why they should choose you.

Setting the Tone and Style

The tone and style of your product description should align with your brand and resonate with your target audience. This can vary by industry. For instance, modern, trendy fashion wear for Gen Z would require a vibrant and chic lingo, while selling suitcases for professionals would demand a more formal and professional tone. If you're unsure about the best style, tone, voice, or language for your messaging, ChatGPT can provide suggestions.

Prompt:

I own a small bakery that specializes in artisan bread and pastries. Our target audience includes local residents, young professionals, and families. Can you suggest the best tone and style for my product descriptions that would resonate with this audience?

Output:

For your artisan bakery, a tone that is warm, inviting, and slightly indulgent would likely resonate well with your target audience. Consider using descriptive language that evokes sensory experiences, such as the aroma of freshly baked bread or the delicate sweetness of pastries. Here's a sample product description for one of your artisan breads:

Country Sourdough Loaf

Indulge in the rustic charm of our Country Sourdough Loaf, lovingly crafted with traditional techniques and premium ingredients. Each bite offers a symphony of flavors, from the tangy notes of naturally fermented sourdough to the subtle hints of caramelized crust.

Hand-shaped and baked to perfection in our ovens, this artisanal bread boasts a chewy interior with a tantalizingly crisp crust – a testament to our dedication to quality craftsmanship. Whether enjoyed fresh with a smear of creamy butter or as the foundation for your favorite sandwich creations, our Country Sourdough Loaf is sure to delight your senses and elevate any meal.

That sounds neat, doesn't it? ChatGPT not only suggests a suitable tone for your product descriptions but also complements them with a sample description to drive home the point.

Refining the Draft

Once you've decided on the message, tone, and style you want, let ChatGPT know and ask it to refine the initial draft of your product description from Step 1 based on these preferences. I'll run a quick test to show you how it works.

First, continuing with our bakery business example, I created a simple description for a chocolate chip cookie:

"Introducing our mouthwatering Chocolate Chip Cookie! Baked to perfection, each cookie is crafted with love and care using the finest ingredients. Enjoy the perfect balance of rich, creamy chocolate chips nestled in soft, golden-brown cookie dough. Whether it's a quick snack or a sweet treat to share with friends and family, our Chocolate Chip Cookie promises to delight your taste buds with every bite. Indulge in the timeless goodness of our classic favorite!"

Then, I gave this description to ChatGPT and asked it to refine it based on the tone that it had suggested in the previous example—warm, inviting, and indulgent.

Prompt:

Can you take the above product description and refine it in a warm, inviting, slightly indulgent tone? I would like descriptive language that evokes sensory experiences.

Here's the response from ChatGPT:

> Step into a world of irresistible delight with our latest creation: the mouthwatering Chocolate Chip Cookie! Picture this: each heavenly morsel is meticulously crafted, baked to perfection with an abundance of love and care, using only the finest ingredients nature has to offer.
>
> As you take your first bite, let the aroma of freshly baked cookies fill the air, tantalizing your senses and beckoning you closer. Sink your teeth into the soft, golden-brown dough, which cradles a symphony of rich, creamy chocolate chips. With every chew, experience the perfect balance of sweetness and indulgence, transporting you to a realm of pure bliss.
>
> Whether it's a midday pick-me-up or a delightful treat to share with cherished companions, our Chocolate Chip Cookie promises an experience like no other. So go ahead, succumb to the allure of this timeless classic, and let its delectable flavors dance on your palate, leaving you craving for more.

Compare it to the basic description I wrote before, and tell me this isn't miles better! That's the power of Generative AI, as long as you offer proper inputs, instructions, and prompts.

The best part is that none of this is too difficult or requires a lot of business expertise or technical knowledge.

Marketing and Sales Using ChatGPT

Marketing and sales are the twin engines that drive your startup or small business off the ground. Marketing gets you in front of people, ensuring your target audience knows about you and can find you. On the other hand, sales turn those people into loyal customers. Without these two crucial elements, your business simply can't see the light of day.

I know that diving into marketing and sales can be daunting for many of you. Indeed, these areas often require some know-how and expertise. But here's the good news: This knowledge isn't out of reach. Marketing and sales are practical skills you can easily learn with a bit of effort. And the best part? It doesn't have to get too technical at the start. Plus, with ChatGPT by your side, crafting a solid marketing and sales strategy has never been easier.

Let's break it down step by step, making these essential skills approachable and manageable for you. But before we dive into marketing specifics, you have to understand some basic concepts and terminologies. Lucky for you, I'm offering a quick crash course right here and now. If you're already familiar with these, feel free to skip ahead a bit. Either way, I promise to keep it short and simple.

Marketing and Sales Basics With ChatGPT

The essence of marketing can be broken down into five basic steps.

Step 1: Visibility

Visibility is about finding ways to put your product, service, or business in front of people who would be interested in buying them or who need them. It's all about getting noticed.

ChatGPT can assist you in brainstorming ideas to enhance your visibility. Whether it's creating eye-catching social media posts, writing engaging blog content, or suggesting effective advertising platforms, ChatGPT can provide you with creative and practical ideas.

Prompt:

> I own a small bakery that specializes in artisan bread and pastries. Our target audience includes local residents, office workers, and families. Can you suggest some creative ways to increase my bakery's visibility in my local area, such as specific social media strategies, local events we could participate in, or other promotional activities?

Output:

> Certainly! Here are several creative strategies to increase the visibility of your bakery in your local area:

Social Media Strategies

  1. **Instagram Stories and Reels:**

  - **Behind-the-Scenes Content:** Share how your bread and pastries are made. This can include kneading dough, baking, decorating pastries, etc.

  - **Customer Spotlights:** Feature photos and stories from your customers. Encourage them to share their own photos and tag your bakery.

  - **Daily Specials:** Use Stories to announce daily specials, fresh batches, or limited-time offers.

  - **Interactive Polls and Q&A:** Engage your audience with polls about their favorite flavors or Q&A sessions about baking tips.

  2. **Facebook Events and Groups:**

  - **Create Events:** Host virtual baking classes or tasting events and promote them through Facebook Events.

  - **Local Groups:** Join and participate in local community groups. Share updates about your bakery, special promotions, and community involvement.

  3. **User-Generated Content:**

  - Encourage customers to share their experiences on social media using a specific hashtag (e.g., #YourBakeryNameLovesLocal). Feature their posts on your profile.

  4. **Influencer Collaborations:**

  - Partner with local food bloggers or micro-influencers to review your products or host giveaways.

Local Events and Community Involvement

   1. Farmers' Markets and Local Fairs:

   - Set up a stall at local farmers' markets or fairs. This is a great way to reach local residents who value fresh and artisan products.

   2. Community Events:

   - Participate in or sponsor local events such as charity runs, school fairs, or holiday festivals. Offer free samples or set up a booth.

   3. Baking Classes and Workshops:

   - Host baking classes or workshops at your bakery. This can attract families and individuals interested in learning new skills.

   4. Collaborations with Local Businesses:

   - Partner with local coffee shops, restaurants, or grocery stores to feature your products. This can help cross-promote each other's businesses.

Promotional Activities

   1. Loyalty Programs:

   - Implement a loyalty program to reward repeat customers. Offer discounts or free items after a certain number of purchases.

   2. Seasonal and Holiday Specials:

   - Create special products for holidays and local festivals. Promote these limited-time offers on social media and through email newsletters.

   3. Sampling Campaigns:

   - Offer free samples in high-traffic areas, such as outside your bakery, local parks, or office buildings. Include a coupon with each sample to encourage a visit to your bakery.

4. **Window Displays and In-Store Promotions:**

- ○ Use your bakery's windows to create eye-catching displays. Inside, have clear signage for specials and featured items.

5. **Local Media:**

- ○ Reach out to local newspapers, magazines, or radio stations to feature your bakery in articles, interviews, or advertisements.

6. **Customer Referral Program:**

- ○ Encourage your existing customers to refer friends and family by offering incentives such as discounts or free items for successful referrals.

Other Ideas

1. **Pop-Up Shops:**

- ○ Set up pop-up shops in different locations around your town to reach new customers.

- ○ These can be in parks, business districts, or community centers.

2. **Recipe Cards:**

- ○ Provide recipe cards for some of your popular items. This adds value to the customer experience and keeps your bakery top-of-mind.

3. **Charity Partnerships:**

- ○ Partner with local charities to donate a portion of your sales to a good cause. Promote these partnerships to attract socially conscious customers.

There are plenty of excellent suggestions and strategies here that you can analyze, consider, and put together in your marketing plan. Let's say you want to note down all these suggestions and work more on them later. Just ask ChatGPT to sum up everything in short.

Prompt:

Can you summarize these pointers into a more compact list?

Output:

Absolutely! Here's a more compact list summarizing the key points:

Social Media Strategies

1. **Instagram Stories/Reels:** Share behind-the-scenes content, customer spotlights, daily specials, and interactive polls/Q&A.

2. **Facebook Events/Groups:** Host virtual events, engage in local groups, and promote updates.

3. **User-Generated Content:** Encourage customers to share experiences with a specific hashtag.

4. **Influencer Collaborations:** Partner with local food bloggers and micro-influencers.

Local Events and Community Involvement

1. **Farmers' Markets/Fairs:** Set up stalls to reach local residents.

2. **Community Events:** Participate in or sponsor local events with free samples or booths.

3. **Baking Classes/Workshops:** Host sessions at your bakery to attract families and individuals.

4. **Local Business Collaborations:** Partner with coffee shops, restaurants, and grocery stores.

Promotional Activities

1. **Loyalty Programs:** Reward repeat customers with discounts or free items.

2. **Seasonal/Holiday Specials:** Promote limited-time offers on social media and through newsletters.

3. **Sampling Campaigns:** Offer free samples with coupons in high-traffic areas.

4. **Window Displays/In-Store Promotions:** Create eye-catching displays and clear signage.

5. **Local Media:** Feature your bakery in local newspapers, magazines, and radio.

6. **Customer Referral Program:** Incentivize referrals with discounts or free items.

Other Ideas

1. **Pop-Up Shops:** Set up in different locations to reach new customers.

2. **Recipe Cards:** Provide value with recipe cards for popular items.

3. **Charity Partnerships:** Donate a portion of sales to local charities and promote the partnership.

This looks like a pretty solid start for marketing and sales, and we didn't have to get our hands into a lot of learning, head-scratching, or technical know-how to come up with it, all thanks to the power of Generative AI.

For this step, I have included an instance of ChatGPT's response to the example prompt just to let you witness how useful and insightful it can be. Moving forward, I won't be showing much of ChatGPT's responses from my conversations. Instead, try these prompts yourself, sticking with our bakery examples first and later using similar prompts for your business ideas.

With that in mind, let's move on to the next stages of a powerful marketing and sales plan.

Step 2: Traffic

Traffic is about getting people who know about your business to somehow come to you, whether in a physical location or digitally on your website or social media.

ChatGPT can help you come up with strategies to drive traffic to your business. From SEO-friendly content for your website to social media strategies and local community events, ChatGPT can offer tailored suggestions based on your business type and target audience.

Example prompt: *My bakery is well-known locally, but I want to attract more customers to visit our shop. Our key products are artisan breads and seasonal pastries. Can you suggest strategies to increase foot traffic, such as specific local advertising tactics, partnerships with nearby businesses, or community events we could host?*

Step 3: Engagement

Engagement means encouraging your traffic to interact with your business, showing that they are interested in what you offer. This could be through comments, shares, likes, or any form of interaction.

ChatGPT can help you draft engaging content that resonates with your audience. It can suggest ways to encourage interaction on your social media posts, design engaging email newsletters, and more.

Example prompt: *I want to increase engagement on my bakery's social media pages. Our followers are mostly young professionals and families. Can you suggest some interactive post ideas, like polls, contests, or questions, that would resonate with our audience and encourage them to comment, share, and like our posts?*

Step 4: Conversion

Conversion is about convincing these engaged visitors to finally make a purchase. This is where your sales strategies come into play.

ChatGPT can assist you in crafting compelling calls-to-action, creating persuasive sales copy, and developing promotional strategies to convert visitors into customers.

Example prompt: *I want to create a promotional campaign for my bakery to convert social media followers into paying customers. Our key products are artisan breads and seasonal pastries. Can you help me draft a compelling offer, such as a discount or special bundle, along with a strong call-to-action that will encourage followers to visit our bakery and make a purchase?*

Step 5: Retention

Retention is about ensuring that your customers keep coming back to you, becoming happy, satisfied, and loyal in the long run.

ChatGPT can suggest ways to keep your customers engaged and satisfied over time. This could include loyalty programs, personalized follow-up emails, and special offers for repeat customers.

Example prompt: *I want to implement a customer retention strategy for my bakery. Can you suggest some ideas for loyalty programs, such as point systems or exclusive member discounts, and draft a follow-up email template to thank customers for their purchase and offer them an incentive for their next visit?*

Advanced Marketing and Sales Strategies With ChatGPT

The five stages of marketing and sales that I explained above are the foundations, and now you know how ChatGPT can help in those areas. But what we have done so far is just the overview of a marketing strategy. Even when your business is still new and small, you need to go a bit deeper than just a basic plan.

So, let's move ahead from the basics, as I'll walk you through a few more advanced concepts and strategies that are still fairly easy to learn and understand while also being essential for promoting your business from Day 1.

Website Optimization

A website is the first thing you would want for your business, and it's not too difficult to set one up these days. Learning to create a website is out of the scope of this book, as ChatGPT can't do that for you. You can ask it for ideas and brainstorm things, but in the end, you need to build the website yourself.

So, I won't talk about it here, but if you want to learn more, the resources below should help.

The Ultimate Guide to Building a Small Business Website in 7 Steps – Bluehost

- https://www.bluehost.com/blog/the-ultimate-guide-to-building-a-small-business-website-in-7-steps/

How To Create A Website For Your Business - Forbes

- https://www.forbes.com/advisor/in/business/software/how-to-create-a-website/

How to Make a Small Business Website Step by Step (2024)

- https://www.wpbeginner.com/wp-tutorials/how-to-make-a-small-business-website-step-by-step/

Now, let's talk about how ChatGPT can help.

Improving User Experience (UX)

A great user experience keeps visitors on your site longer and encourages them to take desired actions, such as purchasing or signing up for newsletters. ChatGPT can provide insights and suggestions to enhance your website's UX.

Example prompt: *I have set up a basic website for my bakery that includes pages for our products, a blog, and contact information. Can you suggest ways to improve the user experience on my website, such as layout improvements, navigation tips, and features that would make it more user-friendly and engaging for visitors?*

Making an SEO Strategy

Search Engine Optimization (SEO) is vital for making your website more visible on search engines like Google. ChatGPT can help you create a comprehensive SEO strategy that includes keyword research, content planning, and backlink strategies to improve your search engine ranking.

Example prompt: *I need to develop an SEO strategy for my bakery's website to improve its visibility on search engines. Can you help me outline a plan that includes keyword research, content planning, on-page SEO tips, and backlink strategies? I would also like some specific examples of keywords relevant to my business and how to effectively use them.*

Generating Call-to-Action (CTA)

A strong call-to-action can significantly increase conversions by guiding visitors toward making a purchase or taking another desired action. ChatGPT can help you create effective CTAs tailored to your audience and goals.

Example prompt: *I want to add a call-to-action on my bakery's homepage to encourage visitors to sign up for our weekly newsletter. The CTA should be inviting and emphasize the benefits of signing up, such as exclusive offers, updates on new products, and special promotions. Can you help me write this in a warm, engaging tone?*

Social Media and Email Marketing

Social media and video marketing have become incredibly powerful channels for reaching and engaging your target audience. For entrepreneurs and small businesses, leveraging these platforms from the start can provide significant advantages in visibility, customer engagement, and brand building. Let's explore how ChatGPT can help you create effective social media and video marketing strategies.

Crafting Engaging Content

Content is king in social media marketing. ChatGPT can assist you in brainstorming and creating engaging posts that resonate with your audience and encourage interaction.

Example prompt: *I want to create engaging social media posts for my bakery. Can you suggest content ideas and provide examples for different types of posts, such as promotional posts, behind-the-scenes content, and customer testimonials?*

Video Marketing Strategies

Video content is highly engaging and can significantly boost your marketing efforts. ChatGPT can help you develop video ideas and scripts that showcase your products and tell your brand story.

Example prompt: *I want to create a short promotional video for my bakery highlighting our unique selling points, such as our use of locally sourced ingredients and our special seasonal pastries. Can you help me outline a script for the video that includes an engaging introduction, highlights our products, and ends with a strong call-to-action?*

Leveraging Influencer Marketing

Collaborating with influencers can amplify your reach and build trust with your target audience. ChatGPT can help you identify suitable influencers and craft outreach messages.

Example prompt: *I'm interested in collaborating with local food influencers to promote my bakery. Can you suggest how to identify potential influencers and provide a template for an outreach message that introduces my bakery and proposes a collaboration?*

Marketing Plan Development

So far, we have discussed ways to use ChatGPT to create a solid marketing strategy. However, these strategies must also be put on paper in your business plan document. So, even in this regard, ChatGPT can help you to turn all the marketing ideas and strategies into an official document that explains your overall marketing and sales approach.

Here's how ChatGPT can help.

Creating a Simple Marketing Plan

A marketing plan outlines your business's marketing strategy and the steps you will take to achieve your marketing goals. ChatGPT can help you draft a straightforward, actionable marketing plan tailored to your business needs.

Example prompt: *I need to create a simple marketing plan for my bakery. Can you help me outline the key components, including identifying my target audience in detail, setting clear marketing objectives like increasing foot traffic and online orders, suggesting specific marketing strategies such as social media campaigns, local partnerships, and in-store promotions, estimating a realistic budget for these activities, and determining metrics for success like sales growth, social media engagement, and customer retention rates?*

Setting SMART Goals

SMART goals are Specific, Measurable, Achievable, Relevant, and Time-bound. Setting SMART goals ensures that your marketing objectives are clear and attainable. ChatGPT can help you formulate these goals for your business.

Example prompt: *For my bakery, I want to set SMART goals related to various aspects of my marketing efforts. For example, I aim to increase our Instagram following by 30% over the next three months by posting daily content and engaging with followers. Another goal is to boost in-store sales by 15% within the next quarter by launching a loyalty program and offering special weekend discounts. Can you help me refine these goals to ensure they are specific, measurable, achievable, relevant, and time-bound, and suggest any additional actions I should take to achieve them?*

Tracking Progress and Adjusting Strategies

Tracking your marketing progress and being flexible enough to adjust your strategies as needed is crucial for long-term success. ChatGPT can guide you on how to monitor your progress effectively and suggest ways to adapt your marketing tactics based on performance data.

Example prompt: *I have implemented a marketing plan for my bakery, focusing on social media marketing, local events, and in-store promotions. I need help tracking the progress of these activities. Can you suggest specific KPIs I should monitor, such as weekly sales figures, social media engagement rates, customer foot traffic, and feedback from local events? Additionally, I would like advice on tools or methods for regularly analyzing this data and actionable tips for adjusting my marketing strategies if I'm not meeting my goals, such as changing content strategies or increasing promotional efforts during peak hours.*

ChatGPT can be an invaluable tool in your marketing and sales efforts. From the foundational steps of visibility, traffic, engagement, conversion, and retention to more advanced strategies like website optimization, social media, email marketing, and influencer collaborations, ChatGPT offers tailored guidance and actionable insights every step of the way.

Whether you're crafting compelling content, developing promotional campaigns, or setting SMART goals, ChatGPT can simplify the process, making it accessible even if you're just starting out. By leveraging these AI-powered suggestions, you can build a robust marketing and sales strategy that drives your business forward, ensuring you reach and retain your target audience effectively.

Key Takeaways

- A detailed business plan is central to guiding your venture toward success. It provides clarity in goals, strategies, and operational frameworks.

- Utilize ChatGPT to simplify business planning tasks, from crafting compelling product descriptions to developing robust marketing strategies.

- Master marketing basics—visibility, traffic, engagement, conversion, and retention—to effectively attract and retain customers.

- Explore advanced concepts such as website optimization, social media, video marketing, and setting SMART goals to enhance business visibility and engagement.

- Implement ChatGPT's insights to brainstorm ideas, refine strategies, and execute actionable plans that resonate with your target audience.

- Take immediate action by refining your product descriptions, drafting a comprehensive marketing plan, and leveraging ChatGPT's capabilities for sustainable business growth.

With your detailed business plan now taking shape—from a clear product or service offering to strategic marketing plans and efficient operational structures—it's time to put these ideas into action. In the next chapter, we'll explore the critical elements of financial planning. With ChatGPT by your side, you'll learn how to forecast, budget, and secure the financial health and growth of your venture. Stay tuned to discover how AI can streamline your financial strategies and empower your business decisions.

Chapter Five

Smart Money Planning

S tarting a business can seem like an exhilarating journey, but you can barely even take off without solid financial planning. Financial planning is one of the backbones of successful businesses, providing the roadmap that guides entrepreneurs through the complexities of budgeting, forecasting, and managing resources. For aspiring business owners, mastering financial planning isn't just beneficial—it's essential for turning dreams into sustainable realities.

Money, or the lack thereof, can be a make-or-break factor for your business. A well-thought-out budget is essential for your business to take off and thrive. Preparing this budget in advance sets the foundation for your financial health and stability. You might be worried that you lack financial knowledge, aren't an accounting expert, or have no experience as a financial analyst. How could you possibly do in-depth, accurate financial planning for your business?

Don't worry—that's precisely why I've written this ebook. I want to show you that what most people think are the intricate aspects of business management and development can now be easily done with the power of Generative AI like ChatGPT.

So, let's dive in. I'm certain by the end of this chapter, you'll feel pretty confident about creating a solid financial plan for your business and performing intelligent budget forecasting.

Introduction to Financial Planning Basics

Before diving into the practical applications of ChatGPT for financial planning, you must grasp the foundational aspects of budgeting and financial forecasting. In this section, I'll provide a quick overview of these crucial topics—enough to get you started confidently.

Whether you're new to financial planning or seeking to streamline your approach with AI assistance, this introduction will equip you with practical insights. You'll learn how to initiate conversations with ChatGPT to create initial budget templates, refine financial plans based on changing scenarios, and project cash flows—all essential steps in launching and sustaining your business.

Let's go through some fundamental aspects of budgeting, which are essential for every entrepreneur aiming to establish financial stability and strategic direction for their business.

Budgeting Basics

Budget is more than just the money you need to start and run your business. It is a financial plan that outlines a business's expected income and expenditures over a specific period. It serves as a roadmap for financial decision-making, guiding how resources will be allocated to achieve business goals effectively.

Budgeting plays a pivotal role in the success of any business by providing several key benefits:

- **Financial Control**: It enables businesses to track their financial performance against predetermined targets, helping to identify areas of overspending or potential savings.

- **Decision-Making**: Budgets facilitate informed decision-making by providing insights into available resources and constraints, guiding strategic initiatives such as expansions, investments, or cost reductions.

- **Goal-Setting**: Budgets help set realistic financial goals and objectives, providing a benchmark for measuring progress and success.

Key Components of a Business Budget

Here are the essential components that make up a comprehensive business budget:

Revenue Forecast

The revenue forecast is a key component of your budget. It projects the income your business expects to generate from sales, services, or other sources over a defined period, typically monthly, quarterly, or annually.

It provides a realistic estimate of the funds that will flow into your business, forming the foundation for financial planning and goal-setting. Understanding your revenue forecast helps you gauge your business's financial health and identify growth opportunities.

Expenses

Expenses encompass all anticipated costs necessary to operate your business effectively. These are typically categorized into two main types:

- **Fixed Expenses**: These are regular costs that remain relatively stable month-to-month, such as rent or lease payments, salaries, insurance premiums, and utilities. Fixed expenses are essential for maintaining your business's operational infrastructure and are usually predictable.

- **Variable Expenses**: These costs fluctuate based on business activities and can include raw materials, production costs, marketing expenses, and sales commissions. Variable expenses are more directly linked to your business's revenue-generating activities and may vary depending on market conditions or seasonal demands.

Understanding and categorizing your expenses helps you allocate resources efficiently, manage cash flow effectively, and maintain financial stability over time.

Cash Flow

Cash flow refers to the movement of money in and out of your business. Revenue and expenses can be broad figures, such as average revenue/expense over a year. However, cash flow bridges those two aspects, breaking down how and when the revenue came in and expenses went out over a specific period, be it a month, a quarter, or a year.

By regularly monitoring your cash flow, you can make smart decisions to keep enough money on hand for your business needs and avoid unexpected cash shortages.

Alright, did that sound a bit boring? Hopefully not, but if it did, bear with me a bit, as these are the bare minimum basics you need to cover. And these are three interrelated aspects.

Here's a simple example:

Based on these factors, you can prepare a simple financial plan as such:

We are projecting an average monthly revenue of $10,000 for the first year, while our estimates for total operational expenses in the same period, considering both fixed and variable costs, come to an average of $6,500 per month. For further analysis, we have prepared a cash flow projection that breaks down the proposed revenue and expenses for each month over the span of the year. Based on these estimates, we are confident that our business will still remain profitable by the end of Year 1.

That would be a nice pitch to present before an investor. Of course, I'm just throwing numbers here as an example, so you'll soon learn how to plan out such numbers and estimates for your business. However, the above example presents a clear correlation between the three basics of budgeting: revenue, expenses, and cash flow.

I'll later come back to putting the above concepts into action for your business with ChatGPT's help. For now, we still have a little more learning to do.

Financial Forecasting Essentials

Now that you've got a handle on budgeting let's talk about another important part of financial planning: financial forecasting. This might sound daunting, but it's basically just about predicting your business's financial future based on what's happening now and what happened in the past. It's like having a financial crystal ball to help you make smarter decisions.

What is Financial Forecasting?

Financial forecasting is predicting how your business will perform financially in the future. It helps you prepare for what's coming so you can make informed decisions and keep your business on the right track.

Why is Financial Forecasting Important?

Financial forecasting is important because it:

1. Helps you set realistic goals and figure out how to achieve them.

2. Gives you insights into potential challenges and opportunities.

3. Ensures you have enough cash to cover expenses and invest in growth.

Types of Financial Forecasts

There are a few different types of financial forecasts you should know about. Here are the key ones.

Sales Forecast

A sales forecast predicts how much money your business will bring in from sales over a certain period. It's based on past sales data, current trends, and what you expect in the future. Accurate sales forecasting helps you plan for things like production, inventory, and marketing.

Cash Flow Forecast

A cash flow forecast estimates how much cash will come in and go out of your business. Ensuring you have enough money to cover your expenses and invest in your business's growth is important. This forecast helps you avoid cash shortages and manage surpluses effectively.

Expense Forecast

An expense forecast estimates the costs your business will have in the future. It includes both fixed expenses (like rent) and variable expenses (like materials). This forecast helps you control spending and identify where to cut costs or invest more.

Scenario Planning

Scenario planning involves creating different financial scenarios based on various assumptions, like changes in the market or unexpected events. This type of forecasting helps you prepare for different possibilities and have backup plans ready.

Sensitivity Analysis

Sensitivity analysis looks at how different factors affect your business's financial performance. For example, it helps you understand how sales volume or pricing changes could impact your revenue and profits. This analysis helps you make more resilient financial plans.

In the next section, we'll explore how to use ChatGPT to create and refine your business budgets. You'll learn how to ask specific questions and use AI-generated templates to kickstart your financial planning process.

Budgeting and Forecasting With AI

Now that you have a good grasp of the basics of financial planning, it's time to take things a step further. In this section, you'll learn how to put together the building blocks of an actionable financial plan for your business with the help of ChatGPT.

Imagine having a knowledgeable assistant at your fingertips, ready to help you create detailed budgets and accurate financial forecasts. With ChatGPT, that's exactly what you get. This powerful AI tool can simplify complex tasks, provide valuable insights, and guide you through the financial planning process with ease.

Whether you're starting from scratch or looking to refine existing plans, ChatGPT can help you generate budget templates, refine financial details, and forecast future performance. By leveraging AI, you can create a solid financial plan to set your business on the path to success.

Budgeting With AI

With ChatGPT, you can simplify the process and create a comprehensive financial plan for your business. In this section, I'll guide you through how to use ChatGPT to combine the key elements—revenue, expenses, and cash flow forecasts—into a cohesive budget.

Step 1: Generating Budget Templates With ChatGPT

The first thing you need to start with your budget plan is a template. If your business has yet to launch or has recently started, you don't have a lot of historical financial data to look back on and plan. You are planning from scratch, and that's why you need a template to give some structure to your budgeting plan.

Luckily, it's super simple. Just ask ChatGPT to do it! Simple and straightforward.

Of course, there's a catch—the more details you provide about your business, the better and more relevant ChatGPT's response will be.

Prompt:

I'm starting a small bakery that specializes in artisan bread and pastries. Our target audience includes local residents, office workers, and families, but I will also do online orders and home deliveries.

Since I don't know much about managing a business, can you help me create a budget template that includes revenue forecasts, fixed and variable expenses, and a cash flow projection?

Output:

Bakery Budget Template

1. Revenue Forecasts

Estimate your monthly revenue from different sources.

Revenue Source	Jan	Feb	Mar	Apr	May	Jun	Jul	Aug	Sep	Oct	Nov	Dec	AT
In-Store Sales													
Online Orders													
Home Deliveries													
Catering Services													
Special Events/Parties													
Total Revenue													

2. Fixed Expenses

List your fixed monthly expenses.

Fixed Expenses	Monthly Amount	Annual Total
Rent		
Utilities (Water, Gas, Electricity)		
Salaries (Full-time Staff)		
Insurance		
Loan Payments		
Licenses and Permits		
Advertising and Marketing		
Internet and Phone		
Accounting/Bookkeeping Services		
Miscellaneous		
Total Fixed Expenses		

3. Variable Expenses

List your estimated variable monthly expenses.

Variable Expenses	Jan	Feb	Mar	Apr	May	Jun	Jul	Aug	Sep	Oct	Nov	Dec	A T
Ingredients													
Packaging													
Part-time Staff Wages													
Delivery Costs (Fuel, Maintenance)													
Cleaning Supplies													
Repairs and Maintenance													
Marketing and Promotions													
Miscellaneous													
Total Variable Expenses													

4. Cash Flow Projection

A summary of your cash flow to ensure you have enough funds to cover expenses.

Cash Flow	Jan	Feb	Mar	Apr	May	Jun	Jul	Aug	Sep	Oct	Nov	Dec	Annu Total
Opening Cash Balance													
Total Revenue													
Total Fixed Expenses													
Total Variable Expenses													
Net Cash Flow (Revenue - Expenses)													
Closing Cash Balance													

Yes, take a moment to let that sink in. With one question and in less than five minutes, I have an impressive budget template in front of me. With complete tables and relevant fields to track revenues, expenses, and cash flow, this template is pretty solid for starters.

Try this out for your business idea right away, and I'm sure you'll love the results!

But this is just a template in the end. And it's no good if you don't know what to do with it. So, the next step is to break down each component of this template with ChatGPT's assistance.

Step 2: Defining Revenue Streams

So, to move ahead with this basic budget plan, you need to define your revenues and expenses. Let's start with the former.

You already know what your main revenue will be—it's your business idea, after all. But more often than not, it's not as simple as selling a single product, and your business will inevitably have a few different sources of revenue.

In the above template, ChatGPT already listed some common revenue sources relevant to our bakery example—in-store sales, online orders, home deliveries, catering services, and special events. I may not do all these things for my bakery or explore new streams of my own.

If you are clear about how you will diversify your products, services, and revenue, that's great. But if you aren't, you know the golden rule – just ask ChatGPT!

Prompt:

I'm still planning the different streams of revenue I could have for my bakery business. I know that at the start, in-store sales will be the main source of revenue, but I do plan to slowly push for online orders and home deliveries. Other than that, what ideas could I consider?

Output:

Sure, let's break it down step-by-step. We'll start with identifying potential revenue streams and estimating your revenue.

Potential Revenue Streams

1. **In-Store Sales:** This includes all sales made directly at your bakery. You can break it down further into:

   - Bread sales

   - Pastry sales

   - Beverages (coffee, tea, etc.)

   - Special items (seasonal products, custom orders)

2. **Online Orders:** Sales made through your website or other online platforms. This can be broken down into:

- Pre-order bread and pastries

- Special occasion orders (birthday cakes, holiday specials)

- Subscription services (weekly or monthly bread delivery)

3. **Home Deliveries:** Orders that you deliver directly to customers. This could include:

- Regular deliveries for local customers

- Corporate orders for office events

- Catering services for events

4. **Wholesale to Local Businesses:** Selling your products to local cafes, restaurants, or grocery stores.

5. **Classes and Workshops:** Offering baking classes or workshops for individuals or groups.

6. **Special Events and Pop-Ups:** Participating in local markets, fairs, or setting up pop-up shops.

7. **Gift Baskets and Packages:** Creating themed gift baskets for holidays, special occasions, or corporate gifts.

Estimating Revenue

To estimate your revenue, you need to make some educated guesses based on your market research and initial business plan. Here's a step-by-step approach:

1. **Market Research:**

- **Competitor Analysis:** Look at similar bakeries in your area. What are their prices? How busy are they?

- **Target Audience:** Who are your customers? What are their buying habits?

1. Sales Projections:

- ○ **Daily Sales Estimate:** Estimate the number of customers you expect each day and the average amount they will spend.

- ○ **Weekly and Monthly Sales:** Multiply your daily sales estimate by the number of operating days in a week and a month.

Example for In-Store Sales

Let's say you expect an average of 50 customers per day, and the average customer spends $10.

- **Daily Sales:** 50 customers * $10 = $500

- **Weekly Sales:** $500 * 7 days = $3,500

- **Monthly Sales:** $500 * 30 days = $15,000

Do this for each revenue stream. For online orders and home deliveries, start with a smaller estimate and increase it gradually as you build your customer base.

Revenue Forecast Template

Here's how you can structure your revenue forecast in your budget template:

Month	In-Store Sales	Online Orders	Home Deliveries	Wholesale	Classes/Workshops	Special Events	Total Revenue
January	$15,000	$2,000	$1,000	$500	$300	$200	$19,000
February	$16,000	$2,200	$1,100	$550	$300	$200	$20,350
March	$17,000	$2,500	$1,200	$600	$300	$200	$21,800
...	...	...	...	...	...	...	...
December	$18,000	$3,000	$1,500	$700	$300	$200	$23,700
Total	$	$	$	$	$	$	$

ChatGPT just gave us potential revenue ideas, showed us some basic guidelines and math to do a bit of starting research and calculations, and threw in an example template to help us understand. I think that it's amazing how one prompt can lead to such deep insights. Sure, I wouldn't copy-paste these things on my budget plan or blindly do what ChatGPT suggests, and neither should you. But from having no business knowledge to brainstorming budget templates with ChatGPT—that's a huge learning curve you have just covered in minutes.

Step 3: Planning Expenses

Let's say I want to start a business, but I'm completely oblivious to what expenses I should consider and prepare for. Sure, everyone knows there will be rent and salary if I hire people, and I can easily make a list of things I may need to buy to start my business. But what if I am not prepared for the day-to-day costs of running my business?

And if I'm not aware of the different types of expenses I might have to consider, how can I estimate how profitable my business would be?

These are the usual struggles of any entrepreneur who is a beginner in business management and development. And guess who's coming to the rescue? You know it—ChatGPT.

Prompt:

I'm starting a small bakery that specializes in artisan bread and pastries. Our target audience includes local residents, office workers, and families, but I will also do online orders and home deliveries.

Since I don't know much about managing a business, can you help me figure out what expenses will be associated with my business that I should consider as part of long-term financial planning?

Output:

Starting and managing a small bakery involves various expenses that you should consider for long-term financial planning. Here are the key categories of expenses you will likely encounter

Initial Setup Costs

1. **Lease/Rent Deposit:** Initial payment for securing your bakery's location.

2. **Renovation and Decoration:** Costs for setting up the interior and exterior of the bakery to create a welcoming environment.

3. **Equipment Purchase:** Ovens, mixers, proofers, refrigerators, display cases, cash registers, etc.

4. **Licenses and Permits:** Health permits, business licenses, food handling permits, etc.

5. **Initial Inventory:** First stock of raw materials like flour, sugar, butter, eggs, etc.

6. **Technology and Software:** POS systems, accounting software, website development, and maintenance for online orders.

Ongoing Operational Costs

1. **Rent/Lease Payments:** Monthly cost for your bakery location.

2. **Utilities:** Electricity, water, gas, and waste disposal.

3. **Salaries and Wages:** Payments for bakers, cashiers, delivery personnel, and other staff.

4. **Ingredients and Supplies:** Regular purchase of baking ingredients, packaging materials, cleaning supplies, etc.

5. **Maintenance and Repairs:** Regular upkeep of equipment and facility.

6. **Marketing and Advertising:** Costs for promoting your bakery, both online and offline, including social media advertising, local flyers, and promotions.

7. **Insurance:** Coverage for property, liability, workers' compensation, etc.

8. **Delivery Costs:** Fuel, vehicle maintenance, and potential third-party delivery service fees for home deliveries.

9. **Professional Services:** Accounting, legal services, and potentially consulting services.

Technology Upgrades

1. **POS System Updates:** Regular updates or upgrades to your point-of-sale system to ensure it remains efficient and secure.

2. **E-commerce Platform Fees:** Monthly or annual fees for maintaining your online store and processing online orders.

Miscellaneous Expenses

1. **Office Supplies:** General supplies like stationery, printing materials, etc.

2. **Bank Fees:** Fees associated with business banking accounts, merchant services, etc.

Long-term Financial Goals

1. **Retirement Contributions:** Setting aside funds for your personal retirement.

2. **Business Savings:** Building a savings buffer to reinvest in your business or for future opportunities.

I don't think there is anything else that needs to be said here. ChatGPT just gave me a long list of diverse expenses I should account for that apply to a bakery business. You can follow up and ask about each of these aspects to learn more about these expenses in detail. There's a gold mine of information waiting to be revealed.

So, with your revenue and expenses planned out, you can then fill them into your cash flow table. With a little time, effort, and, of course, ChatGPT's help, you'll have a solid budget plan for your business.

Forecasting With AI

For beginners, we are focusing on the five basic types of financial forecasts we discussed earlier: sales forecast, expense forecast, cash flow forecast, scenario planning, and sensitivity analysis.

The problem is that historical data is an important element of forecasting. But for startups and entrepreneurs, if their business is just starting or hasn't started yet, how would they look back to past data when there is nothing to look at? Established businesses often review their previous year's performances, strategies, and learnings to plan for the year ahead. New businesses can't do the same.

And that's where ChatGPT comes in.

Prompt:

> I'm starting a small bakery that specializes in artisan bread and pastries. Our target audience includes local residents, office workers, and families, but I will also do online orders and home deliveries.
> I need to do some financial forecasting for my business, but while I'm good at baking, I don't know anything about running a business. So, I have no idea how to make financial forecasts, and I don't even have historical data to look at because my business is only about to start. How can I plan for sales forecasting?

Output:

> Creating a financial forecast for your new bakery involves several steps. Here's a structured approach to help you get started:
>
> 1. **Market Research**
>
>   - **Analyze Local Demand:** Estimate the demand by looking at similar local businesses. Observe their customer traffic and average sales.
>
>   - **Identify Your Target Market:** Segment your audience (local residents, office workers, families) and estimate their purchasing power and habits.

- **Assess Competition:** Look at competitors in your area to understand their pricing, customer base, and sales volume.

2. Define Your Offerings

- **Product List:** Outline all the products you will offer (e.g., types of bread, pastries).

- **Pricing:** Set prices for each item based on your costs and competitive pricing.

3. Estimate Initial Sales Volume

- **Daily Sales:** Estimate the number of customers per day and average spend per customer.

- **Weekly and Monthly Trends:** Consider factors like weekends, holidays, and local events that might affect sales.

4. Calculate Costs

- **Fixed Costs:** Rent, utilities, salaries, insurance, equipment.

- **Variable Costs:** Ingredients, packaging, delivery costs, marketing.

5. Create a Sales Forecast Model

- **Time Frame:** Plan for monthly sales for the first year.

- **Scenarios:** Develop optimistic, realistic, and pessimistic scenarios to account for uncertainty.

6. Use a Simple Spreadsheet

Sales Forecast Template: Create or use a template to input your data. Here's a basic structure:

Month	Expected Customers	Average Spend per Customer	Total Sales Revenue	Fixed Costs	Variable Costs	Total Costs	Profit/Loss
January							
February							
March							
...							

7. Estimate Growth

- **Initial Growth:** New businesses often see a gradual increase in customers as they build awareness.

- **Marketing Impact:** Consider the effect of promotions and advertising on customer growth.

8. Break-Even Analysis

- **Break-Even Point:** Calculate the point at which total revenue equals total costs. This helps in understanding how many sales are needed to cover expenses.

9. Adjust and Refine

- **Review Regularly:** Adjust your forecasts based on actual sales data once you start operating.

Customer Feedback: Use feedback to improve products and services, which can influence future forecasts.

There you have it—plenty of things to look at for your sales forecasting. Dive deeper into these aspects with ChatGPT, or continue your own research. But within minutes, you have a list of relevant things to consider. How long would it take to just plan and consider everything in your head and make this list? Definitely not two minutes!

So go ahead and try out the same prompt for other types of forecasting, and in no time, you'll have enough material to work with that would take even experienced business developers many hours to plan.

Risk Management and Mitigation With ChatGPT

Starting a business is already a bold move, but just launching your venture doesn't warrant a sigh of relief. You will still face many inevitable risks and challenges when running a business, and planning for such things in advance is the sign of a smart and visionary entrepreneur.

So, how can ChatGPT help you get started with this intricate aspect of business management?

Identifying Potential Risks

The first step in risk management is identifying potential risks that could affect your business. These risks can be internal, such as operational inefficiencies, or external, like market fluctuations. ChatGPT can help you brainstorm and list potential risks by considering various aspects of your business.

Prompt:

ChatGPT, what are some common operational risks for a new bakery business?

Output:

Starting a new bakery business involves several operational risks that should be considered to ensure smooth operations and sustainable growth. Here are some common operational risks for a new bakery business:

1. **Quality Control Issues:** Maintaining consistent product quality can be challenging, especially as production scales up or when using perishable ingredients.

2. **Supply Chain Disruptions:** Dependence on suppliers for ingredients and equipment can lead to disruptions due to issues like late deliveries, quality inconsistencies, or supplier bankruptcies.

3. **Equipment Breakdowns:** Malfunctions or breakdowns of baking equipment can halt production and lead to delays in fulfilling orders.

4. **Staffing Challenges:** Finding and retaining skilled bakery staff can be difficult, especially during peak times or in areas with low unemployment.

5. **Food Safety Concerns:** Compliance with food safety regulations and maintaining proper hygiene standards is crucial to prevent contamination and health risks.

6. **Inventory Management:** Overstocking or understocking ingredients and products can impact cash flow, storage space, and freshness of baked goods.

7. **Customer Service Issues:** Managing customer expectations, handling complaints, and ensuring consistent service quality are essential for customer satisfaction and retention.

8. **Cash Flow Management:** Balancing expenses, such as ingredient purchases and equipment maintenance, with revenue from sales can be challenging, especially during seasonal fluctuations.

9. **Competition:** Competing with other bakeries, cafes, and supermarkets in the local area can impact pricing strategies, customer loyalty, and market share.

10. **Regulatory Compliance:** Adhering to local health and safety regulations, zoning laws, and employment laws can involve legal complexities and potential fines if not followed correctly.

Addressing these risks involves careful planning, implementing operational procedures, and having contingency plans in place to mitigate potential disruptions to the bakery business.

Financial Risks

1. **Cash Flow Management:** Ensuring you have enough cash on hand to cover operational costs, especially during slow periods.

2. **Unexpected Expenses:** Unplanned expenses, such as equipment repairs or legal fees, that can impact your financial stability.

Market and Competition

1. **Customer Preferences:** Changes in customer preferences or trends that could affect demand for your products.

2. **Competition:** New competitors entering the market or existing ones expanding their offerings, which could impact your market share.

Regulatory and Compliance Risks

1. **Health Inspections:** Failing health inspections due to non-compliance with local regulations, leading to fines or temporary closure.

2. **Licensing Issues:** Problems with acquiring or renewing necessary business licenses and permits.

Operational Efficiency

1. **Production Bottlenecks:** Inefficiencies in the production process that can lead to delays and increased costs.

2. **Inventory Management:** Difficulty in managing inventory levels, leading to waste or stockouts.

Developing Mitigation Strategies

After identifying and prioritizing risks, the next step is to develop strategies to mitigate them. Mitigation strategies aim to reduce the likelihood of risks occurring or minimize their impact if they do. ChatGPT can provide practical mitigation strategies for different types of risks.

Prompt:

Can you give me some realistic scenarios of supply chain problems for bakery businesses and also provide strategies on solving or mitigating them?

Output:

Certainly! Here are some realistic scenarios of supply chain problems for bakery businesses, along with strategies to solve or mitigate them:

Scenario 1: Ingredient Shortages

Problem:

A key supplier for flour experiences a manufacturing issue, causing a delay in delivery. As a result, your bakery faces a shortage of flour, impacting your ability to produce bread and pastries.

Strategies to Mitigate:

1. **Diversify Suppliers:** Establish relationships with multiple suppliers to ensure you have alternative sources if one supplier fails.

2. **Maintain Safety Stock:** Keep a buffer stock of essential ingredients to cover you in case of short-term shortages.

3. **Long-term Contracts:** Secure long-term contracts with suppliers to ensure a steady supply and possibly negotiate priority treatment during shortages.

Scenario 2: Delivery Delays

Problem:

Due to bad weather or transportation issues, your regular deliveries of perishable goods like eggs and dairy are delayed, risking spoilage and production downtime.

Strategies to Mitigate:

1. **Local Sourcing:** Source perishable goods from local suppliers to reduce transportation time and dependency on long-distance deliveries.

2. **Flexible Scheduling:** Adjust your production schedule to use ingredients that are in stock while waiting for delayed deliveries.

3. **Emergency Suppliers:** Identify emergency suppliers who can provide quick deliveries in case of regular supplier delays.

Scenario 3: Quality Issues with Supplies

Problem:

You receive a batch of butter that does not meet your quality standards, impacting the taste and texture of your pastries.

Strategies to Mitigate:

1. **Quality Assurance Agreements:** Set strict quality standards in contracts with suppliers and enforce penalties for non-compliance.

2. **Regular Inspections:** Conduct regular quality checks of incoming supplies before they are used in production.

Supplier Audits: Perform periodic audits of your suppliers' facilities and processes to ensure they meet your quality requirements.

Okay, I had to stop at three scenarios. ChatGPT gave me 10.

Go ahead and experiment with these prompts and brainstorm with ChatGPT to see what risks could disrupt your business and how you can prepare for them ahead of time.

Using ChatGPT to Learn

Risk management is a complex topic. Some people work for big, billion-dollar companies that only specialize in risk management and mitigation. So, obviously, it's a technical aspect of business, and that is why you need to continuously learn and update yourself on minimizing business risks. And even in this area, ChatGPT can easily help. All you need to do is write the right prompt. Let's see how.

Prompt:

Help me understand the basic steps of risk management in business

Output:

Step 1: Understand the Basics of Risk Management
1. Introduction to Risk Management

- Learn the definition of risk and risk management.

- Understand the types of risks (strategic, operational, financial, compliance, and reputational).

2. Key Concepts and Terminology

- Familiarize yourself with key terms such as risk appetite, risk tolerance, risk assessment, and risk mitigation.

3. Online Courses and Resources

- Enroll in introductory online courses on platforms like Coursera, edX, or Udemy. Look for courses like "Risk Management for Small Businesses" or "Introduction to Enterprise Risk Management.

Step 2: Identify and Assess Risks
1. Risk Identification

- Learn techniques for identifying potential risks in your business (SWOT analysis, brainstorming, expert interviews).

2. Risk Assessment

- Study methods to evaluate the likelihood and impact of identified risks (quantitative vs. qualitative assessment).

3. Tools and Software

- Explore tools and software for risk assessment (Excel for risk matrices, dedicated risk management software).

Step 3: Develop Risk Mitigation Strategies
   1. **Risk Mitigation Techniques**

      o Learn various risk mitigation strategies (avoidance, reduction, sharing, acceptance).

   2. **Business Continuity Planning**

      o Understand the importance of business continuity and disaster recovery planning.

   3. **Case Studies**

      o Study case studies of businesses that successfully mitigated risks. Analyze what they did right and where they could improve.

Step 4: Implement Risk Management Processes
   1. **Risk Management Frameworks**

      o Familiarize yourself with common risk management frameworks (COSO, ISO 31000).

   2. **Policies and Procedures**

      o Develop risk management policies and procedures tailored to your business.

   3. **Training and Communication**

      o Ensure that all employees understand and adhere to risk management practices. Conduct regular training sessions and updates.

Step 5: Monitor and Review
   1. **Regular Monitoring**

      o Set up processes for continuous monitoring of risks. Use Key Risk Indicators (KRIs) to track risk exposure.

1. **Periodic Reviews**

   ○ Schedule periodic reviews of your risk management processes. Update risk assessments and mitigation strategies as needed.

Additionally, here is how you can prompt ChatGPT to identify and mitigate risks:

I'm looking for detailed guidance on how to identify and mitigate risks for my business in [Location]. Can you explain the steps for conducting a risk assessment, creating effective mitigation plans, and recommend tools to help manage risks? Additionally, please provide relevant examples to illustrate these concepts.

A lot more information was provided, but the point is that ChatGPT gives you all you need to start your own research or continue self-learning, even for business aspects that may seem complex for beginners.

Fundraising Strategies With ChatGPT

Securing the necessary funds is often one of the biggest challenges for any new business. Whether you're looking to launch a startup or expand your existing business, having a solid fundraising strategy is essential. In this section, you'll learn how to use ChatGPT to explore and implement various fundraising strategies tailored to your business needs.

Identifying Suitable Fundraising Options

The first step in developing a fundraising strategy is identifying the most suitable options for your business. ChatGPT can help you explore a variety of fundraising methods, from traditional bank loans to innovative crowdfunding campaigns.

Equity Financing

Equity financing involves raising capital for a business by selling shares of ownership in the company. Investors provide funds in exchange for ownership equity, typically through shares of stock. This method allows businesses to obtain capital without taking on debt, and investors may also bring expertise and networks to support business growth. However, it dilutes the ownership stake of existing owners, reducing their control over decision-making and involves sharing future profits with shareholders.

Example Prompt: *ChatGPT, what are the benefits and drawbacks of equity financing for my bakery? Explain the advantages and disadvantages of equity financing for a bakery, including how it impacts ownership and control.*

Debt Financing

Debt financing involves borrowing funds from lenders, such as banks or financial institutions, which must be repaid with interest over a specified period. The borrowed funds do not give lenders ownership in the business but rather create a contractual obligation for repayment. Benefits include retaining full ownership and control over the business, but it also involves regular interest payments and the obligation to repay the principal, which can strain cash flow if not managed properly.

Example prompt: *Should I consider taking out a loan to fund my bakery expansion? Discuss the pros and cons of debt financing for a bakery, considering interest rates, repayment terms, and financial risk.*

Crowdfunding

Crowdfunding is a method of raising capital through small contributions from a large number of individuals, typically via online platforms. It allows businesses to reach a broader audience beyond traditional investors and can generate pre-orders or support from early adopters. Crowdfunding campaigns often offer rewards or early access to products and services in exchange for contributions. However, success depends on effective marketing and the appeal of the business idea to the crowd, and platforms may charge fees or require successful funding thresholds to access funds.

Example prompt: *ChatGPT, how can I launch a successful crowdfunding campaign for my bakery? Provide a step-by-step guide to launching a successful crowdfunding campaign for a bakery, including platform selection and marketing strategies.*

Grants and Competitions

Grants and competitions provide non-repayable funds or prizes to businesses based on specific criteria, such as innovation, social impact, or industry focus. Grants are typically government or foundation-funded and support activities that align with the grantor's objectives. On the other hand, competitions often involve pitching business ideas or plans to judges or panels for cash prizes, mentorship, or networking opportunities. Both grants and competitions can enhance visibility, credibility, and financial resources for businesses, although they often have competitive application processes and specific eligibility requirements.

Example prompt: *ChatGPT, are there any grants or competitions available for small food businesses around my area <insert location>? Identify potential grants and business competitions suitable for small food businesses, including application tips and eligibility criteria.*

Crafting Compelling Fundraising Pitches

A compelling pitch attracts investors and secures funds. ChatGPT can help you craft persuasive pitches by highlighting your business's unique value proposition, market potential, and financial projections.

Elevator Pitch

An elevator pitch is a concise and compelling summary of a business idea, product, service, or oneself, designed to be delivered in the time it takes to ride an elevator—typically around 30 seconds to two minutes. Its purpose is to quickly grab the listener's attention and communicate the essence of what makes the idea or business unique and valuable.

ChatGPT can help refine your business idea or key message by asking targeted questions. By providing details about your business, target audience, unique selling points, and goals, ChatGPT can help distill the core elements into a clear and impactful pitch.

Example prompt: *Help me write a concise and impactful elevator pitch for my bakery, focusing on its unique selling points and market opportunity.*

Pitch Deck

A pitch deck is a visual presentation that accompanies your pitch, providing a structured overview of your business to potential investors. It typically consists of slides highlighting key aspects such as the business model, competitive landscape, financial projections, and team expertise. A well-crafted pitch deck informs and engages investors by illustrating the potential and viability of your business idea.

ChatGPT can help you create a compelling pitch deck by structuring the content effectively. By outlining each slide's purpose and content, ChatGPT can assist in crafting slides that capture attention, convey information clearly, and build a persuasive case for investment.

Example prompt: *Guide me through creating a compelling pitch deck for a bakery, covering slides on the business model, competitive landscape, and financials.*

Investor Meetings

Preparing for and conducting meetings with potential investors is a critical step in fundraising. These meetings allow you to expand on the information in your pitch deck, build rapport, and address specific questions or concerns that investors may have.

ChatGPT can offer tips for preparing effectively, such as anticipating common investor questions about market validation, scalability, revenue streams, and risk mitigation strategies. It can also provide guidance on how to structure your presentation during the meeting, emphasizing key points and tailoring your messaging to align with investor interests.

Example prompt: *Provide tips for preparing and presenting effectively in meetings with potential investors for a bakery, including common questions and how to address them.*

Navigating the Fundraising Process

The fundraising process can be complex, with various stages and requirements. ChatGPT can help you navigate this process, from initial research to closing deals with investors.

Researching Investors

Example prompt: *Suggest ways to research and identify investors who are interested in the food industry, including online platforms and networking events.*

Initial Contact

Example prompt: *Provide guidance on how to make initial contact with potential investors for a bakery, including crafting an introductory email or message.*

Negotiating Terms

Example prompt: *Offer tips for negotiating favorable terms with investors for a bakery, focusing on equity, control, and valuation considerations.*

So, there's a lot we have discussed and a lot of example prompts you can modify and explore. The process is easy—you ask the questions, and ChatGPT does all the heavy lifting. But there are a lot of questions to ask, and you do need to spend considerable time brainstorming, learning, and refining things with ChatGPT. The end results are a clear plan and actionable strategies to raise funds for your business and set it up for success.

Key Takeaways

- Financial planning is indispensable for any business. It provides a roadmap for budgeting, forecasting, and resource management. It ensures financial health and guides decision-making, which is crucial for sustainable growth.

- A business budget goes beyond mere expenditure; it forecasts income and expenses, offering control, informed decision-making, and goal-setting capabilities. Understanding revenue forecasts, fixed and variable expenses, and cash flow is essential for financial stability.

- Forecasting helps predict a business's financial future, which is vital for goal-setting and strategic planning. Types include sales, cash flow, and expense forecasts, alongside scenario planning and sensitivity analysis, which prepare businesses for various market conditions.

- Leveraging AI, such as ChatGPT, simplifies financial tasks. It aids in creating budget templates, refining financial plans, and forecasting accurately, even for new businesses without historical data.

- Identifying and mitigating risks early is essential. ChatGPT can assist in identifying potential risks and developing strategies to minimize their impact, which is crucial for long-term business resilience.

- Securing capital is vital for business growth. ChatGPT helps explore funding options like equity, debt, crowdfunding, and grants, guiding entrepreneurs in crafting compelling pitches and navigating the complex fundraising process.

Mastering financial planning and navigating the complexities of business management are daunting tasks, especially for new entrepreneurs. However, with AI tools like ChatGPT, these challenges become opportunities for learning and growth. When it comes to financial planning, AI can streamline processes, provide valuable insights, and allow you to make informed decisions that lay a solid foundation for your business success. As you embark on your entrepreneurial journey, embrace the power of AI to transform your ideas into thriving realities.

In the next chapter, we'll explore the critical steps for implementing your plan and ensure the vision you've meticulously crafted on paper begins to take shape in the real world, driving toward success and innovation.

Chapter Six

Making It Official

In business, there's a popular analogy: "Running a business is like running a marathon, not a sprint." This means success requires sustained effort over the long haul, covering endless distances.

You've already accomplished a lot by learning the basics of creating a business and financial plan with ChatGPT. Now, it's time for the next crucial step: implementing your plans to bring your business to life. In this phase, your hard work starts to pay off, and your ideas become reality.

And that's what this chapter is about. Here, we'll go over the steps that come after creating a business plan. We'll go over the entire process, from setting up KPIs to optimizing them to ensure your business plan is implemented successfully. And we'll have our partner-in-crime, ChatGPT. Let's navigate the path from plan to reality, transforming our vision into actionable steps with ChatGPT as our guide.

Establishing a Legal Structure: The First Step Toward Reality

So far, everything you've done has been restricted to paper and files. A business plan is nothing but ideas on a sheet of paper. So, the first step after creating a business plan is to put it into a structure recognized by the law and the public. And it starts with incorporating a legal entity.

Establishing a legal entity is fundamental to starting and doing a business in any location. It's how others interact with your ideas and offerings. Think of a legal entity as an ID for organizations, similar to how ID cards are used for individuals.

A legal entity is an organization recognized by the law, such as a business or nonprofit. The legal structure defines how this entity is organized, like a sole proprietorship, partnership, corporation, or LLC, influencing management, liability, and financial operations. Both are important for defining an organization's legal status and operational framework.

A legal structure serves as the bridge between your ideas and your reality in the world. However, such a structure has other purposes, too.

Liability Protection

Having a business means some things will go against you. Perhaps someone gets ill after having a pastry or gets injured at your bakery. In such cases, the liability will fall on you. Different legal structures offer varying levels of personal liability protection for business owners. For example, an LLC or corporation can protect personal assets from business debts and legal actions.

Tax Implications

A legal entity ensures you're taxed appropriately and fairly. Note that the choice of structure influences how the business is taxed. Sole proprietorships, partnerships, and corporations often have pass-through taxation, while C corporations can be subject to double taxation (corporate and personal taxes).

Operational Flexibility

A legal structure will decide how much flexibility you have in how you operate. Some structures allow for more flexible management and ownership arrangements. For instance, corporations have a more rigid structure, with a board of directors and formal meeting requirements, while LLCs offer more flexibility.

Funding and Investment

At some point in time, you may want to raise capital or get a loan. Investors and banks loan out to business entities. They look at various parameters when deciding on who to loan (and at what rate!). So, establishing a legal structure is paramount if you want to access funds.

Compliance and Regulation

Every business must comply with the local rules and regulations. A legal entity is just part of that process. Different structures have different regulatory and reporting requirements. Corporations often have more stringent requirements than sole proprietorships or LLCs.

Credibility and Perception

The legal structure can affect how customers, suppliers, and lenders perceive the business. Incorporation can enhance credibility.

How to Set up a Legal Entity?

Setting up a legal entity was once complex and reserved only for the wealthy. But things have changed, and creating a legal entity is now a matter of a few clicks and filling out a form. Depending on your location, you can have a "real" business within a week or month.

Another thing to note is that creating a legal entity is location-specific. Each state in the US has its own laws governing business structures. For example, the process and requirements to form an LLC in California might differ significantly from those in Texas.

That being said, here's a brief overview of how to create a legal entity.

Evaluate Your Needs and Goals

This is the big picture. What is the goal and vision of Tom's Bakery? A mom-and-pop shop owned by a single person or a vision of a global conglomerate with thousands of outlets across the world? This will determine the legal structure. So give it some thought and consult with others, if possible.

Research Business Structure Options

Businesses are structured differently. In the United States, you have the following business structure options:

- **Sole Proprietorship**: Easy to set up and operate but offers no liability protection.

- **Partnership**: Suitable for businesses with co-founders; offers shared responsibility but also shared liability.

- **Limited Liability Company (LLC)**: Provides liability protection with pass-through taxation. It offers operational flexibility, making it a popular choice for small businesses.

- **Corporation (C Corporation or S Corporation)**: Provides liability protection and different tax options and can raise capital by issuing stock.

As already said, business structures are specific to the location. For instance, if you are in the UK, you may have a different structure. Thus, research your options before proceeding.

Asking ChatGPT

We're here to play smart, not hard. So why not let ChatGPT do the heavy lifting for you? Simply apply this prompt to get a detailed list of options available: *I'm building a new business [name] in [location]. List all the business structures available for the location. Also help me figure out the best option for my case. [Additional Business Information]*

Register the Business

Once you've zeroed in on the structure that's best for your case, the next step is to register the business. This requires you to choose and register a business name. So, if you're thinking of Tom's Bakery, make sure "Tom's Bakery" is available and not in use by another business. Check availability with the state and local authorities.

File the Necessary Documents

A key aspect of registering your business is filing the necessary documents. The information provided becomes the public record of the business. This transparency allows potential customers, investors, and creditors to assess the legitimacy and trustworthiness of the business.

The number and type of documents you need to file depends on the business structure opted for. For sole proprietorship, there's typically no formal registration required with the federal government. However, some documents might be needed depending on your specific situation, which can be easily taken care of online. For an LLC, you're required to file the Articles of Organization with the state's Secretary of State office. For a corporation, you need to file the Articles of Incorporation.

Asking ChatGPT

To get a broad picture of the type of documents you need to file, you can get assistance from ChatGPT. This is not an absolutely required step, but it is useful. Use this prompt to get a detailed answer: *I'm setting up a business [business name] in [location] under the structure [business structure]. Provide a list of documents I need to file to register the business.*

Obtain Required Permits and Licenses

Running a business requires you to have the necessary permits and licenses. These are specific to the business. For someone like Tom's Bakery in the food sector, here are some license requirements:

- **Food Business License**: Required for operating a bakery.

- **Health Department Permits**: Ensure compliance with local health and safety regulations.

- **Sales Tax Permit**: If applicable, for collecting sales tax.

- **Employer Identification Number (EIN)**: Obtain an EIN from the IRS for tax purposes.

Asking ChatGPT

Here is a sample prompt for you to obtain the process of obtaining permits and licenses in your area: *I'm looking to understand the process of obtaining business licenses and permits for my business in [Location]. Can you provide guidance on how to research the specific requirements, the application process, and any examples relevant to my area?*

Here's a prompt you can use to get a detailed list of permits and licenses required: *For [business name] in [business sector], provide a list of permits and licenses required to operate in [location]. Provide references for further reading.* Ask relevant questions, if needed, before answering.

Register for Taxes

As already said, you can't escape taxes. Part of running a business is filing for taxes on time. In the US, you'll be paying two types of taxes:

- **Federal Taxes**: Register with the IRS for federal tax obligations, such as any employment or income taxes.

- **State and Local Taxes**: Depending on the location, you need to register for state and local taxes, including sales tax and employment taxes.

Use this prompt for a better understanding of the taxes you need to file: *For a new business [business name] in [location] operating under [business structure], provide a list of applicable taxes. Provide references for further reading.*

Set up Business Banking and Financial Systems

The last step in setting up a legal structure is having a banking and financial system in place. You surely wouldn't want to transact using your personal account because it would only complicate tax filing and accounting. Here's what you need to do instead:

- **Open a Business Bank Account**: Keep personal and business finances separate.

- **Set up Accounting and Payroll Systems**: Ensure accurate financial management and compliance with tax obligations.

Building the Initial Team: The Second Step

Nowadays, everyone wants to be their own boss and start a business. That's a good thing for yourself and the world. We need more brave-hearted entrepreneurs.

But the picture looks disheartening when you look at the failure rate. According to an article from the U.S. bureau of Labor Statistics, only about 1 in 3 businesses that were started in 2013 were operating ten years later (*34.7 Percent Of Business Establishments Born In 2013 Were Still Operating In 2023*, 2024). However, you may have heard different statistics that are more discouraging than these.

One factor of these start up statistics relates to the importance of having the right team. According to Entropreneur **"23%** of startups mentioned team issues leading to failure" (*A New Study Reveals the 20 Factors That Predict Startup Failure: Do Any Apply to You?*, 2018). Some may not start with a team as they are solo entrepreneurs, but for those businesses that call for more people, it starts in the beginning. So, after registering your business, it is time to build an initial team.

Hiring is Specific to a Business

Every business hires differently based on their needs and requirements.

A sole entrepreneuer may not need anyone except the owner, while a C corporation will have to hire a CEO, CFO, CTO, and so on.

Therefore, you need to figure out what you need. Is Tom's Bakery going to be a multi-floor bakery location? Then, you may have to hire managers, front office staff, and bakers. Depending on the size, you may have to either hire for or outsource accounting, marketing, and food testing operations.

Hire for What You're Not Good At

As an entrepreneur, you have some strengths and weaknesses. Perhaps you're good at analyzing trends, marketing, selling, or programming. Your initial team should complement your skills and make up for what you're not good at. This creates a more well-rounded team that ensures you can successfully implement the business plan.

For Hiring, Company Statements Go a Long Way

Hiring is not about finding people to work for you. Hiring is about hiring the right people who align with your goals and values. On hiring a co-founder, Harj Taggar of Y Combinator, an American technology startup accelerator and venture capital firm, says, "I think you really want to look for is understanding the goals and values someone has for starting a company or wanting to do a startup" (*How to Find the Right Co-founder : YC Startup Library | Y Combinator*, n.d.).

This applies to employees as well. People want to work for a company that aligns with their values and principles, and its mission and vision statements communicate this to the world.

So, before you hire, jot down a strong and authentic mission and value statement that describes your business.

Asking ChatGPT

Here's a prompt you can use to generate a mission and vision statement for your business: *[Business name] is a [business segment] brand that focuses on [business USP]. Create 4-5 mission and vision statements that will appeal to consumers, employees, and investors alike.*

ChatGPT can also help you with hiring. Here is how to use it to extract information about hiring the right people for your business

I'm looking for guidance on how to hire the right people for my business in [Location]. Can you provide a concrete process for job posting, structuring interviews, and onboarding new employees, along with relevant examples?

Build a Strong Culture

Building the initial team can be a lengthy process, depending on the business size. And there's an entire study of Human Resources dedicated to that. That is beyond the scope of this book, but you must know that building a team requires building a strong culture. The culture is what keeps the team members together and drives teamwork. So, foster a culture of collaboration, transparency, and open communication.

Protecting Intellectual Property: Third Crucial Step

What if I told you that even executing your plan flawlessly might not guarantee success? No, I'm not talking about having the wrong plan in the first place. Assume you had the best plan and executed it to perfection, but you still failed. What went wrong? You didn't protect your assets. You didn't protect your intellectual property.

Intellectual property (IP) is like the crown jewel for many startups. It's the embodiment of their innovative ideas, creative concepts, and unique processes that give them a competitive edge.

Most businesses today are built on IPs. Coca-Cola is a billion-dollar business because of its "closely guarded secret recipe." Amazon is a trillion-dollar business because of its patents. The same goes for most Big Tech companies.

If these companies hadn't protected their assets, anyone could have replicated their products and sold them at a discount.

Therefore, to execute your plans, you need to protect your assets. If your business is built on a novel concept, you can patent or trademark it. Names are often trademarked so no one else can misuse them.

Asking ChatGPT

The exact process of trademarking or patenting a product is specific to the location. You can ask ChatGPT to get detailed information. Simply execute this prompt:

[Business name] is located in [location] and operates in the [sector]. It produces [prod-

uct] built on a [novel concept]. Explain the procedure to file a patent on [concept]. Provide resources for further reading.

Advertising and Marketing: Letting the Consumers Know You Exist

You have already created a marketing plan inside your business plan. That's the first thing you should execute because marketing attracts customers.

Once people are aware of your business, you need to convince them to choose you over competitors. Effective marketing strategies attract potential customers and convert them into paying clients. This might involve highlighting unique selling propositions, showcasing product benefits, or offering special introductory deals.

Asking ChatGPT

ChatGPT can help you prepare marketing materials. But you need to create prompts specific to the medium. For example, if you're creating flyers to be distributed at an event, here's a prompt you can use: *[Business name] is a newly opened [business type] in [location]. It specializes in [USP], and its target market is [target market]. Create a flyer to be distributed at a nearby event with the offer [offer details].*

Likewise, you need to recreate the prompts for digital ads, SEO, and other marketing mediums.

Reviewing Business Performance and Progress: Ensuring You're on the Right Path

A business plan is a roadmap but not set in stone. The key to executing a business plan is tracking key metrics continually and making adjustments along the way. Tracking key metrics allows you to see if you're on track to achieve your goals. For example, if your sales figures are consistently below projections, it indicates a need to revisit your marketing strategy or pricing structure.

Also, regularly reviewing metrics allows you to identify unexpected shifts in customer behavior, competitor actions, or industry trends. With this data, you can be proactive and adapt your business plan to stay ahead of the curve.

Last but not least, reviewing business performance helps with managing the business. Business guru Peter Drucker said best: "What gets measured gets managed" (Quriosity, 2014).

So, based on your business plan, set up Key Performance Indicators (KPIs) and measure them continually. Make adjustments as and when necessary and ask your team to follow suit.

Using ChatGPT to Refine and Update Your Plan

ChatGPT's capabilities aren't limited to creating a business plan. It can also help refine and update it.

ChatGPT's underlying model is continually updated with the latest data. Thus, it can refine the business plan with the most relevant information available. As a business owner, this is a valuable skill you can learn and master.

Addressing Changing Market Conditions

You're already aware of ChatGPT's capabilities of summarizing reports and trends. You can use this to stay on top of every trend that hits your industry.

For Tom's Bakery, ChatGPT can provide insights into the latest trends in the bakery industry, particularly in the plant-based segment, such as increasing demand for vegan products or new dietary preferences.

Start with a simple prompt like, *What are the latest trends in the [business sector] that are going to affect [your business niche]?*

You can then compare the results with the market research you already had. Upload the business plan document in ChatGPT's box and use this prompt: *Here's what [business name] knew till now. Summarize what is going to change based on the*

new emerging trends. Also, suggest ways [business name] can cope with those changes.
Update the plan accordingly.

Implementing Feedback Loops

Businesses get better over time as they learn more about their customers. Once you run marketing campaigns and get more customers, you should have feedback systems in place to collect their feedback, opinions, and insights into your business. And ChatGPT can help you create those systems.

Let's start with a simple feedback form. You can prompt ChatGPT to create a survey form to be sent to each customer's email. Here's one you can use: *[Business name] is conducting a feedback survey for customers who recently purchased [the product]. It will be conducted in an online form and a link will be sent to their email. Draft a questionnaire to capture their thoughts, opinions, and satisfaction levels.*

After collecting the data via the feedback system, you can direct ChatGPT to derive key insights from it. Use a simple prompt like, *Here are the responses collected from the survey [responses]. Summarize and list key insights from the responses. List areas where [business name] is doing well and where it needs to improve.*

Utilizing Performance Analytics

You can take the analysis a step further and get a more detailed view of not only the past or present but also the future. You can use ChatGPT to make predictive analyses about what the future holds.

For this, you need to prompt ChatGPT to perform a basic predictive analysis based on the information provided. So supplement it with all the information you have and use the prompt: *Based on the information provided, calculate expected sales in the coming three months.*

Key Takeaways

- Implementing a business plan starts with registering the business and forming a legal entity.

- You need to select a specific business structure, which varies based on location.

- Depending on the business niche, you must also obtain permits and licenses.

- The next important strategy is building a team that can implement the business plan. How to hire and the number of people to be hired depends on the specific organization.

- Things like the company's mission and vision statements and building a strong culture go a long way.

- If you're building a business with novel concepts, you must protect your assets by filing for IP.

- Start implementing the business plan through marketing and advertising. This attracts the first set of customers to your business.

- The success of business plan implementation also depends on how you track and adjust the metrics.

- Use ChatGPT to update and refine your business plan. This includes addressing the changing market conditions, implementing feedback loops, and utilizing performance analytics.

Things are starting to shape up. Your business is now a reality. In the next chapter, I'll guide you through putting everything into practice as we create a business plan from scratch.

Chapter Seven

Mapping the Future

A ll right, future Steve Jobs. We covered some crucial business concepts in this book. It wouldn't be wise to claim those are the only concepts you need to know to succeed. But what we've covered—business and finance planning, to be precise—are absolute basics. Get these two things wrong, and it wouldn't take long for your business to burst into flames (apologies for being blunt!).

Now, let's put everything into practice. After all, knowledge is one thing. Wisdom is another. And wisdom comes only from experience.

For the book, we used the example of Tom's Bakery. It's a fictional bakery startup we're trying to establish from scratch. The hero of our startup is a talented baker who prepares delicious cakes. He has worked in noted restaurants and bakeries but has never started his own business.

Well, we'll help our protagonist in his journey to stardom.

In this chapter, we'll follow through with what we have covered systematically. We'll be developing both a marketing and financial plan in one go. It's important to note that the process of creating a business plan, whether for offline or online ventures, remains largely similar. Our focus here will be on the offline bakery.

So, let's get started!

Tom's Bakery

The protagonist (let's call him Tom Harris) wants to start his bakery. We'll help him develop a business plan and a financial plan in one stretch using ChatGPT.

Provide the Situation and Task

ChatGPT can produce a wide range of tasks, but its effectiveness lies in specificity. To get great results, you need to be specific when asking it to generate anything. That's why you need to provide the situation or scenario.

It is important to include all necessary details clearly and concisely. Be mindful of word choice, as one word can change the result. Also, having too many extra words can confuse the AI into giving you an irrelevant answer.

Market Analysis

Let's start with market analysis. You should ask ChatGPT what it knows about the market and what data it has. Obviously, this will be far from complete or even accurate, but it's a good starting point.

So, for our Tom's Bakery, here's a prompt that provides both the situation and task:

Prompt:

> I want to start a bakery shop in Louisville, Kentucky. I was conducting market research on the area. List some information that would be helpful for my market research purposes. Present some stats and figures from authoritative sources.

Output:

> Conducting thorough market research is crucial for the success of your bakery shop. Here's a list of the types of information that would be helpful for your market research, along with some relevant statistics and figures from authoritative sources:

1. **Demographic Information**

   ○ **Population:** As of the latest estimates, Louisville, Kentucky, has a population of approximately 630,000 people.

   ○ **Age Distribution:** Understanding the age demographics can help tailor your product offerings. For example, younger demographics might prefer trendy, innovative baked goods, while older demographics might prefer traditional items.

   ○ **Income Levels:** The median household income in Louisville is around $53,000. Higher income areas might support premium products.

ChatGPT produced some incredible results, which included the following details:

- Demographic information

- Consumer preference and trends

- Competition analysis

- Economic indicators

- Real estate and location

- Regulatory environment

- Market size and potential

While most of the information was generic, it did provide a framework to work on. You need to conduct your own research and fill in the blanks.

Executive Summary

If you recall from the "The Basics of Writing a Business Plan" chapter, an executive summary is the first component of a business plan. So, the next step is to prepare an executive summary to be included in the business plan.

In this step, you need to provide all the details to ChatGPT. Just to summarize, here are the information you should have readily available:

- Business description

- Mission statement

- Product and service description

- Market analysis

- Financial highlights

- Growth projection

For now, you can skip the last two and provide the rest.

A prompt like the following can create this section for you: *Let's prepare an executive summary for my startup, Tom's Bakery. Use this information for this section: the bakery is founded by Tom Harris, a 34-year-old baker with 15 years of industry experience. Tom started his career at McDonald's and then worked at John's Bakery, the no.1 bakery in Louisville. Tom's Bakery will focus on artisan and plant-based bakery products. Our mission is to make plant-based bakery products mainstream in Louisville and Kentucky. Use the market analysis data prepared above along with the attachment. Make the section crisp and information-rich.*

Note how this section is thorough. You're encouraged to include more specifics if available. You may also be wondering about the attachment. The attachment in the above prompt is the completed market research document. ChatGPT allows you to upload text documents to generate responses.

This should provide you with a pretty good draft for the executive summary section. Edit as per your requirements to make it final.

Strategy

We're done with the analysis and executive summary. Now, onto strategy creation.

Just like you did with market analysis, you let ChatGPT map out a strategy for you. Again, this is not going to be exhaustive or complete. But it'll give you a good framework to work on.

Prompt:

Based on the information provided above, help Tom's Bakery create a strategy to dominate the local market. Prepare a cost-effective strategy that doesn't require much capital investment upfront. Also, the business should start generating revenue from the first day itself and become profitable within a year.

Output:

To help Tom's Bakery dominate the local market in Louisville, Kentucky, we'll focus on a cost-effective strategy that emphasizes immediate revenue generation and profitability within a year. Here's a step-by-step plan:

1. **Market Positioning and Niche Focus**
   Niche Selection:

   - **Artisanal and Specialty Breads:** Tap into the trend for artisanal and specialty breads, such as sourdough, whole grain, and gluten-free options.

   - **Local Ingredients:** Emphasize the use of locally sourced ingredients, which can attract health-conscious and community-oriented customers.

Again, ChatGPT did an awesome job and generated a thorough strategy to work on. In the response, it generated 6sections for strategy:

1. Market positioning and niche focus

2. Location and setup

3. Product offering and pricing strategy

4. Marketing and customer acquisition

5. Operational efficiency

6. Revenue stream and diversification

As any businessperson will tell you, each area is an important component of business strategy. As Tom Bakery is targeting a local market, location, and setup become even more critical in this case.

Toward the end, ChatGPT also generated a financial projection and profitability section:

Output:

Financial Projections and Profitability
Initial Costs:

- Equipment and setup: $10,000

- Lease and renovations: $5,000

- Marketing and promotions: $2,000

- Initial inventory: $3,000

- Miscellaneous: $2,000

- **Total Initial Investment:** $22,000

Monthly Operating Costs:
- Rent: $1,500

- Utilities: $300

- Ingredients: $2,000

- Staffing: $4,000

- Marketing: $500

- Miscellaneous: $300

While detailed, I found this unrealistic, especially for a location like Louisville. The per-square-foot rate varies from $15 to $50, depending on several factors. So let's specify the same to ChatGPT with this:

Prompt:

Recreate the Financial Projections and Profitability section. Equipment and setup is $40,000. The lease and renovation cost is $50,000. Marketing and promotion is $15,000. Initial inventory is $10,000. Miscellaneous is $10,000. Change the numbers accordingly.

Output:

Financial Projections and Profitability
The financial projections for Tom's Bakery include a detailed overview of initial investments, projected revenue streams, and estimated expenses. The primary goal is to achieve profitability within the first year of operations by carefully managing costs and optimizing revenue.
Initial Investment Breakdown
1. **Equipment and Setup:** $40,000
   (Includes ovens, mixers, refrigerators, kitchen utensils, and POS system)

1. **Lease and Renovations:** $50,000

   (Includes lease deposit, interior design, and necessary modifications)

2. **Marketing and Promotion:** $15,000

   (Initial advertising campaign, social media marketing, website development)

3. **Initial Inventory:** $10,000

   (Raw ingredients, packaging materials, and other supplies)

4. **Miscellaneous:** $10,000

   (Licenses, permits, insurance, utilities setup, legal and professional fees)

Total Initial Investment: $125,000

You may have to refine this information and work on it a few times. With some additions and tweaking, your strategy section will be ready.

Marketing and Sales Plan

In the above example, ChatGPT reiterated that "Marketing and customer acquisition" is an essential element of strategy. Therefore, we need to expand on it and make it more thorough and detailed.

Again, let's ask ChatGPT to generate a simple response on marketing.

Prompt: *Create a marketing plan as well. Based on the details provided, generate a marketing plan that details how Tom's Bakery can acquire customers. The monthly budget for marketing is $15,000.*

In this prompt, setting a precise budget did the trick. It generated a thorough marketing plan and even suggested how much money to devote to each medium. Here's how it broke down the $15,000 marketing budget.

Total Monthly Marketing Budget: $15,000

Marketing Channels and Tactics

1. **Digital Marketing** (40% of budget: $6,000)

   ○ **Social Media Marketing** ($2,000): Utilize platforms like Instagram, Facebook, and Twitter to showcase products, share customer testimonials, and run promotions. Partner with local influencers for greater reach.

   ○ **Search Engine Marketing (SEM)** ($1,500): Invest in Google Ads to increase visibility for local searches related to baked goods and bakeries.

   ○ **Content Marketing and SEO** ($1,000): Maintain a blog on the bakery's website featuring recipes, baking tips, and stories about the bakery. Optimize the website for search engines.

   ○ **Email Marketing** ($500): Build an email list to send newsletters, promotional offers, and updates about new products.

2. **Traditional Marketing** (30% of budget: $4,500)

   ○ **Local Advertising** ($2,000): Advertise in local newspapers, magazines, and radio stations to reach a wider audience.

   ○ **Flyers and Posters** ($1,000): Distribute flyers and place posters in high-traffic areas such as community centers, local businesses, and bulletin boards.

   ○ **Local Events and Sponsorships** ($1,500): Sponsor local events, fairs, and festivals to engage with the community and provide product samples.

3. **In-Store Promotions** (15% of budget: $2,250)

   ○ **Grand Opening Event** ($1,000): Host a grand opening with special discounts, free samples, and live demonstrations.

   ○ **Loyalty Program** ($750): Develop a loyalty program offering rewards for repeat purchases, such as discounts or free items.

- **Seasonal and Holiday Specials** ($500): Create limited-time offers and themed products during holidays and special occasions.

4. **Public Relations and Community Engagement** (10% of budget: $1,500)

- **Press Releases** ($500): Issue press releases to local media outlets about new products, events, and achievements.

- **Community Involvement** ($1,000): Engage in community service and charity events to build goodwill and brand reputation.

5. **Online Sales and Delivery Promotion** (5% of budget: $750)

- **Online Ordering Incentives** ($750): Offer discounts or free delivery for first-time online orders to encourage adoption of the service.

Sales Strategy

- **In-Store Sales**: Focus on creating a welcoming atmosphere with friendly staff and high-quality products. Use in-store displays and signage to highlight daily specials and new items.

- **Online Orders and Home Deliveries**: Develop a user-friendly website with an easy ordering process. Partner with local delivery services for timely and reliable deliveries.

- **Custom Orders and Catering**: Promote custom orders and catering services for events, businesses, and special occasions. Offer personalized consultations and tastings.

- **Cross-Promotions**: Collaborate with local businesses and cafes to cross-promote products and expand customer reach.

Measurement and Evaluation

- Key Performance Indicators (KPIs):

- Monthly sales growth (in-store and online)

- Customer foot traffic and online orders

- Social media engagement (likes, shares, comments)

- Email open and click-through rates

- Customer retention rate and loyalty program participation

• Monitoring and Adjustments:

- Track and analyze KPIs monthly to assess the effectiveness of marketing strategies

- Adjust marketing tactics based on performance data, market trends, and customer feedback

It clearly stated how much to spend on each channel and provided the KPIs to track. That's a great response with minimal work to do.

Management and Organization Description

Next up, let's prepare the management and organization section. This is going to be easy. Just provide all the info and ask ChatGPT to prepare the section for you. As a refresher, here's what the section needs:

• Organizational structure (hierarchy within the company or if it's a sole proprietorship)

• Leadership team

• Advisors and board members

• Staffing plan

• Company culture

• HR policies

Depending on how much info you have available or is needed for this section, you should design a prompt accordingly. Here's a sample to inspire you:

Prompt:

The business plan needs a management and organization description. So please create a section to be used in the business plan for Tom's Bakery. Tom's Bakery is founded by Tom Harris, and he is the sole owner. The founding team includes Tom and his wife, Sally, who will serve as the accountant and bookkeeper. The bakery plans to hire 4-5 personnel in the first month of opening. The company culture will be cutthroat in the initial months, but it will be rewarding, too.

Output:

Management and Organization Description
Founder and Ownership:

Tom's Bakery is founded and solely owned by Tom Harris. As the driving force behind the bakery, Tom brings his passion for baking and entrepreneurial spirit to the forefront of this new venture. His vision is to create a bakery that not only offers high-quality, artisanal baked goods but also becomes a beloved part of the Louisville community.

Founding Team:

- **Tom Harris, Founder and CEO:** Tom oversees the overall operations of the bakery, including product development, quality control, and customer relations. His hands-on approach ensures that every aspect of the business meets the high standards he has set.

- **Sally Harris, Accountant and Bookkeeper:** Sally brings her expertise in accounting and financial management to the team. She is responsible for managing the bakery's finances, including budgeting, payroll, and financial reporting. Sally's meticulous attention to detail ensures that the financial health of Tom's Bakery is well-maintained.

As expected, ChatGPT created a well-crafted section for the business plan. It generated the following sections:

- Founding team

- Staffing plan

- Company culture

- Organizational structure

Products and Service Description

Next comes the products Tom's Bakery has to offer. For this section, you provide all the intended products you intend to sell and ask ChatGPT to write a product and service description.

Here's an example prompt:

> Create a product and service description section for the business plan. Initially, Tom's Bakery will sell ten products across two categories: everyday items and delicacies. Under everyday items, there are buns, muffins, sweet rolls, biscuits, and loaf bread. Under delicacy, the bakery will have dishes from around the world. The five products are Japanese rice cake, Indian halwa, Thai lod chong, Belgian speculaas, and Brazilian pao de queijo.

ChatGPT did a great job here and even expanded the products on its own:

Output:

1. Everyday Items
Our Everyday Items category features classic baked goods that are perfect for daily consumption. These products are designed to meet the needs of customers looking for delicious, fresh, and convenient options for breakfast, snacks, or any time of the day.

- **Buns:** Soft and fluffy buns available in a variety of flavors, including plain, whole wheat, and sesame. Perfect for sandwiches or as a stand-alone snack.

- **Muffins:** Moist and flavorful muffins made with the finest ingredients.

Available in popular varieties such as blueberry, chocolate chip, and banana nut.

- **Sweet Rolls:** Deliciously sweet rolls, including classic cinnamon rolls, sticky buns, and fruit-filled rolls. A delightful treat for breakfast or dessert.

- **Biscuits:** Flaky and buttery biscuits, ideal for pairing with coffee or tea. Available in both savory (cheese, herb) and sweet (honey, cinnamon) options.

- **Loaf Breads:** Freshly baked loaf breads in various styles, including white, whole grain, rye, and sourdough. Perfect for sandwiches, toast, or as an accompaniment to meals.

2. Delicacies
Our Delicacies category showcases popular items from around the world, offering customers a chance to experience a variety of international flavors and textures.

Competitive Analysis

Another integral component of business planning is competitor analysis. And Chat-GPT can help you with this. Start with a simple prompt asking it to draft a competitor analysis:

Prompt:

Now, let's create a competitive analysis section for the business plan. List the main bakeries operating in Louisville, Kentucky, along with their details. Analyze the local market and provide a SWOT analysis. List credible sources for further reading.

Output:

Competitive Analysis
Main Bakeries Operating in Louisville, Kentucky
   1. **Heitzman Traditional Bakery and Deli**

- **Details:** Established in 1891, Heitzman offers a variety of baked goods, including cakes, pies, cookies, and deli items. Known for its traditional recipes and long-standing reputation in the community.

- **Location:** Multiple locations in Louisville.

- **Specialties:** Wedding cakes, donuts, and bread.

2. Nord's Bakery
- **Details:** A popular local bakery known for its donuts, pastries, and custom cakes. It has a loyal customer base and a reputation for friendly service

ChatGPT drafted a brief section listing the main bakeries operating in the city. It listed their name, details, location, and specialties and then prepared a SWOT analysis for Tom's Bakery and listed sources for further reading. You should work 30 to 40 minutes to get this section done.

Operations Plan

Lastly, we're supposed to add an operation plan for Tom's Bakery. This will serve as a how-to guide for the managers and employees in the early days. Here's a prompt to generate this section:

Prompt:

Create an operations plan to be included in the business plan. This will serve as a guide for managers and employees. Explain how Tom's Bakery should work in the early days. The focus is on efficiency and faster work. Tom's Bakery will source raw materials from vendors and prepare everything in-house fresh every morning. It will then be stored in ovens and refrigerators to keep everything fresh till night hours.

Output:

Operations Plan for Tom's Bakery

Objective:

To ensure efficient, high-quality production and service that maximizes customer satisfaction and operational efficiency.

Daily Operations Overview

1. **Early Morning Preparations**

5:00 AM - 7:00 AM: Baking and Preparation

- **Baking Team Arrives:** Bakers and kitchen staff begin their shift.

- **Mixing and Preparation:** Start preparing doughs, batters, and fillings for all baked goods. This includes kneading bread dough, mixing cake batter, and preparing fillings for pastries.

- **Baking:** Utilize the ovens to bake the items. Buns, muffins, sweet rolls, biscuits, and loaf breads will be the priority, followed by delicacies.

- **Cooling and Storage:** Once baked, items are cooled on racks. After cooling, they are transferred to display cases or stored in refrigerators and ovens to maintain freshness.

2. **7:00 AM - 8:00 AM: Opening Preparations**

Here, ChatGPT prepared a thorough operation plan by hours of operation. It specified the early morning preparations all the way up to closing procedures, along with vendor and supply chain management protocols. Toward the end, ChatGPT suggested KPIs to track sales volume, customer satisfaction, waste management, and operational efficiency.

Financial Planning

Now, let's prepare the section's crucial element using ChatGPT: a financial plan. As a refresher, here are the key components of a financial plan discussed earlier:

- Revenue forecast

- Expenses

- Cash flow

So, let's put these into a comprehensive financial plan.

Starting with expenses, here's a prompt we used earlier to generate an expense plan; you can reuse it (with some tweaks) to get the desired results for expenses:

Prompt:

Prepare an expense plan for Tom's Bakery. Our target audience includes local residents, office workers, and families, but we will also do online orders and home deliveries. Figure out the main expenses that will be associated with my business that I should consider as part of long-term financial planning. Use the information generated till now for more context.

Output:

Initial Investment Breakdown
1. **Equipment and Setup:**
   Original: $40,000
   Adjusted (20% increase): $48,000
   (Includes ovens, mixers, refrigerators, kitchen utensils, POS system, etc.)

2. **Lease Deposit:**
   Original: $50,000
   Adjusted: $40,000

3. Renovation and Interior Design:
Original: $50,000
Adjusted: $10,000

4. Marketing and Promotion:
Original: $15,000
Adjusted (15% increase): $17,250
(Initial advertising campaign, social media marketing, website development, etc.)

With the expense plan in place, let's move to the next component: cash flow. If you recall, we have already created a cash flow statement in Step 2 of planning, which is defining revenue streams. Here is the prompt used (with some modifications):

Prompt:

Tom Bakery is planning the different revenue streams. We know that at the start, in-store sales will be the main source of revenue, but we do plan to push for online orders and home deliveries slowly. Other than that, what ideas should we consider? Prepare a thorough cash flow statement to be used in financial planning.

Output:

Annual Startup Cost
The initial startup costs for Tom's Bakery encompass all necessary expenses to set up and launch the business. These include equipment, lease and renovation costs, initial marketing efforts, inventory, and miscellaneous expenditures.
Initial Startup Cost Breakdown:
1. Equipment and Setup: $48,000
(Includes essential bakery equipment such as ovens, mixers, refrigerators, kitchen utensils, and a point-of-sale system)

2. Lease Deposit: $40,000
(Covers the initial security deposit for leasing the bakery premises)

3. **Renovation and Interior Design:** $10,000
   (Includes interior modifications, décor, signage, and minor construction as needed)

4. **Marketing and Promotion:** $17,250
   (Initial expenses for launching advertising campaigns, social media marketing, and setting up a website)

5. **Initial Inventory:** $12,000
   (Costs for acquiring the first batch of raw ingredients, packaging materials, and other necessary supplies)

ChatGPT suggested other revenue sources, such as wholesale partnerships, subscription boxes, baking classes and workshops, and merchandising, that you can consider and include in your financial plan.

Time for the last component: revenue forecast. This will be tricky because forecasting requires data, but you don't have any at this stage. In such cases, it's best to provide a rough estimate and let ChatGPT do its job. Also, recall the fact that we discussed five different financial forecasts, namely, sales, cash flow, expenses, scenario planning, and sensitivity analysis.

Here's an example prompt we're reusing from an earlier chapter for this case:

Prompt:

We need to do some financial forecasting for Tom's Bakery. We have no idea how to make financial forecasts, and I don't even have historical data to look at because my business is only about to start. How can I plan for sales forecasting?

Output:

Example Sales Forecast

Everyday Items

Product	Daily Sales (units)	Price per Unit ($)	Daily Revenue ($)
Buns	100	2	200
Muffins	100	3	300
Sweet Rolls	100	2.5	250
Biscuits	100	2	200
Loaf Breads	100	4	400
Total	500		1,350

Delicacies

Product	Daily Sales (units)	Price per Unit ($)	Daily Revenue ($)
Japanese Rice Cake	50	5	250
Indian Halwa	50	6	300
Thai Lod Chong	50	5.5	275
Belgian Speculaas	50	4.5	225
Brazilian Pao de Queijo	50	5	250
Total	250		1,300

Here, ChatGPT prepared a financial forecast based on certain assumptions. While not accurate, it's a benchmark you can use for forecasting future sales and revenue numbers. It also generated the first-year financial forecast template for you to keep track of metrics.

- Factor in the introduction of online orders, home deliveries, and custom orders starting in the second quarter.

Financial Forecast Example

First Year Sales Forecast (Assuming Growth)

Month	In-Store Sales ($)	Online & Delivery Sales ($)	Custom Orders ($)	Total Sales ($)
January	79,500	0	0	79,500
February	83,475	0	0	83,475
March	87,648	0	0	87,648
April	92,030	1,000	2,000	95,030
May	96,631	2,000	3,000	101,631
June	101,462	3,000	4,000	108,462
July	106,535	4,000	5,000	115,535
August	111,862	5,000	6,000	122,862
September	117,455	6,000	7,000	130,455
October	123,327	7,000	8,000	138,327
November	129,493	8,000	9,000	146,493
December	135,968	9,000	10,000	154,968
Total	1,265,386	45,000	54,000	1,364,386

Message ChatGPT

Include the sections that you deem fit in your financial planning.

Now, we're done with the business and financial planning with ChatGPT. Depending on how many edits you have to make, you can get it done within a day or two. That's significant time savings, given that you may have to spend a week or so otherwise.

Key Takeaways

Dave Ramsey, the self-help finance guru, is renowned for his 7 Baby Steps to Financial Freedom. Many people have attained financial freedom simply by following his steps. This suggests you don't have to reinvent the wheel to succeed. Just follow and replicate a tried-and-tested methodology to walk your way to success.

The same applies to when you're starting a business. Running after the shiny objects and trying dozens of different things can be quite tempting. But this distracts you from what truly matters: planning and execution.

As reiterated numerous times throughout this book, business planning keeps you on track to success, and financial planning ensures you don't run out of money before you reach success. So, it's wise to focus more on getting these two right.

Getting these right also means tracking and updating them as the business landscape changes. That's what separates the successful from the amateurs.

So, while we've done the first part of putting a business and financial plan together, the second part hinges on you. You don't have to tread the waters alone, though. This book touches on how to keep the plan updated using ChatGPT. So you don't have to look any further. You have all you need to make your business a success at your disposal. What matters is being disciplined enough to follow the advice discussed.

On the next page, I've attached a sample business plan for Tom's Bakery, which ChatGPT generated based on the inputs I provided.

Chapter Eight

Crafting a Winning Plan Case Study

I n this case study of the fictional Tom's Bakery, you will see how a completed business plan may look. Remember it is critical to always fact-check your numbers for your niche and location as they can vary widely.

Sample Tom's Bakery Business Plan

Executive Summary

Business Name: Tom's Bakery **Owner**: Tom Harris **Location**: Louisville, Kentucky **Business Concept**: Tom's Bakery offers a unique selection of everyday baked goods and international delicacies. The bakery aims to provide high-quality, freshly prepared items, catering to local residents, office workers, families, and tourists. The business will prioritize in-store sales initially, with plans to expand into online orders and home deliveries.

Business Objectives

1. **Revenue**: Achieve monthly sales of $70,000 in the first month, increasing to over $100,000 by the end of the first year.

2. **Customer Base**: Establish a loyal customer base of at least 1,000 regular customers by the end of the first year.

3. **Profitability**: Reach profitability within the first year of operations.

Market Analysis

Target Market:

- Local residents

- Office workers

- Families

- Tourists

- Online customers

Market Research Highlights:

- **Demographics**: A diverse population with a significant number of young professionals and families.

- **Local Competition**: Several established bakeries with varying specialties. Tom's Bakery will differentiate by offering a mix of everyday items and unique international delicacies.

- **Trends**: Growing demand for convenient and unique food options, with an increasing trend toward online ordering and delivery.

Products and Services

Product Categories:

1. **Everyday Items**: Buns, muffins, sweet rolls, biscuits, loaf breads.

2. **Delicacies**: Japanese rice cake, Indian halwa, Thai lod chong, Belgian speculaas, Brazilian Pao de queijo.

Service Offerings:

- In-store sales

- Online orders and home deliveries

- Custom orders and catering for special events

Management and Organization

Founder and Owner: Tom Harris

- **Role**: Overseeing daily operations, product development, and customer relations.

Co-Founder: Sally Harris (Tom's Wife)

- **Role**: Accountant and bookkeeper, managing financial records, payroll, and budgeting.

Staff:

- 4-5 employees (bakers, front-of-house staff)

- Part-time assistants during peak hours

Company Culture: Initially competitive, with a strong emphasis on efficiency and customer satisfaction, rewarding high performers with incentives.

Marketing and Sales Strategy

Marketing Budget: $15,000 per month

Marketing Channels:

- **Digital Marketing**: Social media, search engine marketing, content marketing, and email marketing.

- **Traditional Marketing**: Local advertising, flyers, posters, local events, and sponsorships.

- **In-Store Promotions**: Grand opening events, loyalty programs, and seasonal specials.

- **Public Relations**: Press releases and community engagement.

Sales Strategy:

- Focus on high-quality products and exceptional customer service.

- Gradually expand to online sales and custom orders.

- Utilize cross-promotions with local businesses.

Operations Plan

Daily Operations:

- Sourcing raw materials from local vendors.

- Fresh preparation of baked goods every morning.

- Storing products in ovens and refrigerators to maintain freshness throughout the day.

- Efficient workflow for staff to ensure quick service and product turnover.

Operating Hours:

- Open daily from 7:00 AM to 9:00 PM, with flexible hours during holidays and special events.

Expense Plan

Initial Startup Costs:

1. **Equipment and Setup**: $48,000

2. **Lease Deposit**: $40,000

3. **Renovation and Interior Design**: $10,000

4. **Marketing and Promotion**: $17,250

5. **Initial Inventory**: $12,000

6. **Miscellaneous**: $12,000 **Total Initial Investment**: $139,250

Monthly Operational Expenses:

1. **Rent and Utilities**: $3,600

2. **Salaries and Wages**: $18,055

3. **Raw Materials and Inventory**: $4,200

4. **Marketing and Advertising**: $1,725

5. **Operational Expenses**: $805

6. **Insurance and Professional Fees**: $600

7. **Online Orders and Deliveries**: $600

8. **Total Monthly Operational Expenses**: $29,585

Financial Projections and Profitability

Projected First-Year Revenue: $1,202,192 **Projected First-Year Expenses**: $355,020 **Initial Investment**: $139,250 **Projected Profit (First Year)**: $707,922

Break-Even Point: Expected within 6-7 months of operation, based on current sales and expense projections.

Financial Forecasting and Cash Flow

Revenue Streams:

1. **In-Store Sales**: Primary source of revenue, expected steady growth.

2. **Online Orders and Home Deliveries**: Incremental revenue growth starting from the second quarter.

3. **Custom Orders and Catering**: Additional revenue, especially during holidays and special events.

Sales Growth:

- Initial focus on building in-store sales, followed by online expansion and diversification of services.

Cost Management:

- Monitor and adjust expenses regularly to maintain profitability.

This business plan is a comprehensive guide for Tom's Bakery's management and staff, outlining the business's vision, strategies, and financial outlook. It will be regularly reviewed and updated to reflect the business's performance and market conditions.

One-Page Business Plan for Investors

Tom's Bakery: One-Page Business Plan

Owner: Tom Harris **Location**: Louisville, Kentucky **Business Concept**: Tom's Bakery offers a unique mix of everyday baked goods and international delicacies. The bakery caters to local residents, office workers, families, and tourists, with a focus on high-quality, freshly prepared items.

Business Objectives

1. **Achieve monthly sales of $70,000 in the first month, growing to over $100,000 by year-end.**

2. **Establish a loyal customer base of at least 1,000 regulars within the first year.**

3. **Reach profitability within the first year.**

Market Opportunity

- **Target Market**: A diverse demographic, including young professionals, families, and tourists.

- **Competitive Edge**: Unique product offerings, including international delicacies not widely available in Louisville.

- **Growth Potential**: Increasing demand for convenient, quality baked goods and a growing trend toward online ordering.

Products and Services

- **Everyday Items**: Buns, muffins, sweet rolls, biscuits, loaf breads.

- **International Delicacies**: Japanese rice cake, Indian halwa, Thai lod chong, Belgian speculaas, Brazilian Pao de queijo.

- **Services**: In-store sales, online orders, home deliveries, custom orders, and catering.

Marketing and Sales Strategy

- **Budget**: $15,000 per month.

- **Channels**: Digital marketing (social media, SEO, email), traditional marketing (local ads, events), and in-store promotions.

- **Sales Focus**: Drive in-store traffic initially, expand online presence, and offer custom catering services.

Financial Projections

- **Initial Investment**: $139,250 *(Equipment: $48,000, Lease Deposit: $40,000, Renovation: $10,000, Marketing: $17,250, Inventory: $12,000, Miscellaneous: $12,000)*

- **Projected First-Year Revenue**: $1,202,192

- **Projected First-Year Expenses**: $355,020

- **Estimated Profit**: $707,922

- **Break-Even Point**: Expected within 6-7 months

Management Team

- **Tom Harris**: Owner and Operator

- **Sally Harris**: Accountant and Bookkeeper

- **Team**: 4-5 employees, including bakers and front-of-house staff

Investment Opportunity

Tom's Bakery seeks investors to support its initial setup and operational costs. The business promises a unique market position with substantial growth potential and a clear path to profitability. Investors will benefit from a structured approach to cost management and revenue generation, ensuring a steady return on investment.

For further details and investment discussions, please contact Tom Harris at [contact information].

In summary, Tom's Bakery case study can act as a guide for writing your own master business plan. Each area should be thoughtfully planned out from market analysis and financial projections, along with a one page business plan for investors. The plan shows the importance of properly planning and preparing as it prompts business owners think through possible problems and solutions. Because the sample plan is detailed, it brings to light business objectives and strategies, at the same time it provides a snapshot view for potential investors with all the necessary information. Having a well organized business plan propels the business endevor to growth and profits. You can use this case study as a model for realistic financial goals.

Conclusion

C ongratulations on reaching the end of this journey! You're now equipped with the knowledge and tools to navigate the exciting yet challenging world of starting a business. Together, we've explored the importance of business planning, explored financial considerations, and discovered how AI assistants like ChatGPT can be your secret weapons.

It's perfectly natural if you don't remember or master every detail covered in this book. I faced the same challenge when crafting my first business plan. To overcome this, I recommend revisiting the chapters periodically. Revision helps refine your ideas and ensures your plan remains adaptable as your business evolves. Think of it as sharpening a saw; each review session strengthens your understanding and makes your plans more effective.

Keep this book handy as a trusted reference guide, and schedule regular review sessions to revisit the concepts and update your plan as needed. However, remember that reading and rereading alone won't achieve your goals. Just as sharpening an axe is only useful if you actually chop down a tree, the real magic happens when you take action. Implement the strategies you've learned and turn your vision into reality.

Expect bumps along the way—moments of doubt and unexpected hurdles. These are opportunities to learn and grow. Celebrate small wins, learn from mistakes, and, most importantly, stay connected to the passion that sparked your entrepreneurial journey. Surround yourself with supportive individuals, mentors who believe in your dream, and fellow entrepreneurs who understand the rollercoaster ride of launching a business.

Success rarely happens overnight. It's a marathon, not a sprint. Embrace the journey, stay focused, and be willing to adapt your plans as you learn and grow. With dedication, perseverance, and the insights from this book, you have the potential to turn your entrepreneurial dream into a thriving reality. Take a deep breath, believe in yourself, and get ready to make your mark on the world.

Finally, if you found this book helpful, please share it with others who might benefit from it. Your support can make a difference for more aspiring entrepreneurs. I'd also love to hear your thoughts—it takes less than a minute to make a real difference by leaving a review on Amazon to let others know how this book helped you. Now, go out there and turn your dreams into reality!

LEAVE A REVIEW!

References

10 characteristics of successful entrepreneurs | HBS Online. (2020, July 7). Business Insights Blog. https://online.hbs.edu/blog/post/characteristics-of-successful-entrepreneurs

13+ Reflective Journal Templates - PDF. (2024, March 21). Template.net. https://www.template.net/business/journal-templates/reflective-journal-template/

2xYou Remote Executive Assistant Services. (2023, August 13). How to use ChatGPT for operations as an entrepreneur. LinkedIn. https://www.linkedin.com/pulse/how-use-chatgpt-operations-entrepreneur-2xyou/

34.7 percent of business establishments born in 2013 were still operating in 2023. (2024, January 12). U.S. Bureau of Labor Statistics. Retrieved September 12, 2024, from https://www.bls.gov/opub/ted/2024/34-7-percent-of-business-establishments-born-in-2013-were-still-operating-in-2023.htm

5 examples of responsible technology: a new initiative puts AI to work for communities. (2024, January 17). World Economic Forum. https://www.weforum.org/agenda/2024/01/responsible-technology-ai-initiative/

7 Helpful ChatGPT prompts for growth strategies and scaling the business. (n.d.). Bizway Resources. https://www.bizway.io/blog/7-helpful-chatgpt-prompts-for-growth-strategies-and-scaling-the-business

7 Helpful ChatGPT prompts for risk management and contingency planning. (n.d.). Bizway Resources. https://www.bizway.io/blog/7-helpful-chatgpt-prompts-for-risk-management-and-contingency-planning

911CyberSecurity.com. (2023, March 6). Differentiate your brand with a unique selling proposition: ChatGPT and Bard tailored solutions. 911CyberSecuri-

ty. https://911cybersecurity.com/differentiate-your-brand-with-a-unique-selling-pro position-chatgpt-and-bard-tailored-solutions-for-different-industries/amp/

A guide to data driven decision making: what it is, its importance, & how to implement it. (n.d.). Tableau. https://www.tableau.com/learn/articles/data-driven-decision-ma king

A new study reveals the 20 factors that predict startup failure: Do any apply to you? (2018, February 5). Entrepreneur. https://www.entrepreneur.com/leadership/a-new-s tudy-reveals-the-20-factors-that-predict-startup/308447

A step-by-step guide to using ChatGPT to build a simple risk application. (2023, June 12). Numerix. https://www.numerix.com/resources/webinar/step-by-step-guide-to-usi ng-chatgpt-to-build-a-simple-risk-application

Adams, R. (2024, March 15). 45+ ChatGPT Prompts for Business Plans. AI Habit. https://aihabit.net/chatgpt-prompts-for-business-plan/

Adamson, D. (2023, July 11). Understanding the power of risk Management Chat-GPT prompts for business success. LinkedIn. https://www.linkedin.com/pulse/underst anding-power-risk-management-chatgpt-prompts-business-adamson/

Adapt or die: eight businesses that transformed their business models to survive. (n.d.). Hiscox. https://www.hiscox.co.uk/broker/about-hiscox/news/adapt-or-die-eight-busine sses-transformed-their-business-models-survive

AI + you: How to use ChatGPT for content creation. (n.d.). Learn at Microsoft Cre-ate. https://create.microsoft.com/en-us/learn/articles/how-to-use-chatgpt-for-content-c reation

Akiko Design. (2023, October 17). WORKING WITHOUT a BUSINESS PLAN: ODDS OF SUCCESS! - Kreston Pedabo. Kreston Pedabo. https://krestonpedabo.com /working-without-a-business-plan-odds-of-success/

Alagar. (2023, December 11). The business benefits of artificial intelligence. IABAC®. https://iabac.org/blog/business-benefits-of-artificial-intelligence

Alexander, L. (2024, July 26). How I write SMART goals and make them a reality [+ free SMART goal templates]. HubSpot. https://blog.hubspot.com/marketing/how -to-write-a-smart-goal-template

Amar, A. (2024, July 4). 5 Keys to Budgeting and Forecasting Successfully. Datarails. https://www.datarails.com/budgeting-and-forecasting-top-keys/

Araby. A. (2023, July 31). Navigating the Funding Maze: A survival guide for AI startups. LinkedIn. https://www.linkedin.com/pulse/navigating-funding-maze-survi val-guide-ai-startups-araby-ai/

Arey, D. (2023, April 8). Starting out in Project Management: Leveraging ChatGPT for Risk Management. LinkedIn. https://www.linkedin.com/pulse/starting-out-proje ct-management-leveraging-chatgpt-arey-ieng-miet/

Baker, K. (2023, October 19). How to use ChatGPT for business growth: 10 prompt examples. Podium. https://www.podium.com/article/ways-to-use-chatgpt-for-business/

Barresi, B. J., OD PhD. (2023, July 26). Leveraging ChatGPT to grow value for social enterprises. Medium. https://avplaybook.com/leveraging-chatgpt-to-grow-value-for-s ocial-enterprises-3e01a400d26e

Barresi, B. J., OD PhD. (2023, July 30). Leveraging ChatGPT to build social enter- prises - Accelerate Impact Playbook. Medium. https://avplaybook.com/leveraging-cha tgpt-to-build-social-enterprise-fe0407f53438

Barresi, B. J., OD PhD. (2024, January 30). ChatGPT use cases for social enterprise leaders - Accelerate Impact PlayBook. Medium. https://avplaybook.com/chatgpt-use-c ases-for-social-enterprise-leaders-6d1d076538f3

Bashar, S. D. (2023, July 30). Building a profitable Chat GPT Business: success stories and tips in 2023. LinkedIn. https://www.linkedin.com/pulse/building-profitable-cha t-gpt-business-success-stories-bashar/

Bee, G. (2023, May 29). What are incubators, accelerators, venture capitalists, angel investors, and family offices? LinkedIn. https://www.linkedin.com/pulse/what-incub ators-accelerators-venture-capitalists-angel-investors/

Bennett, K. (2023, July 31). *How to make a budget using ChatGPT. Bankrate.* https ://www.bankrate.com/banking/savings/how-to-make-budget-with-chatgpt/

Blank, S. (2023, April 17). *AI and ChatGPT will revolutionize customer discovery. Entrepreneur & Innovation Exchange.* https://eiexchange.com/content/ai-and-chatg pt-will-revolutionize-customer-discovery

Blystone, D. (2024, June 24). *Who is Elon Musk? Investopedia.* https://www.investop edia.com/articles/personal-finance/061015/how-elon-musk-became-elon-musk.asp

Bogdanov, V. (2023, July 10). *Top Use Cases of ChatGPT Integration into Business Strategies and Operations. rinf.tech.* https://www.rinf.tech/top-use-cases-of-chatgpt-in tegration-into-business-strategies-and-operations/

Bowman, S. (2023, August 3). *The Curious Changemaker: 9 Ways to Cultivate Cu-riosity as a conscious entrepreneur. LinkedIn.* https://www.linkedin.com/pulse/curiou s-changemaker-9-ways-cultivate-curiosity-conscious-sheli-bowman/

Bridges, J. (2024, June 25). *How to write an action Plan (Example included). Project-Manager.* https://www.projectmanager.com/training/make-action-plan

Buchholz, K. (2023, July 7). *Threads shoots past one million user mark at lightning speed. Statista Daily Data.* https://www.statista.com/chart/29174/time-to-one-millio n-users/

Burr, D. (2023, October 26). *Operational efficiency unleashed: ChatGPT's role in streamlining workflows. LinkedIn.* https://www.linkedin.com/pulse/operational-effic iency-unleashed-chatgpts-role-workflows-david-burr-ixcce/

Burton, C. (2023, July 31). *60+ ChatGPT Prompts for Sales: Mastering Sales with AI. Thinkific.* https://www.thinkific.com/blog/chatgpt-for-sales/

Business agility Examples & Case Studies. (n.d.). *Agile Sherpas.* https://www.agilesh erpas.com/blog/business-agility-examples-case-studies

Business plan glossary. (n.d.). https://smartbusinessplan.com/glossary/#ready-to-start

Business plan template | Fill-in-the-blank business plan. (2024, May 2). Five Minute Classes. https://www.fiveminuteclasses.com/worksheets/free-fill-in-the-blank-business -plan-template/

Can ChatGPT write a business proposal? (2023, September 18). PandaDoc. https:// www.pandadoc.com/ask/can-chatgpt-write-a-business-proposal/

Cano, Y. M. Y. (2024, February 5). ChatGPT and AI text generators: Should academia adapt or resist? Harvard Business Publishing. https://hbsp.harvard.edu/inspiri ng-minds/chatgpt-and-ai-text-generators-should-academia-adapt-or-resist

Cartwright, G. (2024, April 18). ChatGPT for customer service: prompts, use cases & more. Klaus. https://www.klausapp.com/blog/chatgpt-for-customer-service/

Case studies - Touchdown ventures. (2022, April 18). Touchdown Ventures. https://w ww.touchdownvc.com/vc-entrepreneur/case-studies/

Case studies of successful investments by angel investors. (n.d.). FasterCapital. https:// fastercapital.com/topics/case-studies-of-successful-investments-by-angel-investors.html

Caudoux, C. (2024, January 3). How to use artificial intelligence for international marketing. Prime Target. https://primetarget.tech/how-to-use-artificial-intelligence-f or-international-marketing/

Chaffey, D. (2023, January 20). How well does ChatGPT understand consumer behaviour? ClickThrough Marketing. https://www.clickthrough-marketing.com/blog/h ow-well-does-chatgpt-understand-consumer-behaviour

ChatGPT prompt to create a value proposition. (n.d.). AI for Work. https://www.aiforwork.co/prompts/chatgpt-prompt-product-marketing-mana ger-marketing-create-a-value-proposition

ChatGPT prompts for risk management. (n.d.). ClickUp. https://clickup.com/templa tes/ai-prompts/risk-management

Chen, C. (2024, May 22). Top 5 generative AI tools to elevate your workflow automation. Bardeen AI. https://www.bardeen.ai/posts/workflow-automation-generative-ai -tools

Chodipilli, K. (2023, July 13). 5 reasons why agility is more important than ever in the enterprise. Leadership Tribe US. https://leadershiptribe.com/blog/5-reasons-why-agility-is-more-important-than-ever-in-the-enterprise

Codecademy. (n.d.). Create a business pitch using ChatGPT. Codecademy. https://www.codecademy.com/article/create-a-business-pitch-using-chat-gpt

Cook, J. (2023, December 21). How to scale your business: 5 ChatGPT prompts for Exceptional growth. Forbes. https://www.forbes.com/sites/jodiecook/2023/11/14/how-to-scale-your-business-5-chatgpt-prompts-for-exceptional-growth/?sh=4ce6d45f7998

Create a distinctive unique selling proposition with ChatGPT. (2023, October 20). Toolify. https://www.toolify.ai/ai-news/create-a-distinctive-unique-selling-proposition-with-chatgpt-655613

Damiongraham. (2023, August 29). The catalyst for change: The role of social entrepreneurship in economic development. Economic Impact Catalyst. https://economicimpactcatalyst.com/social-entrepreneurship/

Deane, M. T. (2024, June 1). Top 6 reasons new businesses fail. Investopedia. https://www.investopedia.com/financial-edge/1010/top-6-reasons-new-businesses-fail.aspx#:~:text=Key%20Takeaways,1.

DeLane, J. (2024, March 7). Importance of agility and strategy in social media marketing. Digital Delane. https://digitaldelane.com/social-media-marketing-the-importance-of-strategy-and-agility

Deng, O. (2023, December 14). A guide to integrating AI tools in your marketing processes [New data + expert tips]. HubSpot. https://blog.hubspot.com/marketing/ai-marketing-processes

Digital Business Development Initiative. (n.d.). Johns Hopkins Carey Business School. https://carey.jhu.edu/partnerships/digital-business-development-initiative

Discuss the importance of adaptability and agility in evolving businesses. (n.d.). TutorChase. https://www.tutorchase.com/answers/ib/business-management/discuss-the-importance-of-adaptability-and-agility-in-evolving-businesses

Dixon, A. (2024, March 1). The 10 components of a business plan. https://smartasse
t.com/small-business/top-components-of-a-business-plan

Do you really need a business plan? (2019, October 28). Duquesne University SBDC.
https://www.sbdc.duq.edu/Blog-Item-The-Importance-of-a-Business-Plan

Dsouza, L. (2023, September 20). Unlocking the power of AI tools for enhanced networking and productivity. LinkedIn. https://www.linkedin.com/pulse/unlocking-pow
er-ai-tools-enhanced-networking-leonardo-dsouza/

Dublino, J. (2024, April 15). 5 tips for setting SMART goals in your business plan. B
usiness.com. https://www.business.com/articles/5-tips-for-setting-smart-business-goals/

Eby, K. (n.d.). Free project milestone templates. Smartsheet. https://www.smartsheet.
com/content/milestone-templates

Ecosystem map. (n.d.). Startup Foundation. https://www.startup-saatio.fi/ecosystem
-map

Enginsoy, S. (2023, October 23). Startup ecosystem analysis. StartupBlink Blog. http
s://www.startupblink.com/blog/startup-ecosystem-analysis/

Entrepreneurial potential self-assessment. (2024, June 12). BDC.ca
. https://www.bdc.ca/en/articles-tools/entrepreneur-toolkit/business-assessments/self-as
sessment-test-your-entrepreneurial-potential

Entrepreneurship: From ancient markets to modern startups. (n.d.)
. Chase. https://www.chase.com/business/knowledge-center/professional-development/
the-history-of-entrepreneurship

Erné, J. (2024, February 29). The Power of AI in Marketing: Navigating the Future
with ChatGPT. LinkedIn. https://www.linkedin.com/pulse/power-ai-marketing-nav
igating-future-chatgpt-jeroen-ern%C3%A9-ocgge/

Exploring the power of ChatGPT: An opportunity for supply chain transformation. (n.d.). Gart-
ner. https://www.gartner.com/en/supply-chain/insights/power-of-the-profession-blog/e
xploring-the-power-of-chatgpt-an-opportunity-for-supply-chain-transformation

Farese, D. (2024, February 21). *Market research: A how-to guide and template. Hub-Spot.* https://blog.hubspot.com/marketing/market-research-buyers-journey-guide

Ferriolo, J. (2023, November 29). *A brief history of business plan. Wise Business Plans®.* https://wisebusinessplans.com/how-did-all-this-business-plan-stuff-get-started/

Follonier, F. (2023, April 23). *What is the business value of ChatGPT and other large generative language models? Relataly.com.* https://www.relataly.com/openai-gpt-chatgpt-in-a-business-context-whats-the-value-proposition/12282/

ForwardAI. (2023, January 20). *80% of businesses fail due to a lack of cash. Here are 4 reasons why cash flow forecasting is so important. ForwardAI.* https://www.forwardai.com/knowledge-center/blog/80-of-businesses-fail-due-to-a-lack-of-cash-here-are-4-reasons-why-cash-flow-forecasting-is-so-important/

ForwardAI. (2023, January 20). *80% of businesses fail due to a lack of cash. Here are 4 reasons why cash flow forecasting is so important. ForwardAI.* https://www.forwardai.com/knowledge-center/blog/80-of-businesses-fail-due-to-a-lack-of-cash-here-are-4-reasons-why-cash-flow-forecasting-is-so-important/

Global Map of Startups & Ecosystem Rankings. (n.d.). *StartupBlink.* https://www.startupblink.com/startups

Gomez, O. (2023, May 26). *Implementing ChatGPT for natural language processing. LinkedIn.* https://www.linkedin.com/pulse/implementing-chatgpt-natural-language-processing-olive-gomez/

GSPANN. (n.d.). *5 data-driven marketing strategies to grow your business in a fast-changing market. GSPANN.* https://www.gspann.com/resources/blogs/how-businesses-use-data-driven-marketing-strategies-to-grow-in-a-fast-changing-market/

Haley, A. *ChatGPT 4 For Data Analysis: Practical Business Uses.* (2024, April 10). *ChatGPT 4 Online.* https://chatgpt4online.org/chatgpt-for-data-analysis/

Hayes, A. (2024, June 27). *Business Plan: What It Is, What's Included, and How to Write One. Investopedia.* https://www.investopedia.com/terms/b/business-plan.asp

Henriques, P. (2024, January 26). *5 steps to scaling up production. Onramp.* https://www.onramp-solutions.com/blog/5-steps-to-scaling-up-production/

Hetler, A. (2024, July 31). *What is ChatGPT? Tech Target WhatIs.* https://www.techtarget.com/whatis/definition/ChatGPT

How businesses are already using ChatGPT: 10 real cases. (2024, May 22). E-commerce Germany News. https://ecommercegermany.com/blog/how-businesses-are-already-using-chatgpt-10-real-cases

How continuous improvement can build a competitive edge. (2019, May 6). McKinsey & Company. https://www.mckinsey.com/capabilities/people-and-organizational-performance/our-insights/the-organization-blog/how-continuous-improvement-can-build-a-competitive-edge

How do you assess the market potential of a foreign country? (2023, August 25). LinkedIn. https://www.linkedin.com/advice/3/how-do-you-assess-market-potential-foreign

How to achieve business adaptability with adaptive strategy execution. (2024, July 3). Quantive. https://quantive.com/resources/articles/business-adaptability

How to find the right co-founder : YC Startup Library | Y Combinator. (n.d.). YC Startup Library. https://www.ycombinator.com/library/8h-how-to-find-the-right-co-founder

How to gather market intelligence: The 8 key steps required. (2024, March 27). Resource Centre. https://www.watchmycompetitor.com/resources/how-to-gather-market-intelligence-the-8-key-steps-required/

How to plan a business infrastructure. (2017, November 21). Small Business - Chron.com. https://smallbusiness.chron.com/plan-business-infrastructure-44972.html

Hughes, C. (2024, August 13). *Maximizing business potential with AI-generated plans: Tools and tips for success.* Forbes. https://www.forbes.com/councils/forbesbusinesscouncil/2023/05/03/maximizing-business-potential-with-ai-generated-plans-tools-and-tips-for-success/

Hughes, D. (2024, May 1). *Best examples of AI in marketing*. Digital Marketing Institute. https://digitalmarketinginstitute.com/blog/some-inspiring-uses-of-ai-in-digital-marketing

Ibars, O. (2023, September 26). *Generative AI meets the Lean Startup: A paradigm shift in entrepreneurship*. Medium. https://bootcamp.uxdesign.cc/generative-ai-meets-the-lean-startup-a-paradigm-shift-in-entrepreneurship-2097d813ef99

Ijaz, H. (2023, December 19). *Competitor analysis using ChatGPT: A tactical guide*. Poll the People. https://pollthepeople.app/how-is-chatgpt-used-for-competitor-research/

In, C. D. (2024, July 17). *7 Use cases of ChatGPT in marketing for 2024*. AIMultiple: High Tech Use Cases & Tools to Grow Your Business. https://research.aimultiple.com/chatgpt-in-marketing/

Indeed Editorial Team. (2023, March 11). *45 Examples of business jargon terms and phrases*. Indeed Career Guide. https://www.indeed.com/career-advice/career-development/jargons-in-business

Indeed Editorial Team. (2023, October 23). *How to conduct a SWOT analysis in 5 steps (With example)*. Indeed Career Guide. https://www.indeed.com/career-advice/career-development/how-to-do-a-swot-analysis

Indeed Editorial Team. (2024, August 16). *10 important components of an effective business plan*. Indeed Career Guide. https://www.indeed.com/career-advice/career-development/parts-to-a-business-plan

InfoDesk. (n.d.). *How to gather market intelligence*. InfoDesk. https://www.infodesk.com/blog/how-to-gather-market-intelligence

Jagtap, A. (2024, January 31). *How ChatGPT can write your business plan?* Upmetrics. https://upmetrics.co/blog/chatgpt-business-plan

Johnson, J. (2023, August 14). *4 Ways ChatGPT can help you build a marketing strategy*. Codecademy Blog. https://www.codecademy.com/resources/blog/chatgpt-marketing/

Jules. (n.d.). *Supply Chain Optimization: 10 Tips to get it right. Easyship.* https://ww w.easyship.com/blog/supply-chain-optimization

K, A. V. (2022, February 10). *Top 5 businesses that AI transformed. Spiceworks Inc.* https://www.spiceworks.com/tech/artificial-intelligence/articles/businesses-that-ai -transformed/amp/

K, C. (2023, May 21). *How has modern strategic planning changed? LinkedIn.* http s://www.linkedin.com/pulse/how-has-modern-strategic-planning-changed-chandan/

Kaluarachchi, D. (2023, October 31). *Mastering the art of ChatGPT's feedback loops - Artificial intelligence in plain english. Medium.* https://ai.plainenglish.io/masteri ng-the-art-of-chatgpts-feedback-loops-88b4b7519db0

Karl, T. (2024, July 30). *Unleashing the power of AI: 6 bene- fits of integrating artificial intelligence into your business. new hori- zons.* https://www.newhorizons.com/resources/blog/unleashing-the-power-of-ai-6-benef its-of-integrating-artificial-intelligence-into-your-business

Kille, C. (2024, August 13). *8 traits that make a successful entrepreneur. Forbes.* https://www.forbes.com/councils/forbesbusinesscouncil/2022/12/01/8-traits-th at-make-a-successful-entrepreneur/

Knight, K. (2021, December 10). *Going global: How to implement a product localiza- tion strategy. Mind the Product.* https://www.mindtheproduct.com/implement-prod uct-localization-strategy/

Lab, N. (2024, February 21). *Custom market research with ChatGPT: NonBounce's approach to eviscerate competitors. Medi- um.* https://medium.com/@melodicwondermusic/custom-market-research-with-chat gpt-nonbounces-approach-to-eviscerate-competitors-cd82408c7c12

Lake, R. (2024, June 3). *Your annual financial planning checklist. Investo- pedia.* https://www.investopedia.com/articles/personal-finance/your-annual-financia l-planning-check-list.asp

Lavinsky, D. (2024). *Business plan checklist. Growthink.* https://www.growthink.com /businessplan/help-center/business-plan-checklist

Leonard, K. (2024, July 9). *The ultimate guide to S.M.A.R.T. goals. Forbes Advisor.* https://www.forbes.com/advisor/business/smart-goals/

Leveraging multilingual ChatGPT for global business expansion. (2024, August 19). Nexacu. https://nexacu.com/id/insights-blog/leveraging-multilingual-chatgpt-for-glo bal-business-expansion/

Leykam, G. (2023, October 24). *Unveiling the triumphs of AI-driven startup success stories. Garrison Leykam, PhD.* https://garrisonleykamphd.com/2023/10/24/unveili ng-the-triumphs-of-ai-driven-startup-success-stories/

Li, Z. (2023, June 2). *Using ChatGPT to make your SEM search term review more efficiently. LinkedIn.* https://www.linkedin.com/pulse/using-chatgpt-make-your-sem -search-term-review-more-efficiently-li/

Lindegaard, S. (2023, April 2). *ChatGPT Implementation and Scaling in an Orga-nization: Your in-depth guide. LinkedIn.* https://www.linkedin.com/pulse/chatgpt-im plementation-scaling-organization-your-guide-lindegaard

Litman, B. P. (2021, March 9). *Importance of market analysis in business growth. The Jerusalem Post.* https://www.jpost.com/special-content/importance-of-market-analysi s-in-business-growth-661433

Liu, H. (2023, June 3). *Embracing the AI Revolution: How SAAS Companies adapt to ChatGPT. LinkedIn.* https://www.linkedin.com/pulse/embracing-ai-revolution-ho w-saas-companies-adapt-chatgpt-heping-liu/

Llc, P. (2023, November 11). *How to use ChatGPT to analyze data? LinkedIn.* http s://www.linkedin.com/pulse/how-use-chatgpt-analyze-data-ptolemay-t6vcf/

Llc, P. (2023, November 11). *How to use ChatGPT to analyze data? LinkedIn.* http s://www.linkedin.com/pulse/how-use-chatgpt-analyze-data-ptolemay-t6vcf/

Looby, J. (2023, September 19). *A Conversation with ChatGPT about segmentation.* KS&R. https://www.ksrinc.com/a-conversation-with-chatgpt-about-segmentation/

Lumoa. (2024, March 19). *What is the role of AI in customer feedback analysis?. Lu-moa.* https://www.lumoa.me/blog/artificial-intelligence-customer-feedback-analysis/

M-Accelerator. (2023, June 12). ChatGPT and startups. M ACCELERATOR. http s://maccelerator.la/en/blog/startups/chatgpt-and-startups/

Macready, H. (2023, August 17). 65 ChatGPT prompts for marketing to make work easier. Social Media Marketing & Management Dashboard. https://blog.hootsuite.com/chatgpt-prompts-for-marketing/

Mailchimp. (n.d.). How to complete a SWOT analysis. Mailchimp. https://mailchi mp.com/resources/how-to-complete-a-swot-analysis/

Mailchimp. (n.d.). SMART goals for your business. Mailchimp. https://mailchimp.com/resources/smart-goals/

Main components of a business plan. (n.d.). The Hartford. https://www.thehartford.com/business-insurance/strategy/writing-business-plan/main-components

Market research and competitive analysis. (n.d.). U.S. Small Business Administration. https://www.sba.gov/business-guide/plan-your-business/market-research-competitive-analysis

Marr, B. (2021, July 13). The 10 best examples of how companies use artificial intelligence in practice. Bernard Marr. https://bernardmarr.com/the-10-best-examples-of-how-companies-use-artificial-intelligence-in-practice/

Marr, B. (2023, June 16). A simple guide to the history of generative AI. Bernard Marr. https://bernardmarr.com/a-simple-guide-to-the-history-of-generative-ai/

MatoW. (2023, September 21). Use the power automate plugin for ChatGPT. Microsoft Learn. https://learn.microsoft.com/en-us/power-automate/use-chatgpt-plugin

Mba, R. S. (2022, October 23). 5 ways AI can improve your product description content. https://www.linkedin.com/pulse/5-ways-ai-can-improve-your-product-description-content-rabin-saha/

Mbongo, N. N. (2023, August 23). The importance of adaptability in today's ever-changing business environment. LinkedIn. https://www.linkedin.com/pulse/importance-adaptability-todays-ever-changing-business-mbongo/

McDowell, M. (2023, October 10). *ChatGPT can now predict fashion and beauty trends.* Vogue Business. https://www.voguebusiness.com/technology/chatgpt-can-now-p redict-fashion-and-beauty-trends/

melp@wp098. (2023, August 15). *Successful Business Development Manager: Key Traits for Growth.* MELP. https://www.melp.us/blog/successful-business-developmen t-manager-key-traits-for-growth/

Milestones Technology Group. (2023, September 10). *Integrating AI into your Business Strategy: Shifting from Exploration to Integration.* LinkedIn. https://www.linkedin. com/pulse/integrating-ai-your-business-strategy-shifting

Milon, B. (2024, April 24). *AI in Logistics: Benefits, Challenges, Case Studies & Best Practices.* www.ilscompany.com. https://www.ilscompany.com/ai-in-logistics/

Miroslavov, M. (2024, February 8). *10 practical examples of SMART goals for work [2024].* OfficeRnD. https://www.officernd.com/blog/examples-of-smart-goals-for-wor k/

Moore, B. D. (2024, April 16). *10 Insightful examples of good business decision making.* Great Work Life. https://www.greatworklife.com/business-decision-making-exa mples-outcomes/

Moroles, J. (2023, July 24). *Using ChatGPT for market research, customer feedback, competitor analysis, and improvements.* LinkedIn. https://www.linkedin.com/pulse/ using-chatgpt-market-research-customer-feedback-analysis-moroles

Mukherjee, S. (2023, November 12). *AI tools in action: Real-world applications and success stories - Business writing/content writing/article writing/blog post/ and consultancy.* LinkedIn. https://www.linkedin.com/pulse/ai-tools-action-real-world-applicat ions-success-post-mukherjee-u1f4c/

Mura, G. (2023, May 23). *Unlocking startup success: Experimenting with Chat GPT for idea validation, user personas, and overcoming resistance.* LinkedIn. https://www.linkedin.com/pulse/unlocking-startup-success-experimenting -chat-gpt-idea-gaspare-mura/

Murphy, J. (2023, October 10). 10 realistic business use cases for ChatGPT. Enterprise AI. https://www.techtarget.com/searchenterpriseai/tip/Realistic-business-use-cases-for -ChatGPT

Murphy, T. (2023, April 27). How to use ChatGPT for customer service. Tech Target Customer Experience. https://www.techtarget.com/searchcustomerexperience/feature/ How-to-use-ChatGPT-for-customer-service

Murray, J. (2020, September 21). Fixed and variable expenses in business budgets. The Balance. https://www.thebalancemoney.com/fixed-and-variable-expenses-in-bus iness-budgets-398512

Nickolas, S. (2024, July 2). Budgeting vs. financial forecasting: What's the difference? Investopedia. https://www.investopedia.com/ask/answers/042215/whats-difference-b etween-budgeting-and-financial-forecasting.asp

Nield, D. (2024, February 22). 17 tips to take your ChatGPT prompts to the next level. WIRED. https://www.wired.com/story/17-tips-better-chatgpt-prompts/

Nimda, & Nimda. (2023, January 11). The importance of market analysis in business growth. PREDIK Data-Driven. https://predikdata.com/the-importance-of-market -analysis-in-business-growth/

Nonprofit Learning Lab. (2023, June 9). ChatGPT for grant writing - unleashing AI to transform nonprofit fundraising. Grantboost. https://www.nonprofitlearninglab.o rg/post-1/chatgpt-for-grant-writing-grantboost

Nunez, A. (2023, June 23). 7 SMART goal examples for business and how to set them (2024). Podium. https://www.podium.com/article/smart-goals-for-small-business/

Nuttall, C. (2023, November 17). Market survey: How to conduct a market research survey. GWI. https://blog.gwi.com/marketing/market-survey/

Nwobodo, C. (2023, August 30). Using ChatGPT to refine your content. LinkedIn. h ttps://www.linkedin.com/pulse/using-chatgpt-refine-your-content-christian-nwobodo/

Ocon, I. (n.d.). FluentU English – English Language and Culture blog. FluentU English. https://www.fluentu.com/blog/english/

Onesto, A. (2023, July 9). AI's impact on organizational structure. LinkedIn. https://www.linkedin.com/pulse/ais-impact-organizational-structure-anthony-onesto/

Orai. (2023, June 22). How to use AI Chatbot to enhance internal communication. LinkedIn. https://www.linkedin.com/pulse/how-use-ai-chatbot-enhance-internal-communication-orairobotics/

Ortiz, S. (2024, June 17). What is ChatGPT and why does it matter? Here's what you need to know. ZDNET. https://www.zdnet.com/article/what-is-chatgpt-and-why-does-it-matter-heres-everything-you-need-to-know/

P, A. (2023, September 27). Success stories of organizations harnessing AI and business intelligence for transformative outcomes. LinkedIn. https://www.linkedin.com/pulse/success-stories-organizations-harnessing-ai-business-phillips

P, R. (2023, March 18). Innovation in business development! LinkedIn. https://www.linkedin.com/pulse/innovation-business-development-rohan-patrick/

Paliwal, A. (2023, January 19). ChatGPT: Way to automate small business processes or workflows. Medium. https://bootcamp.uxdesign.cc/chatgpt-way-to-automate-small-business-processes-or-workflows-ccff36a9c33

Panel, E. (2024, August 13). 16 key factors to consider when budgeting and forecasting for the upcoming year. Forbes. https://www.forbes.com/councils/forbesfinancecouncil/2023/08/11/16-key-factors-to-consider-when-budgeting-and-forecasting-for-the-upcoming-year/

Paris, J. (2023, March 6). Artificial intelligence and continuous improvement. Operational Excellence Society. https://opexsociety.org/founders-desk/artificial-intelligence-and-continuous-improvement/

Parsons, N. (2024, August 1). Do you need a business plan? This study says yes. Bplans: Free Business Planning Resources and Templates. https://www.bplans.com/business-planning/basics/research/

Parsons, N. (2024, August 10). 4 advanced ways to use ChatGPT for better financial Forecasting. LivePlan Blog. https://www.liveplan.com/blog/advanced-chatgpt-financial-forecasting-prompts/

Parsons, N. (2024, August 10). How to use ChatGPT to create a financial forecast for your business. LivePlan Blog. https://www.liveplan.com/blog/create-financial-forecast-with-chatgpt/

Parsons, N. (2024, June 25). Can you use chatgpt to write a business plan? LivePlan Blog. https://www.liveplan.com/blog/write-business-plan-with-chatgpt/

Parsons, N. (2024a, August 1). Do you need a business plan? This study says yes - BPlans. Bplans: Free Business Planning Resources and Templates. https://www.bplans.com/business-planning/basics/research/

Parsons, N. (2024b, August 1). Do you need a business plan? This study says yes - BPlans. Bplans: Free Business Planning Resources and Templates. https://www.bplans.com/business-planning/basics/research/

Patel, S. (2024, May 1). Company growth strategy: 7 key steps for business growth & expansion. HubSpot. https://blog.hubspot.com/sales/growth-strategy

Pawlan, D. (2023, August 8). Top ways to leverage AI/Chat GPT as a startup. Aloa. https://aloa.co/blog/top-ways-to-leverage-ai-chat-gpt-as-a-startup

Pearson, R. (2019, November 1). A history of business plans. LinkedIn. https://www.linkedin.com/pulse/history-business-plans-roger-pearson/

Peck, H. (2024, March 21). Top 10 Project Milestone Templates. ClickUp. https://clickup.com/blog/milestone-templates/

Peppa, P. (2024, February 5). Business in the digital era. Peppa. https://blog.peppa.io/business-in-the-digital-era/

Pereira, D. (2023, March 19). How to do a SWOT analysis in 7 steps (with examples & template). Business Model Analyst. https://businessmodelanalyst.com/how-to-do-swot-analysis/

Periyasamy, R. (2023, August 14). 4 Successful enterprise change management examples. Apty. https://www.apty.io/blog/change-management-examples/

Persinger, M. (2020, March 14). How's your financial health? Our 10-point checklist will give you an idea. EveryIncome Library.

https://library.everyincome.com/plan/hows-your-financial-health-our-10-point-checkli
st-will-give-you-an-idea/?doing_wp_cron=1724133174.913275957107543945312 5

Petruk, M. (2024, February 2). ChatGPT Guide for Startups: How to harness the
potential of AI for your business. WeSoftYou. https://wesoftyou.com/ai/chatgpt-guid
e-for-startups-how-to-harness-the-potential-of-ai-for-your-business/

Phillips, D. (2024, August 8). 34 SMART Goal Examples (+ template) that will help
you succeed. Blueleadz. https://www.bluleadz.com/blog/top-3-smart-goal-examples

Pratt, M. K. (2024, August 6). 12 key benefits of AI for business. Enterprise AI. http
s://www.techtarget.com/searchenterpriseai/feature/6-key-benefits-of-AI-for-business

Prompt, P. A. (2024, May 19). ChatGPT Prompts For Crafting Unique USP's. Pro
AI Prompt. https://proaiprompt.com/chatgpt-prompts-for-crafting-unique-usps/

Proofed. (2023, December 5). 6 tips for editing AI-Generated Content. Proofed. http
s://proofed.com/knowledge-hub/6-tips-for-editing-ai-generated-content/

Pusheva, K. (n.d.). Practical ways to utilise AI in writing product descriptions. https://www.wakeupdata.com/blog/practical-ways-to-utilise-ai-in-writing-pro
duct-descriptions

Quid. (2023, October 31). Top 12 market intelligence tools. Quid. https://www.quid.
com/knowledge-hub/resource-library/blog/market-intelligence-tools

Quiz & worksheet - Entrepreneurial skills & abilities. (n.d.). Study.com. https://stud
y.com/academy/practice/quiz-worksheet-entrepreneurial-skills-abilities.html

Quriosity. (2014, May 2). Who said, "What gets measured gets managed"? A Thinking Person, a.k.a. Cogit8R. https://athinkingperson.com/2012/12/02/who-said-what
-gets-measured-gets-managed/

Ramuthi, D. (2024, July 26). What is an action plan & how to write one [With
examples]. Venngage. https://venngage.com/blog/action-plan/

Reflection journals (n.d.). Notion. https://www.notion.so/templates/reflection-journals

Robbins, D. (2023, December 7). *Revolutionizing Business Planning with AI: A Guide to Using ChatGPT.* LinkedIn. https://www.linkedin.com/pulse/revolutionizing-busi ness-planning-ai-guide-using-chatgpt-robbins-o3dyc/

Robinson, N. (2023, May 9). *Why GPT-powered apps are missing feedback loops - UX Collective.* Medium. https://uxdesign.cc/feedback-loops-how-the-wave-of-gpt-powered -apps-are-leaving-them-behind-1d05c90639c1

Roth, D. (2021, February 9). *How Shake Shack's Danny Meyer built an empire centered on employees.* https://www.linkedin.com/pulse/how-shake-shacks-danny-mey er-built-empire-centered-employees-roth/

Rotman, D. (2023, May 9). *ChatGPT is about to revolutionize the economy. We need to decide what that looks like.* MIT Technology Review. https://www.technologyrevie w.com/2023/03/25/1070275/chatgpt-revolutionize-economy-decide-what-looks-like/

Sachdeva, A. (2023, May 2). *How to use ChatGPT for market research.* GapScout. https://gapscout.com/blog/how-to-use-chatgpt-for-market-research/

Sahlman, W. A. (2023, April 4). *How to write a great business Plan.* Harvard Business Review. https://hbr.org/1997/07/how-to-write-a-great-business-plan

Sarahedwards, & Sarahedwards. (2024, May 1). *What must an entrepreneur do after creating a business plan? Columbia Law Course.* https://execedonline.law.columbia.edu/blog/starting-a-business/what-must-a n-entrepreneur-do-after-creating-a-business-plan/

Scout, H. (2022, September 23). *6 proven strategies for building a customer-centric company.* Help Scout. https://www.helpscout.com/playlists/customer-centricity/

Shafeek, M. (2023, July 10). *Introduction to business development in the digital era.* LinkedIn. https://www.linkedin.com/pulse/introduction-business-development-d igital-era-eng-muhammed-shafeek/

Sheedy, J. (2023, June 20). *The role of artificial intelligence in business innovation.* LinkedIn. https://www.linkedin.com/pulse/role-artificial-intelligence-business-innov ation-dr-jason-sheedy/

Simplilearn. (2024, August 13). *Business planning: it's importance, types and key elements*. Simplilearn.com. https://www.simplilearn.com/business-planning-article

Singh, A. (2021, February 5). *10 Qualities of a successful business development Manager*. LinkedIn. https://www.linkedin.com/pulse/10-qualities-successful-business-development-manager-amandeep-singh/

Smith, I. (2023, November 18). *How to create a business plan using ChatGPT*. HackerNoon. https://hackernoon.com/how-to-create-a-business-plan-using-chatgpt

Smith, J. (2024, August 14). *AI-Driven scenario forecasting and planning*. Brixx. https://brixx.com/chatgpt-ai-for-scenario-forecasting-and-planning/

Staff, P., & Staff, P. (2023, May 8). *3 case studies of successful crowdfunding campaigns to replicate for your website*. Publir - Blog. https://publir.com/blog/2023/05/3-case-studies-of-successful-crowdfunding-campaigns-to-replicate-for-your-website/

Stagno, M. (2023, March 20). *Why self-reflection and self-awareness are vital skills for any entrepreneur*. Entrepreneur. https://www.entrepreneur.com/leadership/why-self-reflection-and-self-awareness-are-vital-skills-for/447154

Storm, A. (2023, May 8). *How to use ChatGPT for market research*. Zapier. https://zapier.com/blog/chatgpt-market-research/

Subbarao, S. (2023, December 11). *Learning from AI-based pitching and its role in startups*. eLearning Industry. https://elearningindustry.com/learning-from-ai-based-pitching-and-its-role-in-startups

Suster, M. (2022, May 17). *Why Reed Hastings Should be Applauded for Netflix Split*. Medium. https://bothsidesofthetable.com/why-reed-hastings-should-be-applauded-for-netflix-split-d2a7df893707

Sutevski, D., PhD. (2024, April 26). *Real-life organizational decision-making examples*. Entrepreneurship in a Box. https://www.entrepreneurshipinabox.com/42395/real-life-organizational-decision-making-examples/#google_vignette

Sychikova, Y., & Sychikova, Y. (2024, March 11). AI in logistics: emerging startups, challenges and use cases [UPDATED 2024]. DataRoot Labs. https://datarootlabs.co m/blog/ai-in-logistics-emerging-startups-remaining-challenges-and-new-models

T, S. (2023, April 24). Data-driven business strategies: Unlocking growth and innovation. LinkedIn. https://www.linkedin.com/pulse/data-driven-business-strategies-unlo cking-growth-innovation-telu/

Team, A. (2024, July 16). How to use ChatGPT to write a business proposal. AI-Pro. org. https://ai-pro.org/learn-ai/tutorials/how-to-use-chatgpt-to-write-a-business-propo sal/

Team, A., & Team, A. (2023, January 28). ChatGPT in advertising: Improving targeting and personalization. AIContentfy. https://aicontentfy.com/en/blog/chatgpt -in-advertising-improving-targeting-and-personalization

Team, A., & Team, A. (2023, January 28). Utilizing ChatGPT for creating more personalized content for customer segmentation. AIContentfy. https://aicontentfy.com/en/blog/utilizing-chatgpt-for-creating-more-personalized -content-for-customer-segmentation

Team, A., & Team, A. (2023, March 5). AI-generated product descriptions: a new approach. AIContentfy. https://aicontentfy.com/en/blog/ai-generated-product-descrip tions-new-approach

Team, E. (2024, January 4). 106 Must-Know startup statistics for 2024. Embroker. https://www.embroker.com/blog/startup-statistics/

Team, E. (2024, January 4). 106 Must-Know startup statistics for 2024. Embroker. https://www.embroker.com/blog/startup-statistics/

The 12 key components of a business plan. (2023, November 17). Shopify. https://ww w.shopify.com/ph/blog/components-of-a-business-plan

The Advantages of Data-Driven Decision-Making. (2019, August 26). Business Insights Blog. https://online.hbs.edu/blog/post/data-driven-decision-making

The dynamic nature of business Edexcel - GCSE Business Revision. (2023, January 20). BBC Bitesize. https://www.bbc.co.uk/bitesize/guides/zm4krj6/revision/1

The importance of data driven decision making in business. (n.d.). RIB Software. https://www.rib-software.com/en/blogs/data-driven-decision-making-in-businesses

The Lean Startup | Methodology. (n.d.). https://theleanstartup.com/principles

Thompson, E. (2024, August 1). Validating with ChatGPT: Step-by-step for AI Etsy shops. 4Fsh. https://www.4fsh.com/harnessing-chatgpt-for-business-idea-validation-a -step-by-step-guide-for-ai-art-stores/

Tina. (2024, July 20). Artificial intelligence (AI) in supply chain and logistics. ThroughPut Inc. https://throughput.world/blog/ai-in-supply-chain-and-logistics/

Tobías, R. G., PhD. (2023, November 11). Integrating ChatGPT into Corporate Risk Management Models. LinkedIn. https://www.linkedin.com/pulse/integrating-chatg pt-corporate-risk-management-models-roberto-zpc2c/?trk=public_post

Tsang, K. (2023, December 8). How artificial intelligence and ChatGPT revolutionize startup business growth. LinkedIn. https://www.linkedin.com/pulse/how-artificial-in telligence-chatgpt-revolutionize-startup-keith-tsang-knldc/

Twin, A. (2024, July 26). How to do market research, types, and example. Investopedia. https://www.investopedia.com/terms/m/market-research.asp

U.S. Small Business Administration. (n.d.). How to write a business plan checklist. Ascent Learning. https://ascent.sba.gov/ae/ad/bcf142814a2281b4bbf155df250d/top ic-1-course-1-howtowriteabusinessplanchecklistpdf.pdf

University Canada West. (2021, October 28). 10 things entrepreneurs must under-stand to be successful. University Canada West (UCW). https://www.ucanwest.ca/bl og/business-management/10-things-entrepreneurs-must-understand-to-be-successful/

Upmetrics. (2024, June 28). A complete business plan checklist - Key points of business plan. https://upmetrics.co/business-plan-checklist

User401d. (2022, July 21). Roadmap for international business expansion. Acvian. https://acvian.com/blog/roadmap-for-international-business-expansion/

Using AI in marketing: Top 5 cases & examples. (n.d.). PostIndustria. https://postin dustria.com/using-ai-in-marketing-top-5-cases-machine-learning-examples/

Uzialko, A. (2024, April 19). How artificial intelligence will transform businesses. Business News Daily. https://www.businessnewsdaily.com/9402-artificial-intelligenc e-business-trends.html

VanBuskirk, A. (2023, April 25). ChatGPT prompt: Create a sales plan. WordBot. https://blog.wordbot.io/chatgpt-prompts/chatgpt-prompt-create-a-sales-plan/

Vintti. (2023, December 24). Fixed cost vs variable cost. Vintti. https://www.vintti.co m/blog/fixed-cost-vs-variable-cost/

Washington State University. (n.d.). 4 ways artificial intelligence is changing modern business. Online MBA. https://onlinemba.wsu.edu/blog/4-ways-artificial-intelligenc e-is-changing-modern-business

Weller, J. (n.d.). Free Fill-In-the-Blank Business Plan Templates. Smartsheet. https://www.smartsheet.com/content/fill-in-business-plan

Wellington, E. (2024, July 8). How to write a value Proposition (+ 6 modern examples). Help Scout. https://www.helpscout.com/blog/value-proposition-examples/

Westwater, S. (2023, November 27). AI Marketing Case Studies – Discover success stories and cutting-edge strategies. LinkedIn. https://www.linkedin.com/pulse/ai-ma rketing-case-studies-discover-success-stories-scot-westwater-ag4ic/

What is generative AI? (2024, April 2). McKinsey & Company. https://www.mckin sey.com/featured-insights/mckinsey-explainers/what-is-generative-ai

Why market research is important | Benefits of market research. (2022, June 2). CintTM. https://www.cint.com/blog/why-market-research-is-important

Wikipedia contributors. (2024, April 15). Business development. Wikipedia. https://en.wikipedia.org/wiki/Business_development

Wikipedia contributors. (2024a, July 31). Sara Blakely. Wikipedia. https://en.wikip edia.org/wiki/Sara_Blakely

Wikipedia contributors. (2024b, September 6). Indra Nooyi. Wikipedia. https://en. wikipedia.org/wiki/Indra_Nooyi

Wikipedia contributors. (2024c, September 24). Howard Schultz. Wikipedia. https: //en.wikipedia.org/wiki/Howard_Schultz

Wikipedia contributors. (2024d, September 27). James Dyson. Wikipedia. https://en .wikipedia.org/wiki/James_Dyson

Wikipedia contributors. (2024e, September 28). Lei Jun. Wikipedia. https://en.wiki pedia.org/wiki/Lei_Jun

Wikipedia contributors. (2024f, September 29). Brian Chesky. Wikipedia. https://e n.wikipedia.org/wiki/Brian_Chesky

Williams, M. (2024, January 26). How to do a market analysis for your business plan. https://www.wolterskluwer.com/en/expert-insights/market-analysis-for-your-bu siness-plan

Wright, R. (2023, March 24). ChatGPT for in-depth PESTLE analysis: A strategic approach to business environment scanning. Communication Genera- tion. https://www.communication-generation.com/chatgpt-for-in-depth-pestle-analys is-a-strategic-approach-to-business-environment-scanning/

Zendesk. (2024, March 8). How to create a customer-centric strategy in 2024. https:/ /www.zendesk.com/blog/customer-centric-business/

Zharovskikh, A. (2023, December 12). ChatGPT use cases for business – How to use the most popular AI tool? InData Labs. https://indatalabs.com/blog/chatgpt-use-cases-fo r-business

Starting a Business Roadmap

The Beginner Entrepreneur's Guide to Be Your Own Boss, Leverage AI, and Achieve Financial Independence

Russel Grant

GET YOUR FREE
PROMPT ENGINEERING
CHEAT SHEET!

SCAN ME

Go to the address below,
or scan the code.

https://cheatsheet.tips

Introduction

Everyone has an idea, but the world belongs to those who execute –
Unknown

I magine waking up each day with the freedom to build something meaningful—a business that reflects your deepest passions and sets you on the path to financial independence. Whether it's creating a groundbreaking product or solving a problem you care deeply about, the spark of inspiration can ignite incredible potential. But here's the truth: passion and ideas alone don't build businesses.

Ideas are only the beginning. Turning them into reality requires more than just inspiration—it takes passion, persistence, and the courage to act. The difference between a fleeting thought and a thriving business is the decision to take that first bold step and the determination to keep going, even when challenges arise. That's the journey this book will guide you through.

My story starts in my hometown, working for a local small business. I was full of ideas about how we could attract more customers, streamline processes, and stand out. But each time I brought my ideas forward, they were dismissed. It was frustrating, sure, but also enlightening. I realized my ambitions outgrew the limits of that workplace, and if I wanted to achieve my dreams, it would not happen there.

That's when the real brainstorming began. I started dreaming up ventures of my own. "Idea of the week," my friends and family called it. They'd listen, nod along, and give a laugh sometimes, but none of them had real business experience to guide me. All of my ideas kept growing, always out of reach, dreams kept safely on paper.

But it wasn't just the lack of experience holding me back, it was also fear.

I had just bought my first house and was terrified of losing it all. Every time I'd come close to starting something, that fear of failure—of losing everything I'd worked for—would stop me in my tracks. And then came some unfortunate life events. I didn't just want to start a business—I needed to. I saw entrepreneurship as the solution, my way of building the life I wanted, and a way to regain control over my future. Rather than being the risky move, it was my only way forward.

I was grateful to live in a time when the internet offered endless resources and opportunities. It allowed me to learn from seasoned professionals, absorb their insights at my own pace, and connect with like-minded individuals. Together, we shared ideas, celebrated successes, and learned from failures, turning challenges into growth.

Now, with artificial intelligence (AI) at your fingertips, starting and running a business has never been more accessible. Imagine launching an online store where AI analyzes market trends to predict your best-selling products or running a marketing campaign that dynamically targets the right audience and optimizes performance in real time. AI takes care of repetitive tasks like managing inventory or scheduling, freeing you to focus on strategy and creativity. With AI as your partner, you gain a powerful tool that accelerates your journey from idea to success.

This book is your guide to turning inspiration into action and building a business that thrives in today's world. Through real-world examples, actionable strategies, and lessons from my experience and others, you'll gain the tools and confidence to take your ideas to the next level. Whether you've been dreaming of this moment for years or just discovered your spark of inspiration, the time to act is now. Let's transform your vision into a reality.

Your amazing adventure starts here.

Chapter One

The Power of the Entrepreneurial Mindset

B eing an entrepreneur is more than just starting a business; it's about embracing a mindset that sees every turn and every event as an opportunity. This mindset is resilient and focused, always working towards a goal despite the obstacles that may arise.

Imagine climbing a mountain: reaching the peak isn't just about wanting it badly enough or having the best tools and equipment. It requires so much more. You need a deep understanding of the terrain, the knowledge to navigate challenges, the right resources, and the mental and physical strength to push forward. Above all, you must possess the will to adapt to the ever-changing environment around you.

The entrepreneurial journey is much the same. The path to building a successful business can feel daunting, much like scaling a towering mountain. However, the road ahead becomes clearer when you start taking those first small steps. And remember, you don't have to climb this mountain alone. Seek guidance, ask for help, and always be open to learning and adapting. Embrace the journey with curiosity and determination, knowing each step brings you closer to your goal.

This book will equip you with the confidence and resources to live your entrepreneurial dreams. With the right mindset, there are no limits to what you can achieve. Keep your eyes on the summit, stay resilient, and trust in your ability to overcome any challenge that comes your way.

Developing the Entrepreneurial Spirit and Overcoming Fears

Becoming an entrepreneur is less about unbroken success and more about cultivating a resilient, entrepreneurial spirit. Few entrepreneurs can boast of an unblemished winning streak. In reality, most successful entrepreneurs have encountered more failures than successes.

These setbacks are not signs of defeat but stepping stones to greater achievements. Take Milton Hershey, who faced three failed candy businesses before he found monumental success with his eponymous chocolate company.

Bill Gates experienced significant failure in his first company. Steve Jobs was famously ousted from Apple, the company he co-founded, before making a triumphant return through another venture. Walt Disney was even fired from a job for not being "creative enough." Every entrepreneur has a journey marked with failures, often more numerous than their successes.

What sets these entrepreneurs apart is their ability to develop an unbreakable spirit and to rise again after every fall. So, what fears are holding you back from taking your first step? Common fears that budding entrepreneurs face include:

- Fear of failure

- Fear of rejection

- Fear of not being good enough

- Surprisingly, even the fear of success

- Fear of financial risks

At first glance, these fears may seem irrational, but they are a natural part of the entrepreneurial journey. Recognizing these fears is the first step toward overcoming them. It is not about eliminating fear but learning to face it and use it as a tool for growth. Embracing your fears can offer valuable insights into your psyche, helping you address the core issues holding you back.

Fear of Failure

As demonstrated by countless entrepreneurs, failure is an intrinsic part of the journey. It's not something to fear but rather something to prepare for. No one can promise guaranteed success; therefore, being ready for setbacks without letting them paralyze your progress is crucial.

Here are some practical ways to overcome the fear of failure:

Set Clearly Defined Goals

Break down your goals into manageable steps and visualize each milestone. Tools like vision boards and journals can keep you focused and motivated.

Address Deep-Seated Emotions

If you have underlying anxieties, phobias, or past traumas, seek the help you need to achieve a balanced and healthy mindset. This could include therapy, meditation, or mindfulness practices. Practicing self-compassion and prioritizing your well-being is essential; don't sacrifice your happiness to pursue your goals.

Rely on Planning and Adaptability

While uncertainty is a given in entrepreneurship, planning can provide a sense of control. Conduct risk assessments and acquire the necessary training and knowledge to build confidence. You may fall and get bruised, like learning to ride a bicycle, but persistence is key. Keep trying until navigating the challenges becomes second nature.

Stay Adaptable

Understand that not all plans will go as expected. The more you work towards your goals, the more adaptable you become. Track your progress using metrics and data to adjust your strategies as needed.

Seek Guidance and Mentorship

Networking with industry leaders and mentors can provide valuable insights and support during uncertain times. Their experience can guide you through challenges more confidently.

Avoid Perfectionism

While planning is important, don't get stuck in the planning phase. The pursuit of perfection can delay progress. It's essential to start somewhere and learn from the process. Take small but steady steps toward your goals.

Fear of Rejection

Fear of rejection often emerges when pitching your ideas to investors or making sales. It can be disheartening when others don't immediately share your vision. However, remember that it's your dream, and you don't need validation from everyone. Rejection, while painful, is not the end. Instead, view it as an opportunity to learn and improve. Gather feedback, refine your approach, and adapt to new opportunities. Each rejection can bring you closer to success when you use it as a learning experience.

Fear of Not Being Good Enough

This fear is often self-imposed. The voice telling you you're not good enough is often yours. But remember, hard work and persistence can often trump innate talent. If you feel lacking in skills, invest time in developing them. Surround yourself with mentors and peers who uplift you and provide constructive feedback. Focus on your strengths and work on your weaknesses. Remember, worrying about things beyond your control is futile. Concentrate on what you can change and improve.

Combat these fears with facts. Emotions can distort your perception, making challenges seem more scary than they are. Use evidence and data to ground yourself in reality. Stop comparing yourself to others and instead focus on building your skills and expertise. Becoming a mentor yourself can also provide a significant confidence boost as you realize the positive impact you can have on others.

Fear of Success

The fear of success is an often-overlooked but genuine concern stemming from feelings of impostor syndrome. When success comes, embrace it confidently, knowing the hard work and dedication that led you there. Tracking your progress and reflecting on your efforts can help you internalize your achievements and recognize that you truly deserve them.

Ultimately, developing the entrepreneurial spirit is about overcoming these fears and moving forward with resilience, adaptability, and a willingness to learn from every experience. This journey is not about avoiding fear but learning to dance with it, using it to fuel your growth and drive your success.

Fear of Financial Risks

The fear of losing money on a business venture can be debilitating, and it is a valid concern. Not everyone has the luxury of risking their life savings or the mental resilience to start over from scratch after a financial setback. Thus, managing your financial risks is essential to alleviate such fears and build confidence in your entrepreneurial journey.

Here are some practical strategies to help you cope with the fear of financial risks:

Prepare A Strong Foundation Before Heavy Investments

Before diving into substantial investments, ensure you have a solid groundwork. This includes:

- Conducting extensive market research to understand short-term and long-term trends and customer needs.

- Clearly define your target audience and validate your business concept with a proof of concept or minimum viable product (MVP).

- Using these insights to build a robust business plan that outlines clear goals and a strategy for achieving them.

Start Small and Scale Gradually

One way to mitigate financial uncertainty is to maintain your regular job while gradually building your business as a side hustle. This approach allows you to:

- Test your business model with minimal financial risk.

- Make incremental investments based on the returns and insights gained rather than committing all your resources upfront.

Utilize Outsourcing and Cost-Effective Resources

Instead of doing everything yourself, leverage external resources to reduce costs:

- Outsource tasks that are not your core competency to freelancers or agencies, often available at competitive rates.

- Use affordable or free automation tools for repetitive tasks, allowing you to focus on strategic areas of your business.

Explore Diverse Funding Options

Reducing your financial burden through external funding can significantly lower your risk. Consider the following options:

- Seek out investors, venture capitalists, or crowdfunding platforms that align with your business vision.

- Look into government grants, public funding, startup incubator programs, or low-interest loans designed to support small businesses.

- Approach friends, family, or potential partners for loans or investments.

- Develop a compelling business plan and pitch to showcase your potential to prospective investors, maximizing your funding opportunities.

General Tips for Overcoming Entrepreneurial Fears

Regardless of your specific fear, the fundamental approach to overcoming any fear starts with understanding and acknowledging it.

Here are some steps to help you deal with various fears:

Identify and Acknowledge Your Fears

Start by identifying your fears and the specific concerns that trigger them. Write them down to confront them more directly, making the process of addressing them more manageable.

Examine the Basis of Your Fears

Analyze whether your fears are based on tangible facts or assumptions. Are they rooted in previous experiences or "what-ifs"? Understanding the underlying causes can help you address these fears more effectively.

Challenge Your Fears Through Exposure

Facing your fears head-on can often diminish its power. Take inspiration from entrepreneurs like Alex Turnbull, who deliberately exposed himself to speaking opportunities to overcome his fear of public speaking. Start with smaller, less intimidating situations, and gradually increase your exposure as you build confidence.

Seek Support and Learn From Others

Learn from others who have successfully overcome similar fears. Join peer communities or find mentors who offer guidance and share their experiences. Books like Do It Scared by Ruth Soukup provide practical advice and strategies for facing fears, especially those common among entrepreneurs.

Replace Negative Self-Talk With Positive Affirmations

Reframe your mindset by replacing negative self-talk with positive affirmations and self-compassion. Encourage yourself the way you would support a friend, focusing on your strengths and potential rather than your fears.

Celebrate Your Achievements

No matter how small your progress, take time to celebrate your accomplishments. Recognizing each step forward as a victory boosts your motivation and reinforces your confidence.

Seek Constructive Feedback

Gain feedback from mentors, peers, and even competitors. Sometimes, an external perspective can help you see beyond your immediate fears and focus on the bigger picture. Use this feedback to refine your approach and grow your business.

Prioritize Your Well-Being

Your mental and physical health is crucial to your success. Practice self-care, maintain a healthy lifestyle, and ensure you have the energy and resilience needed to face challenges and fears head-on.

By understanding and addressing your fears with practical steps, you can develop the courage and resilience necessary to succeed in your entrepreneurial journey. Remember, every successful entrepreneur starts with fears and uncertainties, but what sets them apart is their willingness to confront those fears and keep moving forward.

Conducting thorough risk assessments and building solid business plans are crucial steps when handling the fear of uncertainty and rejection. These activities help manage fears and play an essential role in establishing a robust foundation for your business.

Understanding Risk Assessment

Risk assessment is part of a broader process called risk analysis, which involves analyzing various aspects of a task, identifying potential threats and obstacles, prioritizing them, and devising strategies to mitigate them. It is a key decision-making tool that every businessperson should employ to make informed choices rather than rely solely on gut feelings. The data derived from risk assessments can provide valuable insights to support your decisions, even for the boldest of business ideas.

It's important to note that a risk assessment should not become a perfectionist exercise that hinders progress. Every task has its purpose and scope, and being overly fixated on perfecting one aspect can impede overall progress. The goal is to do your best with the resources at hand and then move on to the next steps based on the outcomes you achieve.

When To Perform A Risk Assessment

Risk assessments should be conducted:

- At the start of any new project or when setting new goals and requirements

- When introducing changes to existing processes or systems

- Periodically, to revisit and update risk parameters, thus ensuring no potential hazard is overlooked

Risk assessments are also a critical part of the auditing process that businesses undergo, helping them stay compliant with regulations and improve operational safety and efficiency. For example, OSHA (Occupational Safety and Health Administration) recommends workplace risk assessments to ensure a safe environment and legal compliance.

Types of Risk Assessments

Risk assessments can vary in scope and scale depending on the specific needs of your business. Common types include:

- **Generic Risk Assessment:** Broad assessments applicable to multiple situations or environments often used for initial evaluations.

- **Large-Scale Risk Assessment:** Comprehensive evaluations that cover a wide range of potential risks across various departments or large projects.

- **Focused Risk Assessment:** Detailed assessments targeting particular aspects of a business, such as specific processes or potential hazards.

Some examples of risk assessments commonly carried out are:

- **Health and Safety Risk Assessment:** Identifies hazards that could impact the health and safety of employees or customers.

- **Workplace Risk Assessment:** Evaluates risks associated with the work environment, such as equipment hazards or ergonomic issues.

- **Fall Risk Assessment:** Focuses on preventing falls, particularly in industries like construction or manufacturing.

- **Construction Risk Assessment:** Identifies risks specific to construction sites, including structural safety and equipment hazards.

Key Considerations for Developing Risk Assessment Procedures

While there are no strict rules for crafting the perfect risk assessment plan, here are some general pointers to keep in mind:

- **Tailor the Assessment to Your Business Needs:** Understand the unique risks associated with your business's operations and environment. Your risk assessment should be specific to these needs.

- **Involve A Range of Stakeholders:** As needed, engage employees, management, and external experts to get a comprehensive view of potential risks.

- **Update and Review Your Assessments Regularly:** Risks can evolve, so revisiting and revising them periodically is essential.

- **Prioritize Risks Based on Impact and Likelihood:** Focus on the risks that pose the greatest threat to your business, balancing potential impact and likelihood of occurrence.

- **Document Everything:** Keep detailed records of all risk assessments, findings, and actions. This documentation will be valuable for audits and future reference.

- **Use Risk Assessments to Drive Continuous Improvement:** Treat risk assessment as a cyclical process. Use the insights gained to improve existing processes and develop new strategies, fostering a culture of continuous improvement.

By following these steps and principles, you can create an effective risk assessment strategy that not only manages potential risks but also supports the growth and resilience of your business.

Mastering Business Plans: Building Confidence and Clarity

Creating a solid business plan can significantly boost your confidence when pitching your business and help eliminate doubts during execution. As I talked about business plans in my last book, The Business Plan Shortcut, a well-crafted business plan serves as a roadmap for your business and a compelling tool to attract investors, partners, and customers.

Key Components of a Traditional Business Plan

A traditional business plan typically consists of the following sections (you might want to refer to the previous book for more):

- **Executive Summary:** A brief overview of your business, its mission, and objectives.

- **Company Description:** Detailed information about your business, including its history, structure, and what makes it unique.

- **Market Analysis:** Insights into your industry, market size, target audience, and competitive landscape.

- **Organization and Management:** Information about your business's organizational structure and the team behind it.

- **Service or Product Line:** A description of the products or services you offer or plan to offer.

- **Marketing and Sales Strategy:** Your plans for reaching and attracting customers, including pricing, advertising, and sales tactics.

- **Funding Request:** If you are seeking funding, include details on how much you need, why you need it, and how you plan to use it.

- **Financial Projections:** Financial forecasts, including income statements, cash flow statements, and balance sheets.

- **Appendix:** Any additional information, such as resumes, permits, or other documents that support your plan.

While these components are foundational, you can tailor your business plan based on your specific needs and audience. For example, a plan for a crowdfunding campaign might be concise; however, one aimed at securing a significant investment might require more detailed documentation.

Utilizing AI Tools to Simplify Business Plan Creation

Creating a comprehensive business plan can be time-consuming. However, AI tools and writing software have made it easier to generate and customize plans quickly.

Here are some top AI-based business plan generators:

- **Upmetrics:** Offers templates and tools to help you write your business plan.

- **NotionAI:** Assists in organizing and drafting plans with AI-enhanced writing tools.

- **Copy AI:** Uses AI to generate text for different sections of your business plan.

- **Grammarly:** Improves the clarity and readability of your business plan.

- **Beautiful AI:** Creates visually appealing presentations for your business plan.

- **15MinutePlan:** Enables quick, effective business plan creation with step-by-step guidance.

- **WriteCream:** Uses AI to help you write persuasive and engaging content.

- **ProAI:** Offers AI-based tools for creating comprehensive business plans.

- **ChatGPT:** Provides AI-generated text and insights for your business plan.

- **CookUp AI:** Helps in drafting business plans with easy-to-use templates.

- **WordKraft AI:** Assists with writing and editing business content.

- **Brixx Plan Software:** Offers planning tools tailored for financial forecasting.

These tools help streamline the process of creating a business plan by providing templates, suggestions, and automated content generation. To get started, you can also refer to resources like the simple business plan template from Smartsheet.

Setting goals and leveraging technology for market analysis

Visualizing Success Through Clear Goals

It is essential to set clear, well-defined goals in order to achieve your business dreams. These goals act as a compass, guiding you toward your vision and providing a framework to overcome fears and uncertainties.

SMART Goals

A proven method to define your goals is to set SMART goals, which are:

- **Specific:** Clearly define what you want to achieve.

- **Measurable:** Establish criteria to measure your progress.

- **Achievable:** Ensure your goals are realistic and attainable.

- **Relevant:** Align your goals with your business objectives.

- **Time-Bound:** Set a deadline to achieve your goals.

Breaking down larger goals into smaller, actionable steps can help you focus on the immediate tasks while keeping the bigger picture in mind. This approach makes even the most ambitious dreams seem more achievable.

Using Data to Strengthen Goals

Data is critical in setting realistic and effective goals. It helps you determine if a goal is achievable within a specific timeframe and provides insights into market conditions and customer behaviors. To set SMART goals, gather as much relevant data as possible using various analytical tools and resources.

Here are some valuable tools and platforms for conducting market research and gathering data:

- **Glimpse:** Provides trends and insights on emerging topics.

- **Statista:** Offers statistics and studies from over 600 industries.

- **Think With Google Research Tools:** Provides data and insights from Google's vast data network.

- **Census Bureau:** Offers demographic and economic data.

- **Make My Persona:** Helps create detailed buyer personas.

- **Tableau:** A data visualization tool that helps interpret complex data.

- **Paperform:** Allows you to create forms and surveys to collect customer insights.

- **GWI:** Provides global audience insights and trends.

- **SurveyMonkey:** An easy-to-use tool for creating surveys and collecting feedback.

- **Typeform:** Creates interactive surveys and forms.

- **Upwave Instant Insights:** Provides real-time data and insights for marketing strategies.

- **Claritas MyBestSegment:** Offers consumer segmentation data.

- **Loop11:** Conducts usability testing and gathers user feedback.

- **Userlytics:** Provides user testing and feedback services.

- **Temper:** Gathers user sentiment and feedback.

- **NielsenIQ:** Provides consumer data and analytics.

- **Ubersuggest:** A keyword research tool that also offers SEO insights.

- **Pew Research Center:** Offers reports on public opinion and demographic research.

- **BrandMentions:** Monitors brand mentions and tracks competitors.

- **Qualtrics Market Research Panels:** Provides access to a broad range of market research data.

- **Qualaroo:** Collects user insights directly on your website.

Using these tools, you can gather the data needed to set SMART goals, refine your business strategy, and enhance your understanding of market dynamics.

With a solid business plan and clear, data-driven goals, you will be better equipped to navigate the challenges of building your business and turn your vision into reality.

Wrap Up

This chapter explored the importance of the entrepreneurial mindset, its resilience, and how it shapes an entrepreneur's journey. You learned about developing an unbreakable spirit, recognizing and facing fears, and using failures as stepping stones toward success.

Action Steps

1. Reflect on your individual fears about starting a business and write them down.

2. Set specific goals that can help you manage and reduce these fears.

3. Find a mentor or join a community of entrepreneurs for support and guidance.

Up Next

The next chapter will explore the foundational elements of building a business. You'll learn about choosing the proper structure, staying legally compliant, and establishing strong financial systems—ensuring your business is grounded on a solid foundation.

Chapter Two

Building A Strong Foundation

There are multiple reasons businesses succeed––or fail, for that matter. However, the common theme among successful ventures is that they enjoy a strong foundation. This stability enables them to withstand market-driven earthquakes and self-inflicted tsunamis such as hiring errors, incorrect budget allocations, etc.

Thus, establishing a reliable base is the next step to building a business.

What does it look like? Among other things, a firm footing is financially sound and legally compliant. No business can exist without capital, and no business can survive by upsetting the regulators.

Take the case of Enron. In the early 2000s, the energy company became synonymous with corporate fraud after it was discovered that the executives engaged in accounting fraud and deceptive business practices. More specifically, Enron created a network of Special Purpose Entities (SPEs) to offload debt and liabilities from its balance sheet, making the company appear more financially stable than it actually was. The scandal led to the company's bankruptcy and the imprisonment of several of its executives.

To prevent such threatening scenarios, you must always keep your business in compliance, requiring you to choose the proper business structure.

If you've never dealt with structuring a business or are unfamiliar with finance, relax––it's not the end of the world. It doesn't mean you should throw in the towel.

Throughout this section, we'll explore the types of business structures that will help you choose the right one. We'll also learn about the essential jargon. Finally, we'll review the basic concepts in accounting and finance that will help you keep your business financially sound.

By the end of the chapter, you will have the knowledge to work with local regulators, audit your business, and handle finances independently.

The Basics of Business Structures

Selecting the appropriate business structure is a foundational decision for any aspiring entrepreneur. This choice can significantly impact your business' legal, financial, and operational aspects. Your chosen structure determines your legal liability, tax obligations, and how you manage your business.

A well-informed decision can provide a secure base for your venture. However, a misstep could lead to unnecessary complications and challenges.

Liability: Your Personal Risk Exposure

Arguably, the main reason why nailing down the proper business structure is important is because of liability.

Liability in business refers to the legal responsibility of a business entity or its owners for debts, obligations, and legal actions, which may include damages, fines, or other financial penalties. Suppose a business or its employees engage in negligent or harmful behavior; the company may be responsible for settling any resulting damages. Each business structure offers various levels of liability protection.

Taxes: How Much You Owe to the State

Every business is required to pay taxes, but tax methods vary widely. Your business's taxation method depends on its structure. Rates for individuals and corporations differ, and your chosen structure directly impacts your overall tax burden.

Additionally, various structures offer unique opportunities for deductions and credits, helping reduce your tax liability.

Capital: The Ease With Which You Can Access It

Funding is a business's lifeblood. Especially when starting, you need access to enough resources to sustain operations until you hit breakeven. This is equally critical during challenging periods like the recent COVID-19 pandemic lockdowns.

The type of business structure you choose significantly impacts your ability to obtain financing. By understanding the factors that influence capital access and developing a strong business plan, you can improve your chances of securing the necessary funding for your venture.

Succession Planning: What Will Happen When You Move On

Nearly 45% of businesses fail within five years, but even those that survive still need a succession plan. This plan legally formulates what will happen to the company once the founder decides to step down. It involves creating a plan for transferring ownership and management responsibilities to family members, other stakeholders, or external parties.

The complexity of this transition largely depends on the business structure. A well-executed succession plan ensures the business can operate smoothly after the founders' departure.

Types of Business Structure

When registering your business, you'll have to choose a structure. In the United States, for-profit businesses generally fit into one of four categories:

- Sole Proprietorship

- Partnership

- LLC or Limited Liability Company

- Corporation

Let's explore each category in more detail.

Sole Proprietorship

A sole proprietorship is the most straightforward business structure to establish and run. As a self-explanatory phrase, it's a business owned and operated by a single individual. There may be a few employees or contractors, but the owner usually does all the heavy lifting. This structure is often suitable for small, home-based businesses or those just starting out.

Here are its key characteristics:

- **Single and Complete Ownership**: The owner owns the business and is the sole operator.

- **No Formal Structure**: Since there are no stakeholders, a sole proprietorship operates without a structure or hierarchy.

- **Unlimited Personal Liability:** No legal separation exists between the business and the owner, making them personally responsible for the business' actions. This means their personal assets, such as their home and savings, can be at risk.

- **Pass-Through Taxation:** Profits and losses are reported on the owner's personal income tax return. This system, known as pass-through taxation, eliminates double taxation.

- **No Separate Legal Entity:** Lastly, understand that a sole proprietorship is not a separate legal entity from the owner. The business is considered an extension of the owner.

Is sole proprietorship a good fit for you?

Pros

- Easy to set up

- Complete control of the business

- Flexibility with operations

Cons

- No liability protection, leaving the owner vulnerable to lawsuits and penalties

- Limited access to capital

- Succession planning can be complicated

Partnership

A partnership is a business structure where two or more individuals share ownership and responsibilities. It is an upgrade from a sole proprietorship business with added complexities and hurdles.

Partnerships are common when the founders have different skills, a shared vision, and are willing to work together. The partners establish an agreement and divide profits and losses based on terms they set, such as equal shares, agreed-upon percentages, or other factors.

There are two main types of partnerships:

General Partnership

- **Shared Ownership:** The partners are co-owners of the business, with equal rights and responsibilities unless otherwise specified in the partnership agreement.

- **Unlimited Liability:** Each general partner is personally liable for all of the partnership's financial obligations, including those caused by the negligence or misconduct of other partners.

- **Shared Profits and Losses:** Based on the predetermined agreement, the partners share both the profits and losses.

- **Joint Management:** In a general partnership, all partners have an equal say in the management of the business unless otherwise specified. This means that significant decisions require consensus among the partners.

Limited Partnership

- **Limited and General Partners:** A limited partnership has at least one general partner with unlimited liability and one or more limited partners whose liability is confined to their investment.

- **Limited Liability:** Limited partners are only responsible for their initial investment amount and are protected from personal responsibility for the partnership's debts. Additionally, they are unable to participate in managing the business.

- **Limited Involvement:** Limited partners typically have limited involvement in business management. Their primary role is to invest funds and share in the profits.

- **Profit Sharing:** Limited partners share in the profits but are not liable for losses beyond their original investment.

Is entering into a partnership a better fit for you?

Pros

- Shared resources and expertise

- Increased capital and funding

- Support network due to the involvement of more partners

Cons

- Higher failure rate due to conflict of interest

- Unlimited liability for general partners

Limited Liability Company (LLC)

The Small Business Administration (SBA) reports that LLCs, Limited Liability Companies, are the most popular business structure for new businesses formed in the US. There are several reasons why new entrepreneurs opt for an LLC over others. But know that it's a hybrid business structure that combines elements of a partnership and a corporation. It offers limited liability protection to a corporation while maintaining the pass-through taxation of a partnership or sole proprietorship.

Here are the key characteristics of an LLC business:

- **Limited Liability:** LLC members are not personally liable for the company's debts and obligations, which protects their personal assets. As an LLC is a separate legal entity, it provides a firmer layer of protection.

- **Pass-Through Taxation:** LLCs are taxed as pass-through entities by default.

- **Flexible Management Structure:** LLCs offer flexibility in terms of management. They can be member-managed, where all members are involved in management, or manager-managed, where designated managers oversee the business.

- **Operating Agreement:** An LLC operates under an operating agreement, a legal document that defines the members' rights, responsibilities, and ownership stakes, serving as a framework for resolving internal disputes.

- **Perpetual Life:** LLCs can exist indefinitely, maintaining continuity even as membership changes and ensuring long-term stability for the business.

Does an LLC align with your business goals?

Pros

- Liability protection

- Perceived as more credible

- Better succession planning

Cons

- Potential for double taxation

- More reporting to regulators

- Ownership transfer restrictions

Corporation

The most complex business structure is the corporation, which is suited for larger businesses with extensive operations and multiple shareholders. While the specific requirements vary by jurisdiction, corporations generally involve more paperwork, legal formalities, and ongoing compliance obligations than sole proprietorships or partnerships.

Here are its key features:

- **Separate Legal Entity:** A corporation is a distinct legal entity, and it can sue and be sued, enter into contracts, and own property under its name.

- **Limited Liability:** This structure allows owners to enjoy protection for their personal assets even when the corporation faces financial difficulties or legal issues.

- **Double Taxation:** Corporations face double taxation. The corporation pays corporate income tax on its profits, and shareholders pay personal income tax on dividends.

- **Management Structure:** Corporations typically have a board of directors and management team that oversee the business's operations.

- **Stringent Regulatory Compliance:** Corporations are subject to various regulatory requirements, including filing financial statements and complying with securities laws.

Is forming a corporation the better fit for you?

Pros

- Better access to capital

- Limited liability

- Can operate at a bigger scale

Cons

- Expensive to set up and maintain

- Double taxation

- Subject to heavy scrutiny

Choosing the proper structure for your business is crucial, so take the time to evaluate your options carefully.

Setting Up A Business Structure

Once you've determined the ideal structure, it's time to navigate the legal maze and register your business. Previously, setting up a business was a challenging and expensive affair. But thanks to technology, it's now much more straightforward. Here's how to get started:

Pick and Register a Business Name

Choosing your business name is like picking your identity, and it's a legal requirement to register it. If you're going to operate under a name different from your LLC or Corporation, you'll need to file for a DBA (Doing Business As).

Before you fall in love with a name, make sure it's available! You can search your state's business registry or the US Patent and Trademark Office (USPTO) database. With over 33 million small businesses in the US, competition for good names is fierce.

Trademark Your Assets

Getting a name isn't enough. You need to trademark it along with other assets like slogans and logos. This ensures others can't copy or misuse your assets.

File with the USPTO. The US Patent and Trademark Office handles this. The process can take a few months, but it's worth it. Think of it as insurance for your brand's reputation.

Apply for Federal Tax ID number (EIN)

Just like an individual's social security number, your business needs a unique identifier—an Employer Identification Number (EIN). It's required if you plan on hiring employees or forming a corporation.

You can get it online directly from the IRS. With your EIN, you can file taxes, open a business bank account, and apply for necessary licenses.

Open a Business Bank Account

Once you have the EIN, you should open a business bank account. Separating personal and business finances isn't just good practice—it's the law if you have an LLC or Corporation. A business account helps you track your revenue, manage expenses, and look more professional. Plus, you may receive credit and loan offers from banks with a bank account!

Determine if You Need a State Tax ID Number

On top of your federal EIN, many states require businesses to get a State Tax ID—especially if you'll be paying state taxes like income or sales tax. Rules vary, so check with your state's Department of Revenue. For example, you'll need this ID in states like California for any sales tax reporting.

Obtain Permits and Licenses

You might need special licenses to operate depending on your industry and location. For example, food services, construction, and other regulated sectors require permits. Skipping this step could lead to hefty fines or even shutdowns.

Get Business Insurance

Approximately 60% of businesses face lawsuits each year. Thus, business insurance is non-negotiable. It protects you from the unexpected—a lawsuit, an accident, or a natural disaster.

There are different types of insurance, but general liability insurance is the most common. It provides the best level of protection for your business. Also, you should consider workers' compensation insurance (if you have employees) and professional liability insurance (if you offer services).

Hire and Classify Employees

Hiring becomes essential if you're not a sole proprietor handling everything yourself. This process includes posting job ads, screening applicants, conducting interviews, and extending job offers. Alternatively, you could collaborate with employment agencies to manage these tasks.

However, the next step in hiring is classifying. Note that 30% of companies incorrectly classify employees, leading to back taxes and penalties. Employees get tax withholdings and benefits, while contractors don't. Be clear on the difference!

Comply With Labor Laws

Labor laws are in place to protect both you and your employees. These laws cover everything from minimum wage to workplace safety standards. Thus, familiarize yourself with the Fair Labor Standards Act (FLSA) and Occupational Safety and Health Administration (OSHA) regulations and make sure you comply.

Keep Good Records

Good record-keeping is crucial for keeping track of taxes, tracking financial health, and avoiding compliance issues. You'll need to maintain clear records of income, expenses, payroll, and tax documents. Invest in an accounting system—whether it's QuickBooks, Xero, or even an Excel spreadsheet.

Consult the Professionals

Professional help goes a long way. Starting a business involves many legal and financial complexities. Working with professionals can save you headaches and money from taxes to contracts. Thus, consult with a lawyer, accountant, or business advisor and seek specialist help in areas in which you fall short.

Basics of Accounting, Bookkeeping, and Financial Management

Evidence shows that a significant number of people lack experience in bookkeeping. Although bookkeeping may seem intimidating and filled with jargon, when broken down and clarified, it becomes much more manageable. And from a finance standpoint, it is super important.

Below, I'll explain some of the most important terms in bookkeeping using everyday examples so you can feel confident handling your business's finances. And from a finance standpoint, it is super important.

Below, I'll explain some of the most important terms in bookkeeping using everyday examples so you can feel confident handling your business's finances.

Assets

Think of assets as everything your business owns that has value. It could be cash, equipment, buildings, or even the computer you're reading this on. Assets are like the tools in your toolbox—they help you run and grow your business.

For example, if you own a bakery, your assets include your oven, the cash in your bank account, and supplies like flour and sugar.

Liabilities

Liabilities are the opposite of assets—what your business owes to others. This could be money you owe suppliers, loans you've taken out, or bills you haven't paid yet. Think of liabilities as your financial "to-do" list.

For example, if you borrowed $10,000 to buy that bakery oven, that loan is a liability.

Equity

Equity is left over after subtracting your liabilities from your assets. In other words, the portion of the business belongs to you (or the owners). Imagine it as the slice of the pie that's yours after everyone else gets paid.

For example, if your bakery has $50,000 in assets and $20,000 in liabilities, your equity is $30,000. That's the value of your business that you own outright.

Single-Entry Bookkeeping

Single-entry bookkeeping is the more straightforward method of tracking your finances. You record transactions like income and expenses once. It's like keeping a checkbook, where you jot down how much you make and spend.

Double-Entry Bookkeeping

Double-entry bookkeeping is a more accurate method where every transaction is recorded twice: once as a "debit" and once as a "credit." This ensures that your books are always balanced (think of it like balancing scales).

Cash Basis of Accounting

The cash basis of accounting is a simple method in which you record income when you actually receive cash and expenses when you pay them. It's like tracking money as it moves in and out of your wallet.

For example, if you sell a cake today and the customer pays you $100, you record that $100 now. If you pay for ingredients tomorrow, you record that payment tomorrow.

Accrual Basis of Accounting

The accrual basis of accounting records income and expenses when they happen, not when the money changes hands. It's like marking a check on your calendar the day you send it, even if it hasn't been cashed yet.

For example, if you deliver a cake today but won't get paid until next week, you still record the income today. The same goes for expenses—if you bought ingredients today but haven't paid for them yet, you record the cost now.

Income Statement

An income statement (sometimes called a profit and loss statement) is like a business report card. It shows your income, expenses, and whether you made a profit or suffered a loss over a specific period.

Your bakery's income statement might show $10,000 in sales and $7,000 in expenses at the end of the month, leaving you with $3,000 in profit.

Retained Earnings

Retained earnings are the profits your business has made over time that you've decided to keep rather than pay out to yourself or other owners. Think of retained earnings like a savings account for your business—money stays in the business to help it grow.

For example, if your bakery made $5,000 in profit last year but left $2,000 in the business instead of taking all of it as income, that $2,000 is your retained earnings.

Setting up Accounting System

Bookkeeping is related to accounting. While the former involves recording transactions, accounting involves analyzing, summarizing, and reporting the data.

Again, this may seem not very easy. But once you know the entire process, things become much more manageable. Here are the steps involved in accounting:

Itemize All Expenses by Department

As your business grows, your expenses will increase, too. To keep things clear, start by itemizing costs by category or department. This could be marketing, operations, inventory, or payroll. Doing this helps you see exactly where your money is going and if any department is overspending.

Adhere to All Income, Employment, and Excise Taxes

Reporting on taxes is the fundamental duty of accounting. Depending on your business type, you'll need to stay on top of income taxes, employment taxes (if you have employees), and possibly excise taxes (for specific goods like alcohol, tobacco, or gasoline).

You'll need to report your business income to the IRS. If you're a sole proprietor, you'll do this on your personal tax return. It gets more complicated for corporations or LLCs, so a CPA might help.

Set Up a Payroll System

If you're hiring employees, one of the first things you need is a solid payroll system. This system should calculate employee wages, withhold the proper taxes, and issue payments on time.

Invest in payroll software that automates calculations, tax withholdings, and even direct deposit, freeing up your time to focus on growing the business.

Identify the Right Payment Gateway

When handling online sales, choosing the right payment gateway is essential. A payment gateway is a service that processes credit card payments for e-commerce. Think of it as the virtual cash register for your online store. PayPal, Stripe, and Square are some popular payment gateways that make it easy to process payments from customers worldwide.

Most payment gateways integrate seamlessly with accounting software, making reporting more accurate.

Some gateways are better for small businesses, while others are designed for higher-volume transactions. So do some homework.

Regularly Review and Evaluate Your Processes

No accounting system is "set it and forget it." Regularly reviewing your processes and financial reports helps you stay on top of your finances. Evaluate whether your current methods are working or if you need to upgrade software, adjust budgeting categories, or hire help.

Consult With a Professional or CPA

Last but not least, don't hesitate to bring in the pros. Consulting a CPA (Certified Public Accountant) or a financial advisor can save you money in the long run. They can help you with taxes, ensure your accounting system is compliant, and even offer advice on scaling your business.

Wrap Up

This chapter walked you through building a strong foundation for your business, from picking the proper structure to navigating legal and financial essentials. With these basics in place, you're setting yourself up for stability and success as you start your journey.

Action Steps

1. Decide which business structure best aligns with your goals.

2. Register your business and obtain any permits or licenses needed.

3. Set up a simple accounting system to track finances from day one.

Up Next

Now that you've set the foundation, it's time to get ready for the big launch! In the next chapter, we'll cover the final steps before going live, from creating your workspace to organizing your operations so you can hit the ground running.

Chapter Three

Launching With Confidence

As your business's launch date nears, you may experience sleepless nights. Staying awake late brooding about the perfect marketing slogan or ideal workstation can be stressful and unproductive.

To get out of this overthinking maze, you must set your ducks in the row for the launch. This involves creating an infrastructure to deliver the products and services to the customers. In other words, you need to set up an office and/or workshop.

When we dream of starting a business, we often imagine the perfect setup: a flawless logo, a stunning website, and a workspace that inspires us to feel like true entrepreneurs. But it's a giant trap—I've fallen into myself, spending far too long on aesthetics instead of just getting started. The reality is that some of the world's biggest companies began with minimal resources. Amazon, for example, famously used desks made from doors to save money, even when they were successful enough to afford more. Large companies like Google and Apple started in garages with basic setups, focusing on testing their ideas rather than perfecting every detail upfront.

Starting lean with a minimum viable product (MVP) allows you to test your idea without a significant upfront investment. If you're starting an internet business, you can even keep your day job, working on your idea during evenings and weekends. This "lean" approach lets you focus on self-sustaining the business before you go all in. Avoiding the setup trap means focusing on growth, customers, and real progress where it counts. I've made these mistakes myself and am here to help you avoid learning it the hard way!

Building an office doesn't have to mean renting a space in an expensive commercial area, which can significantly increase costs. In many cases, particularly in the digital age, a physical space may not even be necessary, depending on your type of business. You can set up a virtual store and manage operations from home, making home-based businesses simple and budget-friendly. Technology must be used effectively to make this work.

This chapter offers clear, practical guidance to help you begin your business confidently. It is organized into three main sections: launching a home-based business, setting up a physical location, and building an online presence.

Additionally, you'll explore strategies to use AI to meet your business goals. Everything is explained in straightforward language with minimal technical terms, so there's no need for advanced technical knowledge to follow along.

A Home-Based Business

With rising rental costs, businesses seek ways to cut costs in this inflated economy. One way smart money managers do this is by cutting their dependence on office space, which is no longer a prerequisite to launching a business.

The home-based business model has become increasingly popular, offering entrepreneurs the freedom and flexibility to operate from the comfort of their own space.

The US Small Business Association reports that 50% of all small businesses begin at home. Tech giants like Apple and Google also started at home. In 1998, Larry Page and Sergey Brin, then graduate students at Stanford University, founded Google in their garage.

The most significant benefit of starting a home-based business is reduced upfront capital. The most significant advantage of starting a home-based business is the lower initial costs. You can avoid expenses for office rent, maintenance, or committing to long-term contracts.

However, there are a few things you need to know before you launch a home-based business.

Zoning Laws

All land in the United States is subject to zoning laws. These laws determine what activities are permitted in different zones, such as residential, commercial, or industrial.

Some areas may have restrictions on home-based businesses, particularly those that involve significant customer traffic or noise.

For example, in a residential zone, you might be allowed to operate a small office-based business but prohibited from running a large-scale or mid-scale manufacturing facility.

Note that zoning laws are local-specific. Thus, checking with your city or county's zoning department is critical to ensure your business activity complies with local regulations.

License and Permits

In most cases, you will need a business license from your city or county to legally operate, even if the business is home-based.

Depending on the niche of your home-based business, you may need to obtain specific licenses or permits from your local government. These can include:

- **Business License:** A general license required for operating a business within a jurisdiction.

- **Home Occupation Permit:** A specific permit allowing you to conduct business activities from home.

- **Professional Licenses:** If you provide professional services (e.g., legal, medical, or accounting), you may need a professional license.

- **Sales Tax License:** If your business sells products, you may need a state sales tax permit.

Ensure you have all the permits in place before you launch.

Home Owners Association (HOA) Rules

It's highly unlikely you're alone in the middle of a wilderness. Chances are you're living in a society. And if you live in a HOA community, their rules may restrict home-based businesses.

HOAs often specify if commercial operations are permitted within the community. And if so, they may have restrictions on:

- **Number of Employees:** HOA may limit the number of employees working from home.

- **Customer Traffic:** HOA might restrict the amount of customer traffic to and from your home.

- **Business Hours:** It may specify the hours you can operate your business.

- **Noise Levels:** HOA may have noise restrictions to prevent disturbances to neighbors.

So, check with the rules and ensure you're not breaching them.

Insurance

Reviewing your homeowner's insurance policy to ensure it covers potential business-related liabilities is essential. You may need additional coverage to protect your assets and business operations.

If a client gets injured on your property while conducting business, your homeowner's insurance may or may not cover the liability.

Mortgage or Lease Impact

If you're renting or have a mortgage on your home, you should check your lease or mortgage agreement for any restrictions on home-based businesses.

For example, your lease might prohibit you from operating a business that involves heavy machinery or frequent deliveries. Alternatively, you might need to notify your landlord or lender before starting a home-based business.

So, unless it is a property you own, you need to communicate with your landlord or mortgage provider.

A Brick-and-Mortar Business

There are times when setting up a home business is not an option. For example, the HOA may not permit you to set up a shop, or your customers may not be willing to travel the distance to your home.

In such cases, your next best (and cost-effective) option is to set up a brick-and-mortar business. A brick-and-mortar business is a traditional business that has a physical storefront or location. These businesses are the soul of the American entrepreneurial spirit and dominate the business landscape.

Some examples of these storefronts include grocery stores, restaurants, salons, gyms, pet shops, etc.

Starting a brick-and-mortar business involves more complexity and regulatory oversight than a home-based business. This is primarily due to using a physical commercial space, which brings additional legal, zoning, and operational requirements.

In addition to the permits required for home-based businesses, you must apply for more. And this depends on the location you're in.

But in general, you'll have to take care of the following:

Building Permits

Brick-and-mortar businesses need a commercial location to operate. These locations must be in line with the local regulations. Whether building new or renovating, permits ensure that your construction adheres to local building codes, zoning regulations, and safety standards.

Authorities will conduct inspections to determine suitability and verify compliance. Moreover, the fire department will inspect the premises to ensure they meet fire safety standards, including having the appropriate fire exits, alarms, and fire extinguishing systems. You must pass a health inspection to ensure sanitary conditions and safe operations in industries like food service, healthcare, or personal care (e.g., hair salons).

After inspection, you'll get the license and clearance needed to launch your brick-and-mortar business.

Employer Identification Number (EIN)

We already discussed EIN, or Employer Identification Number, in the previous chapter, but it's worth reiterating here.

An EIN is a nine-digit number the IRS assigns to US businesses for tax purposes. If you plan to hire employees, you'll need an EIN to report and pay employment taxes. Even sole proprietors often obtain an EIN to keep their Social Security Number private.

Thus, apply for and obtain an EIN. If you're residing outside the US, I recommend reviewing your country's tax laws and taking appropriate action based on them.

You can take ChatGPT's help using this prompt:

Can you help me find the tax laws in [Country/Region]? I'm looking for information on [specific tax topic, e.g., income tax, corporate tax, tax filing requirements, etc.] for businesses in [Country/Region].

Alternatively, asking your tax-law attorney or certified public accountant is highly recommended.

Sales Tax Permit

As a brick-and-mortar business, you're generally responsible for collecting sales tax from your customers and remitting it to the appropriate tax authority.

You'll need to calculate the sales tax amount based on the purchase price and the applicable tax rate. The tax is typically collected from the customer at the time of sale and included in the total purchase price.

However, some goods and services may be exempt from sales tax, such as essential items, charitable donations, or certain types of business-to-business transactions. It's best to familiarize yourself with the sales tax exemptions in your jurisdiction.

Here's a prompt you can use to ask for help with sales tax collection:

> *Can you guide me through the process of collecting and remitting sales tax for my brick-and-mortar business? I need help understanding:*
>   - *How to calculate the sales tax based on the purchase price and applicable tax rate*
>
>   - *When and how to collect the tax from customers during a sale*
>
>   - *How to remit the collected sales tax to the correct tax authority*

After collection, you'll have to file sales tax returns periodically. The frequency will depend on your state's requirements and the amount of sales tax collected. You must also remit the collected sales tax to the tax authority within the specified deadline.

Signage And Adverts Permit

Most municipalities regulate the types of signs businesses can display on the exterior of the building. Brick-and-mortar businesses must navigate these regulations carefully to avoid penalties or having to remove non-compliant signs.

Local regulations often specify the maximum and minimum size of signs allowed for businesses. The type of signage can also be restricted, such as illuminated signs, billboards, banners, sandwich boards, or digital displays.

There are also restrictions and specifications on placement, visibility, height, design, content, and frequency. For example, brick-and-mortar businesses in Stanton,

California, are allowed no more than six annual banner permits. Likewise, Garland, Texas, allows banners within the first 20 days of store opening.

You can visit your local city's website for detailed information on specific permit requirements relevant to your location.

Here is a sample ChatGPT prompt:

> *Can you help me find the permit requirements for [specific activity or business] in [City/Region]? I'm looking for detailed information on local regulations and any necessary permits for this location.*

Environmental Permit

Certain brick-and-mortar businesses will need an environmental permit. These permits are typically required when a business's operations involve air, land, or water emissions, waste management, use of hazardous substances, or activities that may cause pollution.

Businesses that release pollutants into the air - manufacturing plants, auto body shops, and even large-scale dry cleaners - will need an air emission permit.

Similarly, businesses that discharge wastewater or other substances into local water bodies, such as manufacturers, food processors, and breweries, will require water discharge permits.

Developers, construction companies, and other businesses involved in activities that disturb soil or natural habitats—such as excavation, grading, or land clearing—must obtain land disturbance permits. Compliance with environmental regulations, including the Clean Air Act, the Clean Water Act, and the Endangered Species Act, is required. Failure to secure and adhere to these permits can lead to fines, lawsuits, and business closures.

Insurance

Insurance coverage is even more critical if you're opening a brick-and-mortar store. It provides financial protection in the event of unexpected losses or liabilities.

The specific types of insurance needed will vary depending on the nature of your business and the risks involved. The most common ones are property insurance, general liability insurance, commercial auto insurance, product liability insurance, property damage to others (PDO), and workers' compensation insurance.

Here is a sample ChatGPT prompt:

Can you help me determine the types of insurance I need for my business in [Industry/Type of Business]? I want to understand the specific coverage options, such as property insurance, liability insurance, workers' compensation, or others relevant to my business risks.

Labor Laws

If you have employees working at your brick-and-mortar location, you must comply with local labor laws. These laws protect workers' rights and set minimum standards for employment conditions, such as wages, hours, workplace safety, and anti-discrimination practices.

Here is how you can find regional labor laws in the US:

- **Reach out to your state's Department of Labor:** State laws may provide additional protections beyond federal regulations.

- **Contact your local Occupational Safety and Health Administration (OSHA) office:** For more information, call 1-800-321-OSHA.

- Visit the **US Equal Employment Opportunity Commission (EEOC)** website. For further details, call 1-800-669-4000 or visit www.eeoc.gov.

Although many states have higher minimum wages, the Fair Labor Standards Act (FLSA) sets federal minimum wage standards. Likewise, the Occupational Safety and Health Administration (OSHA) enforces safety standards, requiring employers to address potential workplace risks such as machinery, hazardous chemicals, and fire hazards.

Here is a sample ChatGPT prompt:

> *Can you help me find the labor laws specific to [State/Region]? I'm looking for information on [specific labor law topic, e.g., minimum wage, overtime, workplace safety, employee rights, etc.] in that area.*

Remember to keep your employees safe and happy as a business owner.

An Online Business

Now, let's explore the third type of business and how to launch it: online ventures. These businesses offer unparalleled flexibility for both owners and employees. While an online business can be run from home, it doesn't have to be. Some operate entirely remotely, while others blend online operations with a physical presence, depending on their model.

An online business primarily or entirely operates through the Internet, eliminating the need for a physical storefront. It can sell products, services, or digital content directly to customers via websites or online marketplaces. Though many home-based businesses also use online platforms, online ventures are specifically designed to leverage the Internet as their primary operational hub. They may or may not have a physical location, but their core activities and customer interactions occur online.

One significant advantage of online businesses is their potential for global reach. They can serve customers worldwide and are often easier to scale than traditional or home-based businesses, typically limited by geographical constraints. In contrast, home-based companies usually cater to local areas, especially if their services require a physical presence.

Online businesses are generally the easiest to start and manage of the three types. In many cases, you won't need permits either. However, there are key regulations and requirements for online businesses in the US, including:

Business License

Nearly every business in the United States requires some license or permit to operate legally, with a business license being the most common.

Sales Tax

If you sell tangible goods or services to customers, you're generally required to collect and remit sales tax. Similarly, you'll have to file self-employment taxes if you're a sole proprietor or LLC. You must pay federal, state, and local taxes on your earnings. Track all business-related expenses, which can be deducted from your income when filing taxes.

Employer Identification Number (EIN)

You'll need an Employer Identification Number (EIN) from the IRS for tax purposes, even if you don't have employees.

Here is a sample ChatGPT prompt:

> *Can you guide me on obtaining an Employer Identification Number (EIN) from the IRS for tax purposes, even if I don't have any employees? I need to know the process and any requirements for applying.*

Consumer Protection Laws

Online businesses must comply with federal and state consumer protection laws, such as the Federal Trade Commission (FTC) Act and state truth-in-advertising laws. The FTC Act prohibits unfair or deceptive business practices, including false advertising, misleading claims, and deceptive pricing.

Here is a sample prompt through which you can take ChatGPT's help to extract more information:

> *Can you provide an overview of consumer protection laws in [Country/Region]? I'm particularly interested in understanding how these laws apply to [specific industry or scenario, e.g., retail, e-commerce, product warranties, false advertising, etc.] and what businesses must do to ensure compliance.*

Data Privacy Laws

Online businesses collect data regularly. Businesses that collect and store customer data must comply with data privacy laws, such as the General Data Protection Regulation (GDPR) and local-level data privacy laws.

Here is a sample prompt through which you can take ChatGPT's help to extract more information:

> *Can you help me understand data privacy laws in [Country/Region]? I'm seeking information on compliance requirements, particularly regarding [specific aspect, e.g., data collection, storage, sharing, or user consent], and how these laws apply to businesses handling customer data.*

Building a Home Workspace

Companies invest a considerable amount of money in creating the best workplace for their employees. Research has concluded that the office setting directly impacts creativity, productivity, and team environment.

When you work from home, you must create an inspiring workspace. Your home workspace is more than just a workplace; it's a catalyst for success.

In this section, we'll delve into creating a home workspace that inspires, motivates, and elevates your entrepreneurial journey.

Designate A Dedicated Workspace

Any corner of the house may be suitable for working from home. But it's best if you specify a workspace. A dedicated workspace, even if it's just a corner of a room, helps separate your business activities from your personal life. It creates a psychological distinction between "work mode" and "home mode," which improves focus and reduces distractions.

If possible, an entire room is the best option. This ensures you can work distraction-free for hours, especially if you have a family with small children. If not, you can utilize the spare space in the garage, attic, or living room.

Invest In The Right Furniture

Office-specific furniture will support your work for an extended period, ensuring you stay productive. If you already have the furniture, great! If not, we've got some shopping to do.

Invest in an ergonomic chair that supports your back and promotes good posture. Then, choose a desk that suits your work style (standing desks are becoming popular to facilitate movement). As an optional item, consider adding storage units and shelves.

Stable Internet Connection

The Internet will be your gateway to the outside world. It is your lifeline to customers, suppliers, and the digital world.

Thus, invest in a fast and reliable internet connection. If available in your area, consider a fiber-optic connection or cable internet. When prospecting for your options, be aware of any data limits imposed by internet service providers (ISPs). Consider unlimited plans or generous data allowances if your business relies heavily on data usage.

A backup internet connection, such as a mobile hotspot, can be helpful in case of outages. Therefore, also invest in proper data plans.

Ensure Proper Lighting

Imagine a dimly lit, shadowy workspace. Does it inspire you to get up and work? Probably not. Good lighting is more than just a necessity; it's a powerful tool that can transform your home office into a haven of productivity and inspiration.

Poor lighting can also lead to fatigue, headaches, and blurred vision. Adequate lighting helps prevent these problems and keeps you focused for longer.

Backup Power

If you live in an area with constant power outages, you must plan for them through power backup solutions. Think of uninterrupted power supplies (UPSs) and batteries that keep your devices running even after power failure.

Determine your equipment's wattage and power requirements to select the appropriate backup system. Also, consider how long your system needs to provide backup power during outages.

Keep Office Supplies Handy

Maintaining a well-stocked supply closet ensures you have everything you need to stay organized and productive in your home-based office. This eliminates any excuses for not working due to running out of supplies. So, before launching your business, purchase essential office supplies, preferably in bulk. This includes pens, pencils, paper, ink, notebooks, binders, file folders, and more.

Embracing Technology for Business Success

Many people, particularly older entrepreneurs starting their first business, view technology as a daunting obstacle. They cling to the outdated belief that "If you build it, they will come."

However, in today's digital landscape, technology is indispensable. The tech-driven economy doesn't accommodate those who fail to leverage it effectively. This is especially true when launching a home-based or online business where traditional foot traffic doesn't apply.

Here's how you can embrace technology to your advantage:

Build A Website

While a website can be a vital asset for your business, it may not always be necessary, depending on your industry and target audience. Creating one can serve as your digital home, where customers and clients can interact with your brand and learn more about you.

You can use website builders like WordPress, Wix, or Squarespace to create a professional-looking site. These platforms provide customizable templates and intuitive tools for managing your website without advanced coding skills. Alternatively, you can hire a professional WordPress or Wix designer on platforms like Upwork or Fiverr to handle the work for you.

If selling online is part of your business plan, consider upgrading to an e-commerce website to streamline order processing and other transactions.

This revision acknowledges the optional nature of having a website while maintaining actionable advice for those who choose to have one.

Invest In A CRM and Project Management Tool

Depending on your business model, customer relationship management (CRM) software can be incredibly valuable for managing customer interactions and driving growth. While not always essential for every business, a CRM can streamline communication, track leads, and provide actionable insights through sales data analysis. Platforms like HubSpot, Salesforce, or Zoho CRM offer powerful tools to enhance customer service and team collaboration.

For project management, tools like Trello, Asana, or Monday.com can help keep projects organized and ensure timely completion. These platforms are designed to improve workflow efficiency and make managing tasks easier for you and your team.

By carefully evaluating your needs, you can decide whether a CRM, project management software or both are the right investments for your business.

Leverage Social Media

With 5.07 billion people active on social media, leveraging the right platforms can be highly valuable, depending on your business and target audience. Focus on where your ideal customers spend their time. For instance, platforms like Instagram or TikTok might be particularly effective if your audience skews younger. LinkedIn is a strong choice for a professional audience, while Facebook remains widely popular across various age groups. Being active where your audience already engages enables you to effectively showcase your products or services.

Social media activity can also help build trust, especially for new businesses. In a HubSpot survey, 49% of respondents said they trust brands that sell directly on social media platforms.

While there are many platforms to consider, selecting those most relevant to your niche is crucial. Instagram works exceptionally well for the food, lifestyle, and fashion industries, whereas TikTok thrives in entertainment and education niches. LinkedIn is ideal for business-to-business (B2B) networking, and Facebook suits e-commerce and local businesses.

Secure Your Digital Infrastructure

One of the biggest threats businesses face in the digital age is cyberattacks. If sensitive customer information is compromised, cyberattacks can damage customer trust, harm brand reputation, and lead to legal liabilities.

As cyber threats evolve, small businesses must prioritize security measures. This includes securing websites with firewalls and SSL certificates, implementing strong passwords and multi-factor authentication, keeping software up to date, and securing the Wi-Fi network. If all this sounds too technical, seek guidance from a cybersecurity specialist.

If you've employees or contractors, train them to recognize phishing emails, avoid suspicious links, and follow data protection protocols. Here is a sample prompt to take ChatGPT's help to learn more:

Can you help me secure my digital infrastructure? I need advice on best practices for [specific area, e.g., data encryption, network security, user authentication, or backup strategies] to protect my business from potential cyber threats.

Track Everything

The most significant benefit of using tech to run a business is that every action can be tracked. Business owners can gain insights into customer behavior, marketing effectiveness, and sales trends by collecting and analyzing data.

Thus, implement analytics tools like Google Analytics, Crazy Egg, and CRM analytics software to track and measure the effectiveness of your initiatives. Then, take measures to optimize them. Here is how you can take ChatGPT's help:

Can you help me with strategies for analyzing customer data? I want to understand [specific goal, e.g., customer behavior, purchasing trends, or segmentation] and how to use this data effectively to improve my business decisions and marketing efforts.

Using AI to Boost Productivity

Unless you live under a rock, you must have heard of AI and its game-changing capabilities. From writing detailed blogs to generating realistic images, AI is the new tech frontier. And like an astute business owner, you must get AI on your side and leverage it to the fullest.

In my last book, I discussed using AI for business planning. To reiterate, here are some areas where AI can help:

Content Creation

Content is key for digital marketing, but creating high-quality content can be time-consuming and expensive. AI tools can generate content quickly and at a fraction of the cost.

Use AI writing tools like ChatGPT, Copy.ai, or Jasper to create blog posts, social media updates, product descriptions, and ad copy. These tools rely on natural language processing (NLP) to produce engaging content tailored to your audience. They all offer free plans, which are often enough for small businesses. Plus, the time saved by using these tools can quickly offset the subscription cost if you choose a paid plan.

Customer Service

AI-powered chatbots can respond immediately to customer queries, offer support 24/7, and improve customer satisfaction without needing a dedicated support team.

Platforms like Tidio, ManyChat, or Intercom automate basic customer interactions, such as answering frequently asked questions, guiding customers through a purchase, or scheduling appointments. Chatbots can also collect customer feedback and offer product recommendations, enhancing the user experience.

Social Media Management

AI can also help you manage your social media accounts. It can streamline the process by automating content scheduling, engagement, and analytics. Tools like Hootsuite, Buffer, or Loomly utilize AI features to help you schedule posts, optimize posting times, and engage with followers automatically.

Financial Management

Finance is essential to any business, and keeping your venture on solid financial footing is important. While calculated risks can sometimes be beneficial, having a professional accountant on board dramatically increases your ability to make informed financial decisions. Though some small businesses may find hiring an accountant challenging in the early stages, bringing one on as soon as possible can provide invaluable support and guidance that's well worth the investment.

While not a replacement for an accountant, AI tools can automate many accounting and financial tracking aspects. Software like QuickBooks, Xero, or Wave can automate invoicing, expense tracking, and financial reporting tasks. These platforms can also generate insights into cash flow and profitability trends.

By staying on top of finances, you can make better decisions to keep your business afloat.

Task Automation

Automation software can dramatically improve efficiency by handling repetitive tasks, freeing valuable time for more strategic priorities. Tools like Zapier or IFTTT are excellent for automating workflows, such as sending emails, scheduling meetings, or updating CRM systems. These platforms connect with various business apps to perform tasks that would otherwise require manual effort.

I've had a great team of virtual assistants for a while, but their capabilities have dramatically improved with AI integration. Virtual assistants improved through innovative technology to further boost productivity and accomplish tasks previously beyond their skill set. Since incorporating AI capabilities into my team, their performance has reached new heights. They've become not only more efficient at handling routine tasks but also adept at assisting with creative and strategic work. By continually adapting and learning, they can use these tools to tackle challenges with greater intelligence and creativity.

While automation and AI tools offer incredible benefits, they can come with a learning curve. It's essential to prepare for the effort involved in mastering these systems. However, the enhanced productivity and efficiency payoff is undoubtedly worth it.

Wrap Up

You're now prepared to launch your business with confidence! This chapter covered the setup steps for home-based, brick-and-mortar, and online businesses and tips for creating a functional workspace and choosing the right tech tools. You're almost ready to welcome your first customers.

Action Steps

1. Confirm the best setup for your business—home-based, physical, or online.

2. Double-check all required permits, licenses, and insurance.

3. Get your workspace and essential tools ready for day one.

Up Next

In the next chapter, we'll explore digital marketing and branding. You'll learn how to create a standout online presence, develop a memorable brand, and attract the right customers to grow your business.

Chapter Four

Mastering Digital Marketing and Brand Power

E very business owner knows that they need to market their business to succeed. In 2024, the global digital advertising and marketing market reached $667 billion. GlobalNewswire estimates this figure will reach $786.2 billion by 2026, meaning more businesses are pumping more money into digital channels.

However, have you heard the claim that 97% of internet marketing fails? That's actually a popular myth. No one's sure how much marketing money fails, but one thing is for sure: just because you're spending money on marketing doesn't mean you're succeeding. You could be spending money on a losing cause and don't even know it.

Especially new business owners with little or no marketing knowledge are at a greater risk of burning up their hard-earned cash. I don't like to admit it, but I've been there and done that!

The good news is that many of the failures are avoidable. With the proper knowledge and direction, you can use digital marketing to your advantage instead of a money pit.

In this chapter, we'll go over the basics of digital marketing and branding—arguably the most overused and misunderstood concept in marketing. In the first part, you'll learn about the various digital marketing channels and the core concept of branding. The second part is hands-on, where you'll learn how to build an online presence from scratch and use AI in marketing.

By the end, you'll have a working knowledge of digital marketing to a point where you can carry it out on your own or hire a marketer and keep them accountable so they don't throw your money down the drain.

Digital Marketing Fundamentals: Kept Simple for Non-Marketers

The road to mastery starts with mastering the fundamentals. So, let's start at the very basics.

Note that digital marketing is an overarching term composed of various components. Some components are linked, while others are not. In this section, I'll list the core concepts of digital marketing and their components.

In addition to that, there are a few other things that need explanations: branding, marketing, and advertising. These are often used interchangeably, which is not only misleading but also dangerous. You'll come across these terms in the rest of the book. So, you must know what they mean and don't mean.

Understanding Brand

Imagine walking into a store with an extensive collection of wine. You stroll through the selection, inspecting the bottles randomly. Suddenly, a purple-hued bottle with an unusual shape catches your eye. You can't help but pick the bottle up, look at the label, and check its features and packaging. Impressed by the design, you head over the counter to buy it.

That's what a brand does. It helps a product stand out from the rest.

A brand is more than just your business name, logo, or slogan—it's the overall image and feeling people associate with your business. It's how your customers see you and what they think when they hear your name or see your products.

When someone suggests you need to "brand" your business or invest in "branding," they mean creating an emotional connection or association with your company name. If it's about you personally, it refers to building a personal brand.

Phil Knight and the Power of "Why"

This brand concept goes deeper than just appearance or messaging. It's about connecting with people on an emotional level, which is exactly what Nike's founder, Phil Knight, did during a keynote speech. Instead of talking about Nike's cutting-edge technologies or celebrity endorsements, he told a story about the runners who get up at 5 a.m., no matter how cold or wet the weather is, and push themselves to do their best.

He asked the audience, "If you run at least once a week, stand up." Then, he narrowed it down: "If you run 2-3 times a week, regardless of the weather, keep standing." By the end, only a few people remained standing. He pointed to them and said, "We are for you. When you get up to run in the cold and wet, we're standing out there with you, cheering you on. We're the inner athlete. We're the inner champion."

Knight powerfully connected Nike's brand to something deeper—the "why" behind it without mentioning the latest product features or which athletes wear their gear. Nike's "Just Do It" is more than a slogan; it's a rallying cry for those who push through adversity to be their best.

The 'Why' Behind the Brand

It's not what you do that draws people in—it's why you do it. This core motivation is a differentiator in any business, career, or life. Like Nike, your brand must connect on a deeper level with your audience. You can wander through life hoping and waiting for something to click or go through it with intention, knowing your 'why,' and heading straight to where you belong.

If you want to create a brand people can genuinely relate to, if you want them to feel passionate about your product, service, or even you as a person, it starts with knowing your 'why.' Your brand should embody that purpose and resonate with others in a way that's impossible to ignore.

Marketing vs Advertising

Another misconception most people outside the marketing world have is that marketing and advertising are the same. But there's a critical subtle difference.

Marketing is about your activities to get people interested in your product or service. It includes everything you do to understand your customers, tell your story, and attract potential buyers to your business.

Advertising is a part of marketing. It's the specific action of promoting your products or services through paid methods. Take note of the word "paid". Advertising means placing an ad somewhere—like in a local newspaper, on social media, or on a billboard—to make people aware of your brand or encourage them to buy something.

Marketing helps people know you exist, while advertising lets you directly tell them, through paid mediums, about your products.

Let's dive into digital marketing with the definitions out of the way.

So, what is digital marketing? Digital marketing is simply marketing your products or services using the internet. It's how you promote your business online, using tools like websites, social media, emails, and search engines to reach people.

With the rise of the internet, most people are now more engaged in online channels than offline channels. A report by eMarketer reveals that most consumers worldwide prefer searching online over in-store for specific categories like electronics, clothes, toys, books, and more. As a result, a significant portion of marketing budgets is now directed toward digital marketing channels.

The conclusion is that you cannot ignore digital marketing as a business owner.

As already said, digital marketing is an all-encompassing term comprising various components. These are:

- SEO

- PPC

- Content marketing

- Social media marketing

- Email marketing

- Affiliate marketing

- Video marketing

- Audio marketing

Let's unpack each component in more detail.

SEO or Search Engine Optimization

Recall the last time you wanted to learn more about something. What did you do? Chances are you Googled that thing. Googled is colloquial for "searching the internet." In this digital world, acquiring knowledge starts with a search.

Search Engine Optimization (SEO) is the process of improving your website to rank higher in search engine results, like on Google. When people search for something related to your business, SEO helps ensure they find your website first. The goal is to rank your website near the top of the search results so more people visit it.

Google holds 90% of the search market. And ranking higher on Google is the #1 priority for most businesses.

PPC or Pay-per-Click

PPC or Pay-Per-Click is a type of online advertising where you pay each time someone clicks on your ad. In PPC advertising, you create an ad, set a budget, and choose keywords or target settings to decide who sees your ad. Platforms like Google Ads, Facebook Ads, or Instagram Ads allow you to show your ads to people likely interested in your products or services.

In Google, these ads appear at the top of search engine results pages, marked as "Ad." If someone searches for "best bakery in Louisville" on Google, they might see your bakery's ad at the top of the search results. Search ads are effective for reaching people actively looking for something specific. Likewise, social media platforms target ads to people based on their interests, demographics, and behavior.

Content Marketing

Content marketing is a form of marketing in which you use content to gain awareness and generate leads for your business. The content can be blog posts, books, whitepapers, videos, reports, or anything that contains information.

Content marketing aims to provide content your potential customers find helpful, interesting, or entertaining. When people see that your content adds value to their lives, they're more likely to trust your brand and eventually buy from you. In fact, content marketing generates 3x as many leads as outbound marketing (where you reach out to customers) at 62% less cost!

Social Media Marketing

An estimated 5.17 billion people are on social media, accounting for 67% of the world's population. A large number of people will soon join the bandwagon. Social media marketing uses social platforms like Facebook, Instagram, TikTok, LinkedIn, and Twitter to promote your business.

Social media marketing is about creating content your audience finds interesting or entertaining and sharing it where they already spend their time. The goal is to build a community around your brand that is active, engaged, and genuinely connected to your business.

Email Marketing

Email is the old-school way of cost-effectively marketing your business. The top email marketers generate $36 for every $1 spent, making email one of the most effective marketing channels!

Email marketing involves sending targeted messages to subscribers who have willingly signed up to receive updates from your business. These messages can range from newsletters to special offers, product announcements, event invitations, or educational content.

The greatest benefit of email marketing is its reach. Unlike social media, where algorithms determine how many people see your posts, email marketing allows you to reach your subscribers directly in their inboxes. This makes it one of the most reliable ways to communicate your message.

Video Marketing

Video marketing is a powerful way to connect with your audience and promote your business using videos. It lets you tell stories through moving images and sound. With platforms like YouTube and Facebook Live, videos are more popular than text. With smartphones and free editing tools, the cost of creating and distributing videos is at an all-time low.

You can use different types of videos, such as user-generated, product demos, behind-the-scenes, and animated videos.

Audio Marketing

Along with videos, audio has also grown more mainstream. With platforms like Spotify, Apple Music, and Podbean, creators and businesses can host and broadcast audio. Besides podcasts, audiobooks and voice assistants like Siri allow businesses to get in front of users through audio. Audio content can make your content more accessible to people with visual impairments. If that's a niche you're in, take audio marketing seriously.

Affiliate Marketing

Affiliate marketing is a different form of marketing, where you don't do it yourself. Instead, you contract with others who send you leads and customers for a fee. These contractors are known as affiliates. These are the people or companies who promote your products or services. They can be bloggers, influencers, other businesses, or even customers who love what you do.

Affiliates promote their products using special tracking links. When someone clicks on the link and makes a purchase or completes another desired action, like signing up for a newsletter, the affiliate earns a commission.

When done correctly, affiliate marketing can ensure a steady stream of customers for your new business.

Note that digital marketing is a dynamic field that is constantly evolving. New marketing mediums and channels are emerging regularly, offering businesses innovative ways to reach and engage their target audience. This rapid change is driven by technological advancements, shifting consumer behaviors, and changing regulatory environments. So stay updated with the changing times and incorporate the most effective marketing mediums.

Creating a Strong Brand Identity

Before diving into digital marketing in the next section, it's crucial to establish a strong brand identity.

Here's why: Imagine a weight loss business launching a marketing campaign across various digital channels. It runs PPC ads claiming lemon juice aids weight loss, videos featuring a nanny gaining weight from a meat-rich diet, SEO campaigns ranking for dog food, and a podcast about swimming lessons. Without a cohesive brand identity, the message becomes fragmented, confusing the audience and diluting the brand's impact.

Now, unless the different concepts are connected to weight loss, the audience will likely get confused about what the business wants to convey. As Meridith Elliott Powell said, "The Confused Mind Never Buys." Hence, if your brand is unclear, it may be a turn off.

That's why creating a strong and consistent brand identity across all digital channels is crucial. Consistent branding helps build trust with potential customers. When people see that your brand has a cohesive look, feel, and tone across all touchpoints, they perceive it as more professional and reliable. Trust is crucial for small businesses, as consumers often choose brands they feel comfortable with.

A well-crafted brand identity helps your audience recognize your business immediately.

So, how do you create a strong brand identity? That's a task easier said than done. But with the right approach, you can create one. Here are the key components of a brand identity:

- **Brand name:** A memorable and relevant name that reflects your business's essence.

- **Logo:** A visually appealing symbol that represents your brand and is easily recognizable.

- **Tagline:** A catchy phrase that captures the essence of your brand and is memorable.

- **Brand Story:** A compelling narrative that explains your business's purpose, values, and mission.

- **Visual Identity:** Your brand's overall look and feel, including colors, typography, and imagery.

- **Tone Of Voice:** How your brand communicates with customers, whether formal, informal, or humorous.

- **Brand Personality:** The unique character or personality that your brand projects.

- **Brand Values:** The core principles and beliefs that guide your business's decisions and actions.

- **Brand Experience:** Customers' overall impression of your brand, from initial interaction to post-purchase experience.

- **Brand Messaging:** The key messages you want to communicate to your target audience.

When creating a brand experience, consider two things: target audience and authenticity. Will your target market appreciate a business that comes off as aggressive, soothing, cheerful, or alarming? And will you be able to wear that personality for the rest of your business life? Remember, authenticity matters as much as the products, personality, and values. If you're not authentic, you'll soon find yourself in a startup graveyard, a place for failed new businesses.

Looking Upon Freelancers to Assist You With Your Brand

Freelancers have been incredibly valuable to me, offering a flexible and affordable way to accomplish tasks without needing full-time employees. Whether tackling a one-time project or needing ongoing support, freelancers bring specialized skills that can save you time and money. Here's a look at what freelancers can do, how to hire the right one, and what you can expect to pay.

What Freelancers Can Do

Freelancers are skilled specialists who let you pay only for the specific services you need. Here's a quick breakdown of some of what they offer:

Graphic Design & Branding

Need a logo, website, or marketing materials? Freelancers can bring your vision to life. Platforms like 99Designs are perfect; you can run design contests and get several ideas from multiple designers. It's like having a creative team at your fingertips!

Writing & Content Creation

Freelancers can write everything from blog posts and social media updates to newsletters and books. They can also help optimize your content for search engines so your brand gets noticed.

Web Development & Maintenance

Do you need a website built or someone to maintain your existing one? Freelance developers are here to help, whether you need a minor tweak or a full-scale redesign.

Marketing & Social Media

Need help with SEO or running a digital marketing campaign? Freelancers can manage your online presence, including social media accounts, so you can focus on running your business.

Admin & Virtual Assistance

From data entry to calendar management, freelancers can handle the behind-the-scenes tasks that free up your time to focus on what really matters.

Tips for Hiring Freelancers

- Know what you need: Before you start looking, clarify your project's goals, timeline, and budget. The more specific you are, the easier it will be to find the right person for the job.

- Check their work: Take the time to look at a freelancer's portfolio or past work. It'll give you a sense of their style and abilities. Don't forget to read client reviews—these are often the best indicators of their reliability.

- Set expectations: Be upfront about what you expect—project scope, deadlines, and payment terms to avoid misunderstandings down the road.

- Start small: If you're unsure about a freelancer, consider starting with a smaller project first. It's a great way to test the waters before committing to something bigger.

- Time zones matter: If the freelancer is in a different time zone, aligning working hours and communication expectations is important. It helps prevent delays and ensures smooth collaboration.

What Freelancers Charge

Freelance rates vary widely based on experience, location, and the type of work. Here's a general guide to what you can expect to pay:

Graphic Design:

- **Low:** $15–$35 per hour (newbies or offshore designers)

- **Mid:** $35–$75 per hour (experienced designers with a solid portfolio)

- **High:** $75–$150+ per hour (high-end designers or specialists)

Content Writing:

- **Low**: $0.05–$0.10 per word (entry-level or general content)

- **Mid:** $0.10–$0.30 per word (more experienced writers with niche expertise)

- **High:** $0.30–$1.00+ per word (top-tier writers or specialized content)

Web Development:

- **Low:** $25–$50 per hour (junior developers or offshore)

- **Mid:** $50–$100 per hour (experienced developers with strong portfolios)

- **High:** $100–$200+ per hour (specialized or senior developers)

Digital Marketing:

- **Low:** $15–$30 per hour (beginner or offshore marketers)

- **Mid:** $30–$75 per hour (mid-level marketers with proven success)

- **High:** $75–$150+ per hour (highly experienced consultants)

Building an Online Presence

Finishing with theoretical knowledge, we can now begin implementing the acquired knowledge to build an online presence.

Irrespective of whether you're a home-based business, an online business, or a brick-and-mortar business, it's imperative to build an online presence. Establishing an effective online presence involves several steps, each leveraging digital marketing techniques to reach and engage the right audience. Here's a step-by-step guide on how to do it:

Define Your Brand Identity

If you haven't already, you must first define the brand identity. Otherwise, you'll be essentially flushing your marketing money down the drain.

Take a sheet of paper (or open a notepad if you're on PC) and note down the following:

- **Brand Purpose:** Why does your business exist? What problem does it solve?

- **Target Audience:** Who are your ideal customers? Understand their needs, preferences, and online behavior.

- **Brand Voice and Personality:** Establish a consistent tone for communication—whether it's friendly, formal, playful, etc.

- **Visual Identity:** Include elements like a logo, color palette, fonts, and design style that represent your brand across all digital channels.

Here is a sample ChatGPT to help you get started:

Can you help me define my brand identity for my business? I need guidance in establishing a strong foundation by identifying:
- *Brand Purpose: Why my business exists and the problem it solves*

- *Target Audience: Who my ideal customers are and their needs, preferences, and online behavior*

- *Brand Voice and Personality: The tone I should consistently use, like friendly, formal, or playful*

(Continues)

(Continued)

- *Visual Identity: Key elements like a logo, color palette, fonts, and design style to use across digital channels*

I want to make sure this is clear before starting my marketing strategy.

Include this at the top of every digital marketing strategy and report to help you stay on track.

Create A Website

Your website is your business's primary online home, its digital address. Therefore, you must invest in a website that speaks to your brand's image and personality.

To build a website, you can use free platforms like WordPress or SaaS tools like Shopify, Wix, and Site123. Whatever your choice, here are the things to focus on:

- **Domain and Hosting:** Domain is the name of your website, such as Google.com and Amazon.com, while hosting is the cloud server where your website will be hosted, such as CloudFlare.

- **Design and Functionality:** Build a professional, mobile-friendly website that aligns with your brand identity. Platforms like Shopify, WordPress, or Wix make designing a website for non-technical users easy.

- **User Experience (UX):** Ensure your website is easy to navigate, loads quickly, and has clear calls to action (e.g., "Buy Now," "Contact Us").

- **E-Commerce Capability:** If you're selling products, set up an e-commerce platform that allows customers to browse and purchase easily.

It's important not to spend too much time and money creating the website. You can hire a freelancer on Fiverr, Freelancer, or Upwork and get a professional-looking website for as little as $200.

Optimize Your Website With SEO

SEO, or search engine optimization, is the process of improving a website to rank higher in search engine results (like Google). The goal is to make the site more visible to people searching for related topics, which can bring in more visitors. It involves using relevant keywords, creating quality content, and ensuring the site runs smoothly.

Once you have your website ready, it is time to drive internet users to it, and you can do this through SEO. One of SEO's benefits is its organic traffic, which means users are actively looking for specific products or services. Thus, this traffic has a higher conversion rate.

When you optimize your website for search engines like Google, you increase its chances of appearing higher in search results for relevant keywords. This means more people will likely find your website and learn about your business.

SEO is a specialized process requiring research, content, optimization, and maintenance. Therefore, if you don't have the necessary time, skills, and knowledge, hiring SEO experts to handle the task would be better. Platforms like Fiverr and Freelancer have experienced contractors who will do it for you at an affordable price.

Develop A Content Marketing Strategy

Content marketing is a strategy where businesses create and share valuable, relevant content (like articles, videos, or social media posts) to attract and engage their target audience. Instead of directly promoting a product, it focuses on providing helpful information or entertainment and building trust and brand awareness, which can lead to sales over time.

Content marketing is the best way to increase traffic to your website consistently. By providing valuable content, you position yourself as an expert in your field, building trust and credibility with your audience. This is especially important for new businesses.

Therefore, develop and implement a content marketing strategy. Here are the things involved in content marketing:

- **Target Audience Identification:** Clearly define who you want to reach with your content.

- **Content Research:** Research what kind of content you can create and what the competition is like.

- **Content Creation:** Develop a variety of content formats, such as blog posts, articles, videos, infographics, and social media posts.

- **Content Distribution:** Determine the best channels to distribute your content, such as your website, social media, email marketing, and guest blogging.

- **Content Promotion:** Use paid and organic methods to promote your content and reach a wider audience.

Just like SEO, content marketing requires the eye of an expert. Content marketers specialize in this field and can implement the strategy for you.

Run Ads To Acquire Customers Faster

SEO and content marketing are great, but one disadvantage is that they take time to produce results.

Ads are the fastest way to acquire customers for a new business. Digital platforms like Google and Facebook allow you to set up and run targeted ads with a minimal marketing budget.

While the specific steps to run ads vary by the platform, here are some common steps:

- **Define Your Target Audience:** Identify your ideal customer's demographics, interests, and behaviors.

- **Create Compelling Ad Copy And Visuals:** Write persuasive ad copy and design eye-catching visuals.

- **Set Your Budget:** Determine how much you will spend on your ad campaign.

- **Track And Optimize:** Monitor the performance of your ads and make adjustments as needed to improve your results.

Running ads is also an activity that's best left to experts. Thus, hire a digital ads expert from platforms like Upwork and Freelancer to get the best ROI.

Leverage Email Marketing

Email marketing is a high-return marketing medium. It is also an effective way to nurture leads and engage your audience.

Here's how to do email marketing for your business:

- **Build an Email List:** Use lead magnets like discounts, free ebooks, or exclusive content to encourage visitors to subscribe to your email list. Place signup forms prominently on your website and social media channels.

- **Nurture Campaigns:** Create email campaigns that keep subscribers informed about new products, promotions, or valuable content. Platforms like Mailchimp or ConvertKit allow you to design and automate these emails.

- **Personalization:** Segment your email list based on customer interests or behavior to make your emails more personalized and relevant, increasing open rates and conversions.

Emails work well with your website and paid ads. When someone shows interest in your business (a "lead"), building a connection with them before they're ready to buy is important. Regular, helpful emails can keep them engaged and increase their chance of becoming a paying customer.

Partner With Affiliates

Affiliate marketing involves partnering with other businesses and individuals to promote your products or services. This is a great way to get customers without doing the marketing yourself.

If suitable, consider creating an affiliate program. Look for businesses or individuals with relevant audiences who can effectively promote your products or services. You can sign up for platforms like ClickBank to list your affiliate program and find affiliates for your new business.

Track, Analyze, Optimize

Lastly, you need to track every marketing activity and optimize for performance. Tracking is the only way to know if your marketing dollars produce leads. Free tools like Google Analytics and paid tools like SproutSocial enable tracking marketing campaigns. If you're planning to outsource marketing, make sure to ask for reports on a weekly basis. Accountability is the only way to avoid wasting money on marketing.

Using AI for Marketing and Brand Development

Before 2023, it was understandable if you hadn't incorporated AI into your marketing efforts. But by 2024, it's almost unthinkable.

The introduction of ChatGPT in 2023 brought a groundbreaking tool for businesses. It can produce content, create business and marketing plans, manage basic accounting tasks, and write code. Skipping AI now means missing many opportunities.

For beginners, my books "Prompt Engineering and ChatGPT" and "ChatGPT for Business" offer easy-to-follow guidance on using AI in your business, helping you tap into AI's full potential.

Here's what you can use AI for in your marketing:

Generating Marketing Plans

AI tools like ChatGPT can create marketing plans for your business from scratch. All you have to do is provide a prompt and let ChatGPT create a thorough plan. A prompt is nothing but the information you input to AI tools.

For generating a marketing plan, a prompt can look something like this:

"I'm starting an online business that specializes in [niche]. I'll be offering [products] primarily through my website. My audience is [target market]. I plan to market through [marketing channels] with a budget of [marketing budget]. Create a detailed marketing plan for me."

If you input the text in ChatGPT, you'll get a detailed response:

Prompt:

I'm starting an online business that specializes in the online sweaters niche. I'll be offering hand-knit sweaters, primarily through my website. My audience is working women who need sweaters for the office. I plan to market through TikTok and Facebook with a budget of $10,000. Create a detailed marketing plan for me.

Output:

Executive Summary
This marketing plan outlines a strategic approach to launch and promote your online hand-knit sweaters business targeting working women who need stylish and comfortable sweaters for the office. With a budget of $10,000 and a focus on TikTok and Facebook for marketing, this plan aims to build brand awareness, drive website traffic, and generate sales through a combination of organic and paid marketing strategies.
1. Business Overview
* *Product: Hand-knit sweaters designed for professional women.*

(Continues)

(Continued)

- *Sales Channel: Primarily through your dedicated website.*

- *Unique Selling Proposition (USP): High-quality, stylish, and comfortable sweaters that blend professionalism with personal style, hand-knit to ensure uniqueness and quality.*

2. Market Analysis

2.1 Industry Overview

- *Market Growth: The global sweater market is experiencing steady growth, with increasing demand for artisanal and sustainable fashion.*

- *Trends:*

  - *Sustainability: Consumers prefer ethically made products.*

  - *Artisanal Products: Growing appreciation for handcrafted items.*

  - *Workplace Fashion: Demand for professional yet stylish office attire.*

2.2 Competitor Analysis

- *Direct Competitors:*

  - *Other online retailers offering hand-knit or artisanal sweaters.*

- *Indirect Competitors:*

  - *Mass-produced sweater brands targeting professional women.*

- *Competitive Advantage:*

  - *Hand-knit uniqueness.*

  - *Personalization options.*

  - *Storytelling around craftsmanship.*

(Continues on)

Allocating Marketing Budget

You can ask ChatGPT to allocate the marketing budget across various channels.

A good prompt for this can be:

"My marketing budget is [budget]. I want to develop a WordPress website, start a YouTube channel, run Facebook and TikTok ads, and an email campaign using MailChimp. Allocate the marketing budget accordingly."

Prompt:

My marketing budget is $5,000. I want to develop a WordPress website, start a YouTube channel, run Facebook and TikTok ads, and an email campaign using MailChimp. Allocate the marketing budget accordingly.

Output:

With a marketing budget of $5,000, we can create a well-balanced approach that covers building your website, setting up and promoting your YouTube channel, running Facebook and TikTok ads, and launching email campaigns with MailChimp. Here's how to allocate the budget:
Budget Breakdown:

    1. WordPress Website Development: $1,500

    2. YouTube Channel Setup & Content Creation: $1,000

    3. Facebook & TikTok Ads: $2,000

    4. MailChimp Email Campaign: $500

WordPress Website Development ($1,500)Purpose: Establish a professional online storefront for your hand-knit sweaters, where visitors can browse products, learn about your brand, and make purchases.

(Continues on)

Generating Content

AI tools are good at creating content that is on par with that of a human writer. Thus, you can use this capability to create content for your website, YouTube channel, ebooks, product demos, landing pages, etc.

Here's a prompt for this purpose:

> *"My new business's name is [business name]. The business specializes in [niche] and caters to [target audience]. I am [name], and I'm the owner of the company with [specialization and experience]. My business solves [the problem]. Based on the information, create an About Us section for my website."*

Prompt:

> *My new business's name is Tara Sweaters. The business specializes in hand-knit sweaters and caters to working women. I'm Tara Smith the owner of the company with 10 years of expertise in the fashion business. My business aims to make sweaters trendier again. Based on the information, create an About Us section for my website.*

Output:

> *About Us:*
> *Welcome to Tara Sweaters!*
> *I'm Tara Smith, the founder of Tara Sweaters, and I've spent over a decade in the fashion industry perfecting my craft. My passion for timeless style and handcrafted quality led me to create Tara Sweaters—a brand dedicated to making sweaters trendier again for the modern working woman.*
> *At Tara Sweaters, we believe that office wear can be both comfortable and fashionable. Our hand-knit sweaters are designed to add a touch of warm elegance and trendiness to your everyday work wardrobe. Each piece is crafted with care, combining classic techniques with contemporary styles to create garments that are both unique and versatile.*

Optimizing Content For SEO

You can instruct ChatGPT to make the content SEO-friendly. All you have to do is specify the main keyword (a word or phrase people type into search engines (like Google) when they're looking for specific information, products, or services), related keywords, and keyword density. ChatGPT will handle the request accordingly.

An example prompt could be:

"Optimize the About Us page for "[main keyword]" as the main keyword and "[secondary keyword]" as the secondary keyword. Keep the keyword density at 3%."

Prompt:

Now optimize the About Us page for "trendy sweaters" as the main keyword, and "sweaters for winters" as the secondary keyword. Keep the keyword density at 3%.

Output:

About Us
Welcome to Tara Sweaters, where trendy sweaters meet timeless style!
I'm Tara Smith, the founder of Tara Sweaters, with over 10 years of experience in the fashion industry. My passion for quality and handcrafted design led me to create Tara Sweaters—a brand dedicated to making trendy sweaters that cater to the needs of working women. We believe that office wear can be both comfortable and fashionable, and our trendy sweaters are crafted to fit seamlessly into your work wardrobe.

Creating SOPs To Outsource Marketing Activities

A Standard Operating Procedure (SOP) is a detailed, written document that outlines the steps to complete a specific task or process consistently and efficiently. It ensures uniformity, compliance, and quality in operations across an organization.

As your business grows, you may need to hire marketers to handle your marketing activities. But hiring is not the be-all and end-all of marketing. You need to negotiate with them and keep them accountable. ChatGPT can help you with this.

Here's a prompt you can use:

"I'm planning to hire a [marketing domain]. Create a SOP that I can share with him and keep him accountable."

Prompt:

I'm planning to hire a Google Ads expert. Create a SOP that I can share with him and keep him accountable.

Output:

Standard Operating Procedure (SOP) for Google Ads Expert
Objective: To manage and optimize Google Ads campaigns effectively, ensuring optimal use of the budget, increased conversions, and a positive return on investment (ROI).
Role and Responsibilities:
    1. Account Setup and Management

- *Set up the Google Ads account, including linking Google Analytics and conversion tracking.*

- *Ensure accurate billing and access permissions.*

- *Regularly update and manage account settings for optimal performance.*

(Continues on)

These are just some of the ways AI can aid your marketing efforts. As your business grows, you can ask it to act as a virtual assistant and perform mundane tasks like updating the marketing plan, checking for compliance, and generating ROI reports.

Paid AI tools are even more beneficial. Thus, explore the possibilities and use AI to your advantage.

Wrap Up

This chapter gave you a deep dive into digital marketing fundamentals, from building a brand identity to mastering channels like SEO, social media, and content marketing. With a clear brand and marketing strategy, you're ready to make a lasting impression on your audience.

Action Steps

1. Define your brand's core message and design a look that reflects your values.

2. Choose a few digital channels to focus on first, like social media or email.

3. Develop a simple marketing plan to guide your early campaigns and build brand awareness.

Up Next

Next, we'll get into the heart of customer acquisition. Learn to identify your target market, hone your sales approach, and turn potential leads into loyal clients—setting you up for lasting growth.

Chapter Five

Smart Money Moves

A s a small business owner, I've felt the pressure to scale quickly. It's easy to get swept up in the excitement of expansion, to dream of what could be when the numbers grow and opportunities flood in.

Unfortunately, I've learned through experience that pursuing growth purely for its own sake can be risky. In my case, it came at a significant cost to both myself and my business. I constantly chased the next goal without stopping to assess whether I was truly prepared. It's like pushing forward faster than your legs can handle, hoping not to stumble.

Wag, the dog-walking startup, is a perfect example of what happens when growth outpaces a business's foundation. Wag was an ambitious idea in its early days—"Uber for dogs"—and gained significant venture capital funding to scale quickly. However, as the company grew, it became clear that the focus on speed and size was far more important than building a sustainable business. And that's when things started falling apart.

Instead of focusing on the problems in their business model, Wag pushed forward with global expansion, hiring a new CEO, Hilary Schneider, to handle the growth. But as the company expanded, the cracks started to show. Wag relied heavily on independent contractors to provide the service, but they had no system for vetting or training them properly. And as the volume grew, so did the incidents: lost dogs, abuse, even deaths. Customer service couldn't keep up, and the reputation began to crumble.

The worst part? The company's leaders weren't listening. They were too focused on becoming the next unicorn. They wanted to be big, but they didn't have the foundation to support it. When thousands of workers sued for misclassification, the company faced the consequences of not caring for its people or business.

Wag's story is a painful reminder of the dangers of chasing growth without considering the long-term impact. In the end, the company wasn't sustainable despite the flashy funding and the desire to become a household name. It was a lesson in the brutal reality of blitz scaling, where scaling too fast and too big can unravel everything you've built.

However, this doesn't mean that funding is not important. Lack of capital is one of the main reasons new businesses fail. Cash flow is the lifeblood of any business. When the funds run out, operations shut down, and the business fails.

In the early phases of a startup, capital acts as a catalyst for Innovation and experimentation. It provides the necessary resources to develop new products, hire talented individuals, and explore uncharted territories. As Peter Drucker famously stated, "Innovation is not about technology. It's about people and ideas." Capital enables startups to assemble the right teams and nurture the creative minds that drive groundbreaking business ideas.

The importance of money doesn't surface when you build a team. Even when going solo, you'll realize the importance of having money in the bank to fund operations.

In other words, take money flow seriously from day 1 of your business, irrespective of the team or operation size. That's why this chapter is important.

Chapter 5 is dedicated to ensuring your newly started business stays healthy financially. We'll review the various funding options available, especially for small business owners. Some are more easily accessible than others, but you should know they exist.

In the second part of this chapter, we'll delve deeper into financial forecasting. This is to help you calculate how much money you'll actually need to run your business. Both under and over-funding are bad for business health. Again, we'll be using the latest AI techniques in this regard. Various specialized tools have made financial forecasting easier, more accurate, and affordable.

So grab your favorite drink, and let's dive in.

10 Ways to Fund a New Venture

The landscape of entrepreneurship has undergone a dramatic transformation, with access to capital becoming more accessible than ever before. In the past, obtaining funding was often daunting and time-consuming, requiring extensive documentation, collateral, and a proven track record. Banks were notoriously conservative, usually hesitant to lend to startups with limited financial histories.

Over time, a confluence of factors, including technological advancements, regulatory changes, and increased investor interest, has democratized the funding process. Today, a plethora of options are available.

Of course, not all funding options are suitable for a particular business. The founder's job is to determine the best sources and secure the funding.

There are over 15 ways to fund a business, typically grouped into three categories:

- Self-Funding

- Investor Funding

- Loans

Self-funding is when you use your own money to raise liquidity. Note that self-funding also includes money borrowed from friends and family. Investor funding is when you bring in investors to your business, and they provide the financing. Lastly, there's a loan, which a bank or financial institution often issues.

Now that you know the types, let's review the ten most common funding options for new businesses.

1. **Personal Savings:** Start with What You Have

2. **Credit Cards:** Lifeline or Trap?

3. **Friends and Family:** Your First Supporters

4. **Personal Loans:** Pros and Cons

5. **Crowdfunding:** Turn the Crowd into Investors

6. **Angel Investors:** Life Savers?

7. **Venture Capital:** A Step Up

8. **Small Business Administration (SBA) Loans:** The Small Business Option

9. **Business Line of Credit:** Flexible Funding

10. **Grants:** The Power of Free Funding

Personal Savings

Many businesses start with personal funding, where the founder uses their savings to kick-start the venture. It's a straightforward and quick way to finance a business.

For example, Sara Blakely, founder of Spanx, used her personal savings of $5,000 from her job as a door-to-door salesperson. With this initial capital, she created prototypes, filed a patent, and found a manufacturer, ultimately building Spanx into a billion-dollar company.

Pros

- Fast and easy to access

- Full ownership (no equity dilution)

- No interest or repayment obligations

Cons

- Limited by personal savings

- Personal financial risk if the business fails

- May limit funding available for growth

Credit Cards

Credit cards are a common tool for startup funding, offering immediate access to funds. Many entrepreneurs share stories of using credit cards to cover initial expenses. One advantage is the flexibility only to borrow what's needed up to the credit limit, helping bridge cash flow gaps.

Pros

- Quick access to funds

- Flexible borrowing up to credit limit

- Useful for short-term expenses

Cons

- High interest rates, if not paid off monthly

- Can lead to debt accumulation if the business struggles

- Not ideal for long-term or significant funding needs

Friends and Family

Funding from family and friends is a common early-stage option. They may offer support through loans, gifts, or equity investments, providing financial help and emotional encouragement. However, carefully managing expectations is essential to avoid straining personal relationships.

Pros

- Flexible terms (low or no interest, relaxed terms)

- Emotional support from trusted individuals

- No strict repayment schedules

Cons

- Potential strain on personal relationships

- Risk of losing both financial support and trust

- May limit future funding options if significant capital is required

Personal Loans

Personal loans allow founders to borrow based on personal credit, often without requiring a business income history. These loans provide lump sums that can cover startup costs but also hold the founder personally liable if the business does not succeed.

Pros

- No need for an established business history

- Fixed payments and interest rates

- Useful for initial costs like inventory

Cons

- Personal liability if the business fails

- May have higher interest rates than business loans

- Limited by personal creditworthiness

Crowdfunding

Crowdfunding platforms like Kickstarter allow businesses to raise funds from the public, often in exchange for rewards or early product access. For instance, Oculus VR used Kickstarter to raise nearly $2.5 million, surpassing its initial goal of $250,000 and gaining significant traction in the tech community.

Pros

- No repayment obligation if the business fails

- Engages public interest, often building a customer base

- Can offer rewards instead of equity

Cons

- Highly competitive; not all campaigns succeed

- Limited funds for businesses with less public appeal

- Typically, a one-time funding solution

Angel Investors

Angel investors provide early-stage funding in exchange for equity. They often bring valuable industry experience, which can be crucial for product development and early marketing. Angels are valuable mentors but can be selective about where they invest.

Pros

- Access to significant early capital

- Mentorship and strategic guidance

- No repayment obligation

Cons

- Equity dilution (part of the business ownership)

- Finding suitable investors can be challenging

- Investors may have input in business decisions

Venture Capital

Venture capital (VC) firms invest in businesses with high growth potential, often through funding rounds (Series A, B, etc.). For example, Airbnb secured early VC support from Sequoia Capital, helping it scale rapidly.

Pros

- Large amounts of funding

- Support with scaling and strategic growth

- Access to networks and resources

Cons

- Significant equity dilution

- Complex approval and selection process

- Pressure to meet high growth expectations

Small Business Administration (SBA) Loans

The U.S. Small Business Administration (SBA) offers government-backed loans, which are less risky for lenders and often more affordable for borrowers. SBA loans require extensive documentation but provide long-term, lower-cost financing.

Pros

- Favorable terms due to government backing

- Good for more significant, long-term funding needs

- Supportive of various business types

Cons

- Extensive paperwork and time-consuming process

- Requires good credit to qualify

- Strict usage restrictions

Grants

Grants are non-repayable funds from governments or nonprofits, often awarded to innovative or socially beneficial projects. Ginkgo Bioworks, for example, received a $100,000 grant from the Department of Energy for bioengineering.

Pros

- No repayment required

- May offer substantial funding amounts

- Support for innovative and community-focused projects

Cons

- Highly competitive application process

- Specific rules often restrict how organizations use funds

- Limited to particular industries or initiatives

Business Line of Credit

A business line of credit functions like a flexible loan, allowing companies to borrow up to a specific limit and repay as needed. It's ideal for covering short-term expenses like payroll or inventory and provides a revolving source of capital.

Pros

- Flexible and revolving credit source

- Good for managing cash flow

- Borrowing just the required amount of funds

Cons

- May have higher interest rates for smaller businesses

- Can lead to debt if not managed responsibly

- May require good business or personal credit

Each funding source has unique advantages and limitations. Consider your startup's needs, growth stage, and risk tolerance to choose the best option for success.

Financial Forecasting: How Much Money Will You Need?

You're familiar with the various funding sources. Given your expertise and current circumstances, you will likely utilize a mix of these sources. However, a more pressing question remains: How much should I aim to raise? Will $100,000 be enough? Or will I have to secure a $300,000 loan deal?

Both under and over-funding are bad for new business. In under-funding, you're at the risk of running out of money before turning profitable. Over-funded companies often end up taking a lot of initiatives, most of which end up failing. That's why it's important to know how much to raise.

You can answer this question through financial forecasting.

Financial forecasting predicts future economic conditions and performance based on historical data, market trends, and other relevant factors. It helps business owners anticipate their financial needs, set realistic goals, make informed decisions, and plan for both short-term operations and long-term growth.

While big corporates often employ forecasting, it's equally important for small enterprises. Small businesses frequently operate with limited resources, meaning financial stability is vital for survival. Small businesses can face fluctuating sales based on local events, seasonal demand, and customer preferences.

The Financial Forecast Process

As a business owner, it's essential to maintain a high-level understanding of the financial forecasting process, even if finance isn't your area of expertise. This perspective allows you to safeguard the financial viability of your new venture.

The process of financial forecasting typically involves these steps:

- **Collect Historical Data:** Reliable and accurate data are essential in forecasting. Gather past sales data, expense records, and other relevant information to serve as the basis for the forecast.

- **Establish Assumptions:** Create projections regarding market trends, customer growth, cost fluctuations, and seasonal variations. These are the building blocks of a forecast.

- **Create Different Scenarios:** Create a base-case forecast, an optimistic forecast, and a pessimistic forecast. This helps the business understand how different situations will impact finances.

- **Develop A Financial Model:** Use tools like spreadsheets or forecasting software to create financial models that predict income, expenses, and profits.

- **Review and Update Regularly:** A forecast is not a one-time task; it should be reviewed and updated regularly based on the latest data and market conditions.

Here's a prompt you can use to ask for help with financial forecasting for your business:

> *Can you guide me through the financial forecasting process for my business? I'd like to understand how to:*
> - *Collect and use historical data, like past sales and expenses, for accurate forecasting*
>
> - *Set assumptions on market trends, customer growth, and costs*
>
> - *Create different financial scenarios (base, optimistic, and pessimistic) to anticipate varied outcomes*
>
> - *Develop a financial model to project income, expenses, and profits using tools like spreadsheets*
>
> - *Regularly review and update the forecast based on current data and conditions*
>
> *I want to ensure financial viability and be prepared for different market situations.*

Tools for Financial Forecasting

Today, a variety of tools are available to help businesses create financial forecasts, including:

- **Excel or Google Sheets:** Great for small businesses that need basic forecasting without a lot of bells and whistles.

- **Forecasting Software:** Platforms like QuickBooks, Float, and PlanGuru provide more advanced forecasting features and integration with other financial data sources.

- **CRM Integration:** With platforms like HubSpot, integrating CRM data into forecasts can give insights into how customer leads and conversions will impact future revenue.

Budgeting for Business Success

Now, let's focus on another critical aspect of financial planning: budgeting. Simply put, budgeting involves creating a financial plan to monitor income and expenses over a defined period. However, it goes far beyond just tracking money. Effective budgeting involves strategizing, exercising control, and ensuring every financial decision supports your overarching business goals.

Operating without a budget increases the risk of overspending, particularly in high-cost areas like marketing or inventory. In contrast, a well-crafted budget establishes clear spending limits for you and your team, enabling you to prioritize investments that deliver the greatest value.

Budgeting Process 101

Creating a budget doesn't have to be complicated. The best approach is to keep it simple. Here's a step-by-step guide to help small businesses get started with budgeting:

1. Set Your Goals

Begin by setting financial goals for your business. These goals might include increasing sales by 20%, saving for an equipment purchase, or maintaining a certain profit level. The budget should align with these goals to guide the overall direction of your spending.

2. Estimate Your Income

The next step is determining how much money you expect your business to make over a specific period—usually a month, quarter, or year.

3. Identify Fixed and Variable Costs

To effectively budget, you need a clear understanding of your costs. Costs can generally be categorized as:

- **Fixed Costs:** These are expenses that don't change significantly over time, such as rent, insurance, utilities, and salaries for permanent employees. These bills must be paid regardless of how much revenue is coming in.

- **Variable Costs:** These are costs that fluctuate depending on your level of business activity. They include raw materials, shipping, packaging, commissions, and marketing expenses. As your sales increase, your variable costs will also go up.

4. Create a Cash Flow Projection

Cash flow is the movement of money into and out of your business. A cash flow projection helps determine if you'll have enough cash on hand at any given point to cover your expenses.

5. Analyze Your Breakeven Point

Calculating your breakeven point—where total revenue equals total costs—helps determine how much you need to sell to cover all expenses. Understanding the breakeven point is vital for pricing products, planning promotions, and knowing when you're in profit territory.

6. Adjust and Rebalance

Once you've laid out income and expenses, compare them. If expenses exceed income, you must cut unnecessary expenses or reconsider your priorities. Look for areas where you can cut costs without affecting the business's core operations. Decide the most critical expenses and consider deferring or reducing spending on less essential items.

7. Monitor and Update the Budget Regularly

A budget isn't a static document—it should be revisited and updated regularly. Actual performance will inevitably differ from your initial estimates. By monitoring the budget, you can identify which costs exceeded expectations and which revenues were under or overestimated. Updating the budget allows for more accurate forecasting and better management.

Budgeting and Forecasting with AI

There's some good news if you're a finance-averse person who dislikes crunching numbers. AI is here to lend a helping hand.

As stated in the previous chapter, AI has rapidly become a game-changer in many aspects of business, like marketing and content creation. With the latest advancements, you can use AI as an accountant, helping you with budgets and forecasting.

At its core, AI uses data and data analysis to uncover patterns that are too resource-intensive for humans. Humans can then inspect the patterns and make more informed decisions faster. In other words, with AI, decisions are based on data, not gut feelings. And this happens twice or thrice as fast.

AI Tools to Use for Budgeting and Forecasting

There are several AI tools that you can use to create budgets and forecast sales and revenue. Here are some tools I recommend:

PlanGuru

PlanGuru is built for financial planning, budgeting, and forecasting with unlimited budgeting flexibility. This means you can create a multi-department AI budget or forecast without restriction.

PlanGuru allows businesses to create detailed financial budgets by analyzing historical data and forecasts by simulating future scenarios. AI-powered insights help companies to spot trends and adjust their budgets accordingly.

Jirav

Jirav is designed to handle financial planning with AI-driven insights for small and mid-sized businesses. One of the best features is that it automates the budgeting process by integrating existing data sources and creating dynamic budgets that adjust with real-time inputs.

Xero

As a core accounting software, Xero uses AI and machine learning to analyze financial data and create budget templates based on historical data trends. It automatically updates budgets as financial transactions are logged, making it easy to keep budgets up to date.

Vena Insights

Vena Insights is an AI-powered financial tool that integrates with existing systems to automate data collection, analysis, and reporting. Vena can pull data from multiple sources, such as Excel, ERP, and CRM systems. With AI-powered insights, Vena offers customized reports to monitor budget progress and performance.

Domo

Domo is a cloud-based platform that offers business intelligence (BI) and data analytics with AI-powered insights. Designed for small and mid-sized businesses, it claims to increase revenue by almost $1 million through its AI-driven data analysis and reporting services.

Wrap Up

In this chapter, you learned the essential steps for making smart money moves to support your business. From exploring funding options to creating realistic financial forecasts, you now have a roadmap for managing finances strategically and securing the resources you need to grow.

Action Steps

1. Identify potential funding sources that best fit your business model.

2. Create a basic financial forecast for the next 12 months to guide spending and revenue goals.

3. Set up a process to monitor your finances regularly and adjust as needed.

Up Next

With funding and financial planning in place, you're ready to start thinking bigger. In the next chapter, we'll focus on scaling your business—covering expansion strategies, reaching new markets, and optimizing processes to grow sustainably.

Chapter Six

Scaling to New Heights

O kay. So you're up and running, and sales are coming in. There's some word-of-mouth among your first users, and more people are lining up to learn more about your products and services. You may have hired an employee or two to carry out specific tasks, and life's great.

But here's a thing about business: your customer base doesn't remain the same. The people buying from you won't necessarily buy tomorrow. Some move on, others pass away. In other words, regardless of the quality of their products, businesses always lose customers.

The only cure for it is to add new users and convert them into customers. This is often done through scaling. Scaling refers to growing a business's operations and increasing its output or reach. It involves expanding existing operations, such as increasing production capacity, hiring more employees, or entering new markets.

While answering why scaling is important for businesses, Brian Rothenberg, a venture capitalist and a Partner at Defy.vc, wrote, "Scaling is critical because sustainable growth tends to be the cure for everything else that can and does go wrong at a startup."

Scaling offers another crucial advantage: unlocking your business's full potential. For example, if your startup is projected to generate $5 million in annual revenue, reaching that goal may require more than sticking to your current approach. Scaling is the key to turning those projections into reality.

But there's a more lucrative and enticing reason why scaling a new business is so important.

More Time For Yourself

Why do people start a business? One common reason is to escape the 9-to-5 routine and embrace a lifestyle with more freedom and time. However, many first-time entrepreneurs quickly realize they've swapped the 9-to-5 for a grueling 7-to-10 schedule. The business consumes their lives, turning dreams into stress and leaving little time for personal fulfillment.

Scaling the business becomes crucial to reclaiming control. This involves growing your team, hiring or training skilled leaders, and establishing efficient systems. By delegating responsibilities, your business can operate more autonomously. These leaders can oversee essential tasks and ensure processes run seamlessly, minimizing your daily involvement. You can set healthier boundaries between work and personal life with robust leadership and efficient systems. This helps your business flourish and supports a better work-life balance, giving you more time with loved ones.

This chapter is all about scaling your business to new heights. If you're stuck in sales, revenue, growth, or day-to-day chores, it could mean the time has come to scale and unlock your full potential.

In the next section, you'll learn about startup founders' steps to scale their businesses and reach their goals.

What is Scaling a Business Exactly?

Many business owners think scaling a business means increasing headcount or expanding to new locations. While those are components of scaling a company, they are not the whole story. Therefore, let's start with a good definition of scaling a business.

Scaling a business is like expanding a house. Just as you add more rooms to accommodate a growing family, you scale a business to handle increased demand, reach more customers, and generate higher revenue. But unlike building a house, scaling a business involves more than just physical expansion. It's about growing your operations while maintaining efficiency, profitability, and sustainability.

Remember these three key terms: efficiency, profitability, and sustainability. They define the ultimate objectives of scaling up a business.

Scaling can involve various aspects of your business, such as:

- **Hiring More Employees:** As your business grows, you'll need additional staff to handle increased workload and responsibilities.

- **Expanding Your Product or Service Offerings:** Introducing new products or services can attract new customers and boost revenue.

- **Entering New Markets:** Expanding your geographic reach can expose your business to new opportunities and customer bases.

- **Improving Your Technology Infrastructure:** As your business grows, you may need to upgrade your technology systems to handle increased data and workload.

- **Optimizing Your Operations:** Streamlining processes and improving efficiency can help you scale your business more effectively.

Remember, scaling is not just about getting bigger; it's about growing sustainably and profitably. It requires careful planning, strategic decision-making, and maintaining quality and customer satisfaction. By understanding scaling principles, you can position your business for long-term success and growth.

Key Ingredients to a Successful Business Scale-Up

Scaling a business requires a few raw ingredients—just like baking a pizza. You combine the separate ingredients to achieve your end goals.

However, just as different types of pizza call for various recipes, not every business requires the same ingredients for scaling up. For example, a corporation may require third-party financial audits before regulators approve the expansion. There's no such requirement for a small or midsize business. Therefore, the exact prerequisites to scaling a business vary.

That being said, there are some commonalities. Researchers have long studied what businesses that scale successfully have in common. Based on the research, they have come up with frameworks. One such framework is the Six Sigma framework proposed by Harvard Business School Professor Jeffrey Rayport.

Six Sigma stands for:

Staff

Staff is the first element, emphasizing the importance of having the right people in place. As the business grows, hiring talented individuals who fit the company's vision is crucial. These employees should be trained and developed to take on more responsibilities as the company expands. Strong leadership is essential to manage the growing team and oversee daily operations.

Shared Values

Shared values refer to the company's culture and core principles. These values guide decision-making and behavior. As the business scales, maintaining a consistent culture ensures that everyone in the company, including new hires, is aligned with the company's mission. This consistency is important for both internal operations and customer relations.

Structure

The third S is about your business structure and adjusting to support growth. Clear roles, responsibilities, and processes allow the business to function smoothly as it grows. Even with a larger team, standardizing key processes helps maintain quality and efficiency. However, it's also important to keep the structure flexible so the company can adapt to new challenges.

Speed

Speed focuses on the company's ability to act quickly. Businesses that scale successfully are agile in decision-making and execution. Streamlining operations and removing unnecessary steps can increase speed and efficiency. Using technology and automation to handle routine tasks can also help the company respond faster to customer needs.

Scope

Scope refers to expanding the company's reach. This might mean offering new products or services, entering new markets, or targeting different customer segments. Increasing the scope of the business helps diversify revenue streams and reduce reliance on a single market or product.

Series X

Finally, Series X focuses on financial resources. Whether through investment rounds or reinvesting profits, having enough capital is critical for scaling a business. This allows the company to invest in marketing, hire more staff, and expand its operations, among other things. In addition to funding, forming partnerships and alliances can provide resources and expertise to help the business grow.

The Six Sigma framework ensures that all aspects of the business are working together during the scaling process. Companies can grow effectively by focusing on these six areas while maintaining stability and alignment.

As previously mentioned, the Six Sigma framework is just one way of looking at the components of scaling a business. There are alternate models as well. As an example, here's a more simplified model that you can use to determine whether your company is ready to scale:

Product-Market Fit

Arguably, the most important requisite to scaling is product-market fit. It's like ensuring your house is built in a location where people want to live. Otherwise, you'll be building a home in an inhabitable environment. Before scaling, conduct market research to understand your target audience's needs and preferences.

A Solid Business Model

A business model is the blueprint for your business. It outlines your value proposition, revenue streams, and cost structure. A well-defined business model provides a clear roadmap for growth. Identify multiple revenue streams to reduce your reliance on a single source of income. Analyze your costs and find ways to reduce expenses or improve efficiency.

Lead Acquisition and Nurturing System

Scaling involves generating consistent sales, preferably at a lower cost. Develop a comprehensive marketing strategy to attract and generate qualified leads. Create a well-defined sales funnel to guide leads through the customer journey and convert them into customers. Use a CRM system to track leads, manage interactions, and analyze sales performance.

A Strong Leadership and Team

Right people are crucial for driving growth. A visionary leader can inspire and motivate employees to achieve common goals. Foster a positive and collaborative work culture where employees feel valued and empowered. Invest in employee training and development to ensure your team has the skills and knowledge to support scaling.

Proper Finance

Money is essential for sustainable growth. Maintain accurate financial records, create budgets, and track your financial performance. Secure adequate funding to support growth initiatives. Develop financial projections to anticipate future needs and make informed decisions about resource allocation.

Partnerships and Alliances

Partnering with non-competing businesses can help you expand your reach, access new markets, or leverage complementary resources. You can also consider joint ventures to share risks and rewards. Build strong relationships with suppliers to ensure a reliable supply of goods or services.

There may be other prerequisites to scaling a business besides the ones discussed above. Thus, understand your business at the basic level and ensure you have them covered prior to scaling.

Scaling Any Business in 10 Steps

With theoretical knowledge, let's proceed to practical work. Once you've established a business and gained traction, it's time to scale.

As with anything, it's important not to complicate matters and keep things simple. With a focus on simplicity, here are the 10 steps to successfully scaling a business:

1. Establish Product-Market Fit

2. Develop A Scalable Business Model

3. Secure Funding

4. Build A Lead Generation and Nurturing System

5. Streamline Operations

6. Build A Strong Team

7. Consider Outsourcing

8. Leverage Technology

9. Expand Market Reach

10. Monitor Key Metrics

Establish Product-Market Fit

If you're at the scalability stage of business, chances are high that you've found product-market fit. If not, you should seriously reconsider the decision to scale. Scaling efforts will likely fail without this alignment because there won't be enough demand to sustain growth.

Achieving product-market fit involves deepening your understanding of your customers' needs, refining your offerings, and testing how well your product resonates in the market.

Some areas where you should get clarity are:

- Ideal customers

- Ensuring minimum viable profit (MVP) resonates with the customers

- Profit margin

Dropbox is a well-known example of a company that achieved product-market fit before scaling. When Dropbox first launched, the company didn't invest heavily in marketing or growth. Instead, it focused on creating a minimum viable product—a simple file-sharing service that solved a real problem: the difficulty of sharing files across different devices.

Develop a Scalable Business Model

Successful scaling requires a business model that can support rapid growth. Therefore, you need to develop a scalable business model.

A scalable business model can grow and handle increased demand without a corresponding rise in costs. Developing this model ensures that your expenses don't grow at the same rate as your customer base.

A good example is King Digital Entertainment, the creator of Candy Crush Saga. The company scaled the game from mid-2012 to mid-2013. During this timeframe, its revenue increased by 12-fold while cost increased only by 6-fold, ensuring the game remained profitable after the scale.

When developing a scalable business model, focus on these things:

- Unit economics

- Revenue streams

- Fixed and variable costs

- Cost per customer acquisition

With a profitable model in place, you ensure that scaling operations won't burn cash faster than revenue growth.

Secure Funding

Scaling a business isn't without cost. Depending on the business size and scope of scale, you will likely see a significant rise in expenses. To make this happen, ensure you have sufficient funding.

As your business grows, so do the financial demands, whether for hiring staff, expanding marketing efforts, developing new products, or entering new markets. Adequate funding ensures that you have the resources to scale without sacrificing quality.

Start by calculating how much capital is required to scale. This involves looking at your current financial situation and forecasting future expenses related to growth. Consider costs such as:

- Hiring additional staff

- Increasing inventory

- Expanding marketing efforts

- Upgrading infrastructure (e.g., technology, office space)

- Developing new products or services

Break down these expenses over a set timeline to determine how much capital you need at each stage of scaling. This will help you avoid raising too little or too much (which could dilute your ownership unnecessarily).

Build a Lead Generation and Nurturing System

To scale a business, having a consistent way to generate and nurture leads is essential. A lead generation system focuses on attracting potential customers to your business. In contrast, a lead nurturing system engages and guides those leads through your sales funnel until they become paying customers. Together, these systems ensure a steady flow of prospects, fueling growth.

You may have to tweak your marketing and spend more money on advertising. But it's not the only way. When Hotmail wanted to scale operations, it included the following message on every email sent via Hotmail:

```
PS: I love you.Get your
free e-mail at Hotmail
```

Within 1.5 years, it grew to 12 million users, literally for free. Later, Hotmail was acquired by Microsoft for a sweet $400 million.

So, get creative with your lead gen system and try different tactics.

Streamline Operations

When you scale, you must ensure there are as few bottlenecks as possible. Otherwise, your business will be unable to scale quickly. This is done by streamlining operations.

Streamlining operations means refining your internal processes, reducing inefficiencies, and automating repetitive tasks. This is done across the board, from marketing to production to HR to finance. If you're a one-person company, streamlining operations means automating as much as possible.

Start by conducting a thorough review of your existing operations. Break down each function of your business, from production to customer service, and identify areas where time, money, or resources are wasted. Then, steps can be taken to optimize or eliminate the inefficiencies.

Build A Strong Team

Above all, building a company is about its people—not just the products or services. A committed, skilled, and motivated team drives innovation, overcomes challenges, and meets growing demands. Recruiting the right talent and nurturing their leadership potential as your business grows becomes essential for long-term success.

When hiring, look for candidates with the technical skills required for the job that resonates with your company's vision and mission. Zappos, the online shoe retailer, is famous for hiring employees based on cultural fit. They emphasize aligning new hires with the company's core values. Zappos even offers employees money to quit during onboarding if they feel they're not a good fit. This approach ensures that only those committed to the company's culture stay and thrive.

Consider Outsourcing

Employees are not the only way to get things done. The other method is outsourcing. Outsourcing – delegating tasks to an outside firm or freelancers – can be a key strategy when scaling your business. It allows you to access specialized skills, reduce overhead costs, and focus on core activities that drive growth.

Determine what parts of your business are most valuable to keep in-house—typically functions related directly to your product or service. You can outsource tasks that take time and resources but don't directly contribute to your company's growth. For example, if you're in a bakery business, consider accounting.

Leverage Technology

Technology has changed the way businesses scale. On a positive note, it has made scaling faster. The impact of technology on business scaling is so profound that investors have started distinguishing between a scalable and non-scalable business based on how tech-savvy a business is. Generally, a tech-heavy business is considered more scalable than a company that relies on physical stuff.

Technology should be at the core of scaling. Implement technology in every business operation, whether project management, sales, marketing, customer service, or delivery. By leveraging technology, you can automate processes, increase efficiency, and improve customer experience, all essential for managing growth.

Expand Market Reach

Scaling requires broadening your offerings and tapping into new segments, geographic regions, or product categories to increase your customer base and grow revenue.

Tesla initially targeted the luxury electric car market with its flagship Tesla Roadster but expanded its reach by developing more affordable models, such as the Model 3, to attract a broader customer base. This strategic move enabled Tesla to expand into new market segments and significantly increase its customer base. Today, Tesla is among the most valuable companies.

To apply this strategy, identify areas where you can expand and roll out products and capitalize on those opportunities.

Monitor Key Metrics

The final step to scaling a business is setting up and monitoring key metrics. These help you determine whether you're on the right path or need to pivot to a new strategy.

Before scaling, you must determine the key performance indicators (KPIs) that are most important to your business. These metrics should be aligned with your business goals and growth objectives. Financial KPIs such as revenue growth, profit margins, and cash flow are critical for all businesses. However, other metrics, such as customer acquisition cost (CAC), customer lifetime value (CLV), and churn rate, can be equally important for evaluating how efficiently your business is scaling.

Wrap Up

This chapter guided you through the process of scaling your business strategically. You learned how to assess your current capacity, streamline operations, and enter new markets without losing quality or focus. Scaling effectively demands a balance of strategic planning and decisive action.

Action Steps

1. Review your operations and identify key areas where efficiency can be improved.

2. Set specific growth goals and timelines, such as expanding to a new market or increasing production capacity.

3. Build a support system—whether through hiring, partnerships, or outsourcing—to manage increased demands.

Up Next

In the next chapter, we'll explore strategies for seizing new markets. You'll learn how to analyze market opportunities, tailor your approach, and position your brand to make a substantial impact in unfamiliar territories.

Chapter Seven

Seizing New Market Opportunities

I n the previous chapter, I taught you how and when to scale a business. To reiterate, scaling is the only way to maximize your business potential and make the biggest impact in the world.

Here, we will niche down and focus on something specific: finding new market opportunities.

Finding new opportunities is one way of scaling a business—in some cases, it's the best. There are times when growth seems elusive in one market segment. INSEAD business theorists Renée Mauborgne and W. Chan Kim call these segments "Red Oceans." Seizing new market opportunities is the best way to achieve growth and scale.

As with most things in running a business, it's easier said than done. But with proven strategies, the correct information, and lady luck, you can find winning markets and capitalize on them.

When to Find New Markets

The thought of expanding into new markets is tempting. But it's important to time your jump. Jump too soon or too late, and you may miss the mark.

Fortunately, there's a way to assess the ideal moment for entering new markets. You need to look for sure signs. If they're green, you're good to go. Let's have a look at those signals.

Meeting Your Metrics

The US Chamber of Commerce is the world's largest business federation, with over 3 million members. It advises both new and expert business owners on trends and tactics.

One of the blog posts, "6 signs your company is ready to expand," lists "you're meeting your metrics" as the number one sign. I strongly agree with that.

Expanding into new markets should only be done if your KPI or key performance indicators say so. It's a data-driven way to grow your business rather than solely on gut and instincts. Time and again, data-based companies have a higher chance of success.

The exact metrics you'd track are specific to the business. But generally, you'd want:

- Cost and Expenses

- Profit Margin

- Cash Flow

- Customer Acquisition Cost

- Customer Lifetime Value

- Churn Rate

- Inventory Turnover

- Market Penetration

You Have A Solid Team of Employees

Expansion requires a team that can handle more responsibility. If your staff is well-trained, reliable, and eager for new challenges, that's a strong indicator that your business can grow without falling apart.

In retail, for example, your team has been with you for years, and they've become experts in handling day-to-day operations. They're even leading new initiatives, like suggesting ways to improve customer service or streamline inventory management. When your team is ready to step up, you have the support system in place for expansion.

Inability to Meet Customer Demand

Business owners often think you need to expand when sales are plateauing. But the best expansion frequently happens when your sales are exploding. Not meeting demand means you're leaving money on the table. And to capture those customers, you should expand your operations.

Let's say you run a busy hair salon. You've been booked solid for weeks and can't accommodate new clients. You're turning away business because you don't have enough chairs or stylists. This is a clear sign that you've outgrown your current setup, and it's time to consider hiring more staff or opening a second location.

Your Customers Demand More

The best signals come right from your customers. After all, the customer is always right.

If your users approach you with requests for more features or services, you should know you've hit the "expansion" jackpot.

Top companies leverage customer feedback as a powerful tool to drive product innovation and enhance user experience. Take Netflix, for example. It initially started as an online DVD rental company. User feedback led to the introduction of features like personalized recommendations, offline viewing, and multiple profiles.

You need requests like these to know you need to expand.

You've Built A Strong Brand and Reputation

Expanding becomes less risky when your business has a solid reputation and loyal customer base. Positive reviews, word-of-mouth referrals, and repeat customers are all signs that your brand is ready to grow.

Without the reputation, you'll have a hard time convincing new customers and likely experience longer sales cycles. This is considered inefficient and cost-intensive. Thus, ensure trust is in place among your existing users.

You've Identified A Market Opportunity

The celebrated venture capitalist Ben Horowitz once said, "Markets that don't exist don't care how smart you are." And you should keep that in mind when expanding.

If you've identified an underserved market or see a new trend emerging that fits your business, it's worth exploring expansion to capture that opportunity.

For example, a fitness studio owner may notice a growing interest in virtual workout classes. While they may have traditionally only offered in-person classes, expanding into the virtual space could allow them to tap into a whole new market—people who prefer to work out from home.

You Feel Ready for New Challenges

Sometimes, it's about you, the business owner. It might be time to scale up if you feel comfortable in your current operations but crave a new challenge or see more potential for your business.

Backed with data and information, you should take up the challenge and expand your other market opportunities.

However, be wary of Shiny Object Syndrome (SOS). SOS is the constant pull to chase after every new opportunity or trend that seems exciting without fully thinking about whether it's the right fit for your goals. It's like being distracted by the next "shiny object" that catches your attention, often at the cost of what's already working or what truly matters.

In business, this means jumping from one idea, tool, or project to the next, lured by the promise of quick success or instant rewards. The problem? You spread yourself too thin, leaving important tasks unfinished and missing out on the more profound progress that comes from staying focused and committed.

While innovation is key to growth, Shiny Object Syndrome can waste resources—time, energy, and money—on things that might not be the best move for your business in the long run. It prevents you from honing in on what truly drives success, leaving you with many half-finished projects and no clear direction.

Market Research: The Secret Weapon for Seizing New Opportunities

Growing up, I always admired superheroes (I'm sure you do too). I was in awe of the web-shooters of Spiderman and Superman's immense power. Soon, I realized that their powers make them unique. It's what enables them to do magical things.

Likewise, when you seize new market opportunities, you need your secret weapons—and that is market research.

In today's fast-changing world, customer preferences, industry trends, and market dynamics constantly shift. Businesses can make informed decisions about when, where, and how to expand by consistently gathering and analyzing data.

More specifically, there are good reasons why businesses widely adopt continuous market research.

Staying Ahead of Customer Needs

One of the most significant benefits of ongoing market research is the ability to anticipate customer needs. Consumer expectations constantly evolve, and what worked a year ago may no longer be relevant today.

For instance, according to a report by PwC, 73% of customers say that experience is a key factor in their purchasing decisions. This shift in consumer behavior highlights the importance of businesses tracking what their customers want in real-time. By doing so, they can ensure that their expansion plans align with current market demands.

Spotting Emerging Trends Early

Continuous research also helps businesses identify and respond to emerging trends. Technological advancements and market trends can present both opportunities and challenges for businesses. Companies that do not adapt risk being outpaced by their competitors. A good example is the rise of e-commerce.

According to Statista, global e-commerce sales accounted for over 19% of total retail sales in 2023. Companies that quickly recognized this shift and invested in online shopping infrastructure gained a competitive edge. On the other hand, businesses that hesitated lost out on substantial market share. Regular market research helps companies spot these trends early and adjust their strategies accordingly.

Mitigating Risk In New Markets

Expanding a business is always risky. Uncertainties about new markets, customer behavior, and local competition exist. Continuous market research can help companies mitigate these risks by providing valuable insights into market potential, competitive landscapes, and customer expectations in new areas.

For example, if a restaurant chain is considering opening new locations in a different city, market research can reveal local food preferences, spending habits, and competitors. With this information, the chain can tailor its menu and marketing efforts to meet the needs of the new customer base, reducing the likelihood of failure.

Efficient Resource Allocation

Market research also plays a vital role in helping businesses allocate resources effectively. Expansion requires investment in areas such as marketing, staffing, and infrastructure. Without proper data, companies may spend resources inefficiently.

According to a report by the Harvard Business Review, companies that rely on data-driven decision-making are 5% more productive and 6% more profitable than their competitors. By continually gathering market data, businesses can make informed choices about where to allocate funds, ensuring they get the best possible return on their investments.

Staying Competitive

Finally, continuous market research helps businesses maintain a competitive edge during expansion. Competitors are always looking for ways to capture more market share. Regular research allows businesses to monitor their competition's strategies and adjust accordingly. This proactive approach will enable companies to stay competitive and seize opportunities before their rivals do.

Continuous Market Research Methodology

The global market research sector generates billions of dollars in revenue annually. While exact figures can vary, it's estimated to be worth over $80 billion.

Market research companies provide valuable insights into consumer behavior, market trends, and industry dynamics. The people working in this sector drive significant business decisions worldwide through their research and findings.

They spend years honing their skills. But fortunately, people like you and me don't have to. You can use their techniques to conduct continuous market research to seize new opportunities. Below are some core techniques researchers use to evaluate and understand their markets.

Surveys

Have you ever received an email from your favorite brand asking you to "take a quick survey"? That's continuous market research in action.

Surveys are arguably the most commonly used method in market research. They provide businesses with direct customer feedback and help identify consumer behavior trends. Companies use online, phone, or in-person surveys to collect data about customer preferences, product satisfaction, and purchasing habits.

Imagine a coffee shop chain that wants to expand into a new city. The company surveys potential customers about their coffee preferences, how often they visit cafes, and which locations are most convenient. By analyzing the responses, the business can tailor its offerings to the preferences of the new market before opening its doors.

Focus Groups

The second most common method is focus groups, which involve gathering a small group of people to discuss a product, service, or concept in depth. Businesses can gain rich, qualitative data by observing how participants react and interact with each other's opinions. Focus groups provide insights that numbers alone can't, such as emotional responses and personal motivations.

The main concern with focus groups is they tend to be expensive. It takes effort to sort out the best candidates for focus group sessions, agree on a time, and reward them for their efforts. However, with a bit of strategy, you can complete a focus session without spending much.

All you need is past customer data. Then, you can select the best candidates for an interview and set up a Zoom session. You can gift them a discount or priority access to upcoming products as a reward.

Qualitative Interviews

Along with focus sessions, qualitative interviews with a single person work best. In these interviews, you sit down with a single person and talk like you would at a coffee shop with a friend.

One-on-one interviews allow businesses to dive deep into the customer experience. This method involves detailed conversations that help understand customers' motivations, desires, and frustrations. It provides more in-depth insight than surveys and can uncover pain points that weren't previously considered.

Social Media Listening

Social media is more than a place where you update your status. It's a goldmine for businesses looking for insights into their customers. And there are dedicated apps that enable you to do that. This is called social media listening.

Social media listening involves tracking and analyzing online conversations about a brand, product, or industry. Platforms like Twitter, Instagram, and Facebook allow businesses to gauge public sentiment, spot emerging trends, and respond to customer concerns in real-time.

A fashion brand like H&M uses social media listening to track customer reactions to new collections. If they notice customers frequently discussing a particular style or trend, they adjust their inventory or marketing strategy to capitalize on what's trending, ensuring they remain relevant and on-trend.

Observations

Observational research involves watching customers interact with a product or service in a real-world setting. This method helps businesses see what customers do rather than relying on what they say, providing insights that might not come out through direct questioning.

Grocery stores often conduct observational research by watching how customers navigate the aisles. For example, they might observe that customers spend more time browsing organic products.

This insight can prompt them to expand their organic offerings or reposition these products for better visibility, improving sales.

Field Trials

Field trials involve testing a product or service in a small, controlled environment before fully launching it. This method is beneficial for expansion because it allows businesses to assess the real-world impact of their product or service without committing too many resources.

A fast-food chain might test a new menu item in a few select locations before rolling it out nationwide. If the new item sells well and customer feedback is positive, the chain can confidently introduce it in more locations. On the other hand, if the item doesn't perform as expected, they can modify the recipe or marketing before investing heavily in it.

Competitive Analysis

Ongoing market research involves closely tracking competitors. Companies can evaluate competitors' actions, such as product launches, pricing strategies, and marketing approaches, to refine their methods.

A good example of a competitive analysis is Netflix. Netflix closely watches competitors like Disney+ and Amazon Prime to see how they price their services, what content is trending, and how customers respond. By analyzing competitors' actions, Netflix can adjust its own strategies, such as focusing on original content or tweaking subscription tiers to stay competitive in the streaming market.

Public Data

Public data from government reports, industry studies, or trade associations provides valuable insights that can inform expansion decisions. The best part is that this data is often freely available and can reveal trends in demographics, spending habits, and broader economic conditions.

A real estate company might use census data to determine population growth in different areas. If the data shows a particular city is growing rapidly and has many young professionals, the company might target that area for new property developments.

Purchased Data

In some cases, businesses purchase data from third-party providers like Adobe and Nielsen. These are usually market research organizations that gather and compile data. This method is handy for gathering difficult or time-consuming insights to collect independently. Purchased data often includes detailed consumer profiles, spending habits, and industry-specific reports.

While the reports tend to be expensive, they are often reliable and worth the investment, especially as you're entering new markets.

Sales Data Analysis

You might be sitting on a pile of rich information without even knowing. The sales figures that you've got saved on Excel sheets or CRM can offer valuation information on future growth prospects.

Analyzing past sales performance helps companies spot trends, identify popular products, and understand seasonal patterns. It also reveals areas for improvement, such as reducing inventory costs or adjusting pricing strategies.

Amazon uses its massive sales data to recommend products based on customers' past purchases. The company's ability to analyze millions of transactions helps it identify customer preferences, seasonal trends, and successful products, guiding future inventory management and marketing strategy decisions.

The most successful companies use a mix of methods to gauge market opportunities. You should prioritize the ones that are within your comfort level and budget.

Identifying and Capitalizing on New Market Opportunities

Finding new opportunities starts with identifying them. Your entrepreneurial eyes find opportunities at every nook and corner of the street. But it's not worth, nor feasible, to chase every moment. Thankfully, a few ways help you spot the feasible ones.

Not All That Glitters Is Gold

Business owners and investors are always searching for the so-called "Next big thing." They are everywhere, from flying cars to quantum computers to anti-aging technology.

But savvy investors know something others don't (or perhaps ignore on purpose): not all that glitters is gold.

The latest example is crypto and NFT or non-fungible tokens. While Bitcoin and other cryptocurrencies are still around, the world-changing potential they once claimed is all but gone. And as it turned out, NFT collectibles were nothing but another digital gold rush.

As a responsible business owner, you should always be skeptical of overhyped trends and fads that do not bring any business value, especially in the long run.

Just because NFT collectibles are in the news doesn't mean you should expand into it. You can experiment, but considerable investment is always a big no.

Conduct A Gap Analysis

Specific gaps exist in any industry that existing players are not meeting. By carefully analyzing and identifying these gaps, you can expand into them to grow your business.

Identifying gaps in the market involves looking for unmet needs or underserved customer segments. Gaps might include product features that customers desire but competitors don't offer them or geographic regions with little competition. Look for inefficiencies in your industry and find ways to fill those voids.

Monitor Industry and Consumer Trends

Our world rarely stays the same. New inventions, technology, ideas, and customer choices alter how things are done, invariably creating new market and consumer trends.

For example, the surge in remote work increased the demand for virtual collaboration. Businesses like Zoom and Slack fulfilled this market need and became unicorns. Other companies, too, adapted to the growing trend by offering related products, such as office supplies for home setups, contactless delivery, etc.

By understanding emerging trends, you can identify new market segments that align with your offerings.

Monitor Related Industries

Many business executives make the mistake of overtly scrutinizing their industry for growth and expansion opportunities. However, research shows that the best opportunities sometimes come from outside your industry.

This is evident when four in ten companies look outside their domain for new ideas. Developments in one sector can create demand in another. For instance, the growth of e-commerce has fueled demand for logistics services, packaging, and online marketing tools.

Thus, monitor adjacent industries. Look for innovations, customer needs, or new technologies that could influence your market and identify opportunities in them.

Keep An Eye On The Political Landscape

The political environment plays a significant role in shaping business opportunities. Changes in regulations, tax policies, and trade agreements can open up new markets or create barriers in existing ones.

When the European Union imposed stricter regulations on data privacy (GDPR), players that were quick to adapt gained a competitive advantage. Many businesses also offered GDPR-complaint services and saw immediate success.

Businesses Can Mitigate Risks Or Leverage New Opportunities By Staying Informed About Political Developments.

Low-End Market Opportunities

There's a business theory that goes, "Incumbent players always try for the highest-margin segments of a market and underserve low-margin segments. New players can exploit low-end market opportunities without drawing the ire of incumbents who don't fight back due to lower margins."

Clayton Christensen calls this theory the low-end market opportunity theory. Using this theory, you can analyze existing industries and find low-end opportunities for expansion. And you won't have to fight the existing players either, thereby keeping costs down.

Using ChatGPT to Find New Market Opportunities

There are specialized AI tools that you can use to find new opportunities in the market. But the simplest of them all is ChatGPT. ChatGPT is trained on a massive text dataset, enabling it to analyze patterns, trends, and emerging opportunities within your industry. By feeding it with relevant data, you can gain valuable insights into consumer behavior, market trends, and competitor activities.

ChatGPT can help you spot underserved niches or unmet needs in the market. Analyzing customer feedback, social media conversations, and industry reports can identify gaps where your business can differentiate itself and offer unique solutions.

You can begin with a simple prompt like this:

> *"I operate in the [niche] in [location]. I want to expand my business. Help me find new and related opportunities based on the latest data. Use the Internet to find the latest information."*

In this case, you're directing ChatGPT to search for new information, which currently requires a paid version.

Alternatively, you can feed data to ChatGPT via attachments. Use your original market research and the latest market trends and ask ChatGPT to find relevant opportunities.

> *"I've attached my original market research and a business report on the latest trends. I operate in [niche] and want to expand. Find relevant opportunities for me."*

With few iterations, you should figure out unmet needs in an industry with AI.

Wrap Up

This chapter explored strategies for entering new markets. From conducting market research to positioning your brand effectively, you can take confident steps into new areas, attract a fresh audience, and expand your reach.

Action Steps

1. Research potential new markets and identify the ones with the most promise.

2. Tailor your marketing and sales approach to resonate with this new audience.

3. Set clear goals and timelines for entering and growing in these markets.

Up Next

In the final chapter, we'll look at the future of business with AI. You'll learn how to integrate AI into your operations, from enhancing customer experiences to streamlining internal processes, and prepare your business to stay competitive in the age of technology.

Chapter Eight

The Future with AI

In the previous chapter, under the "How to identify and capitalize on new market opportunities" section, I cautioned against the latest trends sold as "gold." Not all that glitters is gold.

Many people put AI in the same glittery bracket. They claim AI is nothing but a new concept sold by greedy Silicon Valley venture capitalists. While some criticism and a healthy dose of skepticism are valid, AI is something that cannot be unseen.

Artificial Intelligence (AI) is everywhere. Whether you're running a local coffee shop or managing a growing e-commerce store, AI is starting to shape how we do business in ways that were hard to imagine just a few years ago. For small and mid-sized business owners, it can seem like AI is something reserved for big companies with huge tech budgets, but that's not the case anymore.

I remember when I first started hearing about AI. Like many, I thought it was something out of a science fiction movie—futuristic robots and machines doing all the work. But then, I started seeing it pop up in real-world situations. Take email marketing, for example. My friend, who owns a small online retail store, spent hours figuring out the best time to email her customers. Then, she discovered an AI-powered tool that did it all for her. Not only did it save her time, but it also boosted her sales by sending personalized recommendations based on customer behavior. She couldn't believe how simple it was, and neither could I.

Since then, I have become increasingly interested in AI and its latest developments. I've distilled what I've learned into this chapter.

Here, you'll learn about the future of AI, how to distinguish between AI hype and reality, and how to use AI for your business. We have already covered many of the business applications of AI tools, from content creation to market research. In the sections below, we expand on them.

AI: Hype vs Reality

It's easy to get caught up in the media buzz about AI. Headlines boast about how AI will revolutionize everything from healthcare to retail, and you've probably heard talk about how AI will either solve all our problems or take over our jobs.

The truth, however, lies somewhere in between. AI has immense potential, but there's also a lot of hype that can cloud its real value for businesses, especially for small and mid-sized ones. The top dogs have the budget to experiment with AI, lose money, and remain profitable.

So, the big question is how to differentiate between AI hype and reality. There's no proven system or methodology. But you can get to the truth by answering a few fundamental questions.

- Does it solve a real problem? AI should address a specific need within your business, like reducing manual labor, improving customer service, or increasing sales.

- Is it proven? Look for AI tools that have demonstrated success in similar businesses or industries.

- How does AI compare to human performance on the same task? The key benefit of AI is its speed, allowing it to complete tasks faster than humans. Compare the outcomes and time required.

- Can you scale it? AI solutions should grow with your business, offering room for expansion without the need for constant updates or a tech expert on staff.

- What are the potential risks and challenges associated with this AI? AI systems often collect and analyze vast amounts of personal data, raising privacy concerns. Thus, inspect potential drawbacks.

AI expert Andrew Ng, one of the pioneers of machine learning, once said, "AI is the new electricity." He means that AI, like electricity, will soon be woven into the fabric of everyday business, powering systems in the background without us even noticing.

This grounded perspective highlights AI's potential to improve business operations, but it also suggests that AI's value comes from its usefulness, not its flashiness.

Emerging Trends in AI For Businesses

Since its public release, ChatGPT has sparked widespread fascination with AI, captivating both individuals and organizations. Interest in AI technology has only continued to grow.

So, let's explore the latest AI trend and some real-world applications demonstrating how AI delivers tangible results for businesses of all sizes.

GenAI

Generative AI refers to AI systems that can create new content with simple inputs. Unlike traditional AI, which primarily analyzes or recognizes existing data, generative AI can produce novel outputs. These systems are often based on advanced machine learning techniques, particularly Generative Adversarial Networks (GANs) or large-scale transformer models like GPT, which OpenAI, the creator of ChatGPT, uses.

Businesses are already using tools like ChatGPT or Jasper AI to automate the creation of blog posts, social media updates, email campaigns, and more. GenAI can produce draft content that human writers can refine, dramatically speeding up content production.

In the coming years, GenAI is poised to influence many more aspects of businesses.

Multimodal Machine Learning

Multimodal machine learning refers to AI models simultaneously processing and understanding multiple data types, such as text, images, video, and audio. This means you can upload an audio sample and ask AI to create a document with text input. How cool is that?

Multimodal machine learning uses several neural networks to process different types of data streams and then combines the insights from each. For instance, an AI system could analyze a video by interpreting its visual content and spoken words to understand its full context.

YouTube uses multimodal AI to recommend videos by analyzing visual content (thumbnails), descriptions, and tags. This ensures more personalized recommendations by understanding what is shown in the video and how it is described. This opens up a new era in how tech works.

AI-Powered Automation

AI will have the most impact on automation. Redundant, manual processes that do not involve creative thinking will eventually be automated with AI.

Today, Robotic Process Automation (RPA) tools like UiPath or Blue Prism can handle repetitive tasks such as invoicing, payroll, and order processing with minimal human intervention.

Accounting software like Xero uses AI to automatically categorize transactions, match invoices, and generate financial reports. This reduces the need for manual data entry, allowing accountants to focus on more complex tasks like financial planning.

Automation is also being widely adopted in marketing. Subscribing to a newsletter triggers a steady flow of emails, automatically managed by tools like HubSpot and MailChimp.

AI Assistant

In a blog post, Bill Gates predicted that everyone online will have an AI-powered assistant working for them. He said, "In the near future, anyone who's online will be able to have a personal assistant powered by artificial intelligence far beyond today's technology." He predicted the timeline for the next five years (starting from 2023).

On his prophecy, he added, "Agents are smarter. They're proactive- capable of making suggestions before you ask for them."

This voice is echoed by the NVIDIA CEO, who on the NVIDIA blog said, "Every single company, every single job within the company, will have AI assistance."

With billions of dollars being poured into the development of AI assistants, it makes sense to follow and keep pace with the trend.

AI-Powered Customer Support

Just like users will have AI-powered assistants, businesses must equip themselves with an army of AI assistants to handle their customers.

AI-driven support systems typically combine chatbots, voice assistants, and algorithms to process customer inquiries. These systems can analyze customer messages or queries in real-time and respond appropriately by pulling information from a database of pre-programmed responses or learning from past interactions.

Some AI systems are also self-learning, meaning they get smarter over time by analyzing customer interactions.

A significant benefit of AI in customer support is its 24/7 availability, helping customers at any time. AI chatbots and voice assistants can handle customer queries outside of regular business hours, ensuring customers get the help they need whenever they need it.

Predictive Analytics

Besides automation, another area where AI will have the most impact is future prediction through predictive analytics. AI-powered systems can better predict the outcome and help businesses make better future investments.

At its core, predictive analytics leverages large datasets to identify patterns and relationships that can be used to forecast future outcomes. Businesses use it for revenue forecasting, demand planning, and financial performance.

For example, by analyzing previous sales data, retailers can forecast demand for specific products, helping them optimize stock levels and reduce inventory costs.

Predictive analytics also finds applications in cybersecurity, application processing, fraud detection, and operational efficiency.

Natural Language Processing (NLP)

NLP enables meaningful interactions between humans and machines by allowing machines to understand, interpret, and generate human language effectively.

For businesses, NLP is revolutionizing communication, customer service, data analysis, and decision-making by allowing machines to process text and speech just as humans do.

In everyday life, NLP-powered voice assistants like Amazon Alexa, Google Assistant, and Apple's Siri allow users to interact with devices through voice commands.

This trend will expand and become even more helpful to users and businesses.

AI-Driven Decision-Making

As businesses increasingly deal with complex and ever-changing environments, AI-driven decision-making becomes a powerful tool to reduce uncertainty, streamline operations, optimize processes, and drive growth.

One high-risk area where AI-driven decision-making is leaving a mark is trading. JPMorgan Chase uses an AI platform, LOXM, to make high-speed trading decisions, executing trades based on real-time market conditions and historical data. This helps the bank optimize trade timing and execution, maximizing profits while minimizing risk.

Another area is supply chain logistics. DHL uses AI systems to predict demand fluctuations, optimize warehouse operations, and even automate route planning for delivery drivers, improving operational efficiency and reducing costs without human decision-makers.

The future of AI-driven decision-making is likely to involve a combination of AI systems and human expertise. Rather than replacing humans, AI will serve as a decision-making assistant, providing data-driven insights that empower humans to make better, more informed decisions.

Ethical and Explainable AI

With the rise of AI, skeptics often point out its ethical side—and rightly so. Research has found that while AI can streamline recruitment and applicant processing, there is a risk of algorithmic bias, which results in discriminatory hiring practices based on gender, race, color, and personality traits.

Ethical AI refers to the responsible and ethical development and deployment of AI systems. It involves considering AI's societal impact, addressing biases, and ensuring fairness and transparency.

Along with Ethical AI, there's a growing trend of explainable AI.

Explainable AI focuses on making AI models more interpretable and understand-able. It involves techniques that allow humans to understand the decision-making process of AI models. In other words, it asks how the AI model arrived at the findings. This enables better inspection of the AI models and ensures no inherent bias.

Low-Code/No-Code Machine Learning

Machine learning, a branch of AI, teaches computers to learn from data. It's like training a dog – instead of giving it specific commands, you show it examples and let it figure out the pattern.

Traditionally, building ML models requires a deep understanding of programming, data science, and advanced analytics techniques. However, with the rise of low-code and no-code platforms, businesses can build machine learning applications without specialized coding or data science expertise.

The primary trend driving the adoption of low-code and no-code ML platforms is the democratization of AI and machine learning. As these tools become more accessible, businesses empower more employees—beyond data scientists and engineers—to create ML models. This is breaking down the barrier of entry to AI, enabling business leaders and other non-technical stakeholders to leverage the power of machine learning for decision-making.

Staying Current With AI

AI is evolving rapidly, and new trends and technologies are constantly emerging. For businesses to remain competitive, they must stay informed about the latest developments and integrate them strategically.

However, with the fast-paced nature of AI advancements, it can be a challenge to keep up. Here are some strategies businesses can use to stay updated on AI trends and ensure they don't fall behind.

Establish A Continuous Learning Culture

One of the most effective ways businesses can stay informed on AI trends is by fostering a culture of continuous learning. This means encouraging employees, especially those in leadership and technical roles, to regularly update their knowledge through training, certifications, and research.

Offer access to online courses, workshops, and certifications focused on AI and related technologies. Platforms like Coursera, edX, Udacity, and LinkedIn Learning provide AI, machine learning, and data science courses.

Also, create an environment where employees can share new insights and developments they've come across in the AI space. This could be through regular team meetings, presentations, or internal knowledge-sharing platforms.

Subscribe to AI News and Journals

Who better to rely on for the latest developments than journalists? Several industry-leading publications, journals, and websites publish regular updates on AI innovations, challenges, and opportunities.

Follow websites that track the latest developments in AI, such as TechCrunch, VentureBeat AI, Wired, and The Verge. These sites often feature news, interviews, and expert opinions about new AI trends.

Additionally, many technology companies, research organizations, and consulting firms publish blogs focusing on AI trends within specific industries. For example, McKinsey, Gartner, and Forrester publish research and insights about AI's impact on business and industry-specific applications.

If you're more academia-focused, keep an eye on AI research published in academic journals like the Journal of Artificial Intelligence Research or Nature Machine Intelligence. Reading papers can give businesses an in-depth understanding of the latest research and innovations that may impact their operations.

Attend AI Conferences and Events

Conferences, webinars, and workshops are excellent opportunities to hear directly from experts, discover cutting-edge technologies, and network with other professionals at the forefront of AI innovation.

You can attend or participate in AI-related conferences like the AI Summit, CES (Consumer Electronics Show), Google I/O, and NVIDIA's GPU Technology Conference (GTC). These events often feature announcements about the latest AI trends, product launches, and research breakthroughs.

Conferences provide a platform to meet AI innovators, researchers, and thought leaders. Building relationships with people in the AI field can help businesses get first-hand knowledge of trends and innovations.

Many AI companies and organizations host workshops or webinars on emerging AI trends and technologies. These sessions can offer practical, hands-on experience and exposure to tools and platforms.

Collaborate With AI Consultants and Partners

Hiring consultants with AI expertise can help you assess the latest AI trends and understand how they can apply them to solve their unique challenges. Consultants often guide companies through integrating AI into their operations, recommending the most effective tools and platforms.

Along with experts, you can collaborate with AI technology providers or third-party platforms, such as Google Cloud AI, Microsoft Azure AI, or IBM Watson. These partners often provide updates, white papers, case studies, and hands-on training for businesses looking to implement AI solutions.

Monitor AI Applications In Competitor Markets

Keeping an eye on competitors and their use of AI can help businesses understand which trends are gaining traction and how to adopt similar technologies to improve their operations.

You can use AI tools to track competitors' AI strategies, such as how they are applying AI in customer support, marketing, sales, or product development. Companies like CB Insights and Crunchbase monitor industry innovations and the AI technologies companies are using. You can leverage the data.

Also, reading real-world case studies about how businesses successfully implement AI can provide practical examples and inspiration. Many AI platforms publish detailed case studies showcasing how companies from different industries benefit from AI.

You can stay ahead of the curve by investing in continuous learning, staying connected to the right sources of information, attending industry events, and working with AI technology partners. And in this ever-evolving world, that's an edge.

Making Your Business AI-Ready

One of the most exciting ways to enhance your business's potential is by embracing AI rather than living in denial. From improving customer service to streamlining operations, AI can help you expand more efficiently and intelligently.

The good news is you don't have to be a tech expert or have a large budget to get started. Becoming AI-ready is all about taking strategic steps to prepare your business, your team, and your processes to harness the power of AI.

A few strategic baby steps will make your business AI-ready.

Understand the Value of AI for Your Business

The first step toward becoming AI-ready is understanding what AI can do for your business. AI isn't a one-size-fits-all solution, and it's essential to focus on the areas where it can have the most significant impact.

Looking to boost sales numbers? Consider starting with AI-powered sales processes. If delivery is backed up, AI can help streamline supply chain management, improve inventory control, and even automate manual tasks to save time and money.

Adopting AI begins with clearly understanding your business and identifying areas for improvement and potential gaps.

Build A Solid Data Foundation

For AI to work effectively, it needs to learn from high-quality, relevant data. Small and mid-sized businesses often overlook the importance of having sound data systems in place, but this is crucial for AI implementation.

For data, Start by gathering customer data, sales data, website interactions, and other business data you already have. Ensure it's clean, structured, and easily accessible. The more consistent your data collection methods, the more effective your AI will be.

Invest in software or systems that can organize and store your data effectively. This could include cloud storage solutions like Google Cloud, which provides data infrastructure.

As your data collection grows, you can invest in data warehouse tools.

Invest In AI Talent

As your business grows and you begin exploring more advanced AI opportunities, having the right talent can make all the difference. Therefore, you should double down on hiring employees proficient in AI tools.

At the bare minimum, look for talent acquainted with prompt engineering. Prompt engineering is about conversing with AI to get the desired results. A marketer with prompt engineering skills uses tools like ChatGPT and CoPilot to generate marketing materials faster. Likewise, accountants with similar skills can crunch numbers faster and be more productive.

Besides that, ensure you provide adequate training through platforms like Udemy and Coursera. This will ensure your people are ready to leverage your business's upcoming AI capabilities.

Start AI Pilot Projects

As a new business with limited budgets, you don't need to dive into complex AI projects right away. Start small with solutions that can provide immediate value. Many accessible and affordable AI tools can easily integrate into your current operations.

Start with something cost-effective like AI-powered chatbots. Implementing the chatbots on your website can improve customer service and lead generation. Platforms like Tidio, Intercom, or Drift offer easy-to-implement chatbot solutions that don't require a technical background.

Then, you can move to AI-driven marketing and content creation with free tools like ChatGPT.

Begin small and see what works and what doesn't.

Monitor and Scale Your AI Solutions

Once you have AI tools in place, monitoring their performance and impact on your business is important. AI systems need ongoing tuning and optimization to remain effective.

Track key performance indicators (KPIs) like customer satisfaction, sales growth, operational efficiency, or employee productivity to gauge the impact of your AI solutions.

Over time, you may need to adjust or retrain your AI models based on new data and trends. Work with your team or AI partners to refine these models and ensure they align with your business objectives.

Once you start getting measurable positive results, scale operations and improve productivity.

Checklist: Preparing Your Business for AI

There are many checklists you'll find on the internet that help you determine your business's AI readiness. You're free to use any of them. But for your convenience, I'm providing you with my own.

Use this checklist to ensure your business is fully prepared to integrate and benefit from AI technologies. Whether you're just starting or looking to expand, these steps will guide you toward becoming AI-ready.

1. Understand AI's Potential for Your Business

Identify key areas where AI can benefit your business (e.g., customer service, sales, operations, data analysis).

- Research AI applications relevant to your industry.

- Define business goals for AI. (e.g., increasing efficiency, improving customer experience, enhancing decision-making).

2. Build a Solid Data Foundation

- Collect and organize business data (customer, sales, website analytics, etc.).

- Ensure data quality (clean, accurate, and up-to-date).

- Implement a data management system (cloud storage, CRM, etc.).

- Ensure compliance with data privacy regulations (e.g., GDPR, CCPA).

3. Start with Small, Scalable AI Solutions

- Select easy-to-implement AI tools (e.g., chatbots, email automation, customer analytics).

- Test AI tools on a small scale before full deployment.

- Choose AI solutions with scalability to grow with your business.

4. Invest in AI Talent or Partnerships

- Consider hiring AI professionals (e.g., data scientists, machine learning engineers) if budget allows.

- Work with AI consultants to guide your AI adoption and strategy.

- Explore partnerships with AI firms that specialize in providing solutions for small businesses.

5. Select the Right AI Tools

- Choose AI tools based on your business needs (e.g., CRM software, marketing automation, data analytics tools).

- Evaluate AI platforms that integrate with your existing systems (e.g., POS, eCommerce platforms, marketing tools).

- Ensure the tools are user-friendly, scalable, and secure.

6. Focus on Ethical AI and Transparency

- Ensure your AI tools comply with data protection and privacy laws.

- Select AI tools that are explainable and transparent.

- Be proactive in preventing bias in AI models and algorithms.

7. Establish a Continuous Learning Culture

- Invest in training programs for employees to learn about AI and its applications.

- Encourage employees to stay updated with AI trends and innovations.

- Create a knowledge-sharing platform for team members to exchange insights on AI.

8. Monitor and Optimize AI Performance

- Track KPIs to measure the success of AI implementation (e.g., customer satisfaction, sales growth, operational efficiency).

- Continuously evaluate the effectiveness of AI tools and solutions.

- Optimize and adjust AI models based on new data or business needs.

9. Ensure AI Solutions Are Scalable

- Choose AI platforms and tools to handle increasing data and complexity as your business grows.

- Plan for AI infrastructure scalability (e.g., cloud computing, modular AI systems).

- Implement AI solutions that can be easily expanded to new departments, products, or markets.

10. Stay Updated on AI Trends

- Subscribe to AI news sources and industry publications (e.g., TechCrunch, Wired, AI-related blogs).

- Attend AI webinars, conferences, and workshops to stay informed on the latest trends and technologies.

- Network with AI thought leaders and influencers to learn about cutting-edge developments in AI.

Wrap Up

In this final chapter, you explored AI's incredible potential to future-proof your business. From automating tasks to enhancing customer experiences, integrating AI isn't just about staying competitive—it's about unlocking new efficiencies and creating a business that can adapt to rapid change.

Action Steps

1. Identify one or two areas in your business where AI tools could make an immediate impact.

2. Research and select accessible AI tools to start with, whether for customer service, marketing, or internal processes.

3. Keep learning and adapting as new AI technologies emerge, staying curious about how they can support your business goals.

Up Next

Congratulations! You can run and grow your business confidently with all these tools and insights. Remember, each chapter has given you strategies to face challenges, seize opportunities, and continuously improve. Embrace your entrepreneurial journey with resilience and keep moving forward, knowing you have a solid foundation to build. Here's to your success!

Conclusion

N ow that you've acquired all the knowledge you need to start and scale your business, it's important to recall the crucial adage, *"Business is a marathon, not a sprint."* This adage conveys that you should always think long-term and run your business with a vision.

As emphasized in Chapter 2, a strong foundation is essential to your vision. It acts as a buffer, absorbing the impact of the inevitable mistakes you will make along the journey. Successful entrepreneurs internalize this principle, while those who falter often learn it through difficult experiences.

While the foundation provides stability, it is bland and uninspired without confidence and charisma. The leaders you admire in business, politics, or sports often possess a magnetic presence that draws people in. While not mandatory, this is an essential game-changing quality.

Successful leaders take responsibility. They set high standards for accountability and make sure everyone on the team, including themselves, meets those standards.

Speaking of everyone, you revisit another business adage: *"Take care of your people, and they will take care of the business."* The people on your team are more than just a group of individuals. When nurtured and empowered, they collectively become a dynamic force capable of achieving extraordinary results.

So invest time in building trust, fostering open communication, and recognizing and rewarding achievements. Lead by example, empower your team members, and create a positive and supportive work environment. Remember, a high-performing team is a valuable asset that can propel your business to new heights.

We've also touched deeply on AI concepts. It's important to remember that technology, while powerful, is merely a tool. The true magic lies in how you wield it. AI combines technological prowess, strategic thinking, and human ingenuity. By understanding the core principles of AI and its potential applications, you can unlock a universe of possibilities for your business.

AI will become even more essential as your business inevitably grows. The ability to scale and seize new market opportunities is what distinguishes thriving businesses from those that fail.

As we talked about in Chapter 7, seizing new opportunities starts with deep and continuous market research. To reiterate, because I see business owners making this mistake time and time again, market research isn't merely a box to tick; it's the compass that guides your business toward uncharted territories. You can gain a competitive edge by consistently monitoring industry trends, analyzing consumer behavior, and staying abreast of emerging technologies.

As we wrap up this book, my final advice is to enjoy the journey. If you don't, the daily struggles may wear you down. One day, you might find yourself giving up and returning to the job market, abandoning the dreams that once inspired you to take this path.

So march ahead enthusiastically, plan diligently, be grounded, and deliver the best possible service to your customers.

If the insights I've shared in this book have brought you any value and enjoyment, please consider leaving a review. It will not only support me as an author but also help others discover the content they might be searching for!

LEAVE A REVIEW!

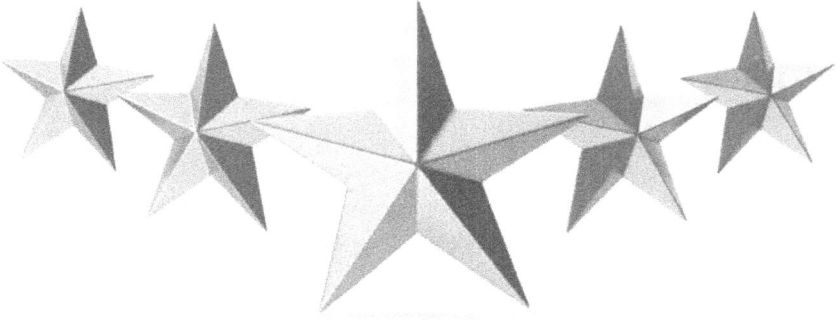

References

3 Inspiring Startup Success Stories | HBS Online. (2023, August 31). Business Insights Blog. https://online.hbs.edu/blog/post/startup-stories

4 financial indicators every entrepreneur should monitor. (2024, October 29). *B DC.ca*. https://www.bdc.ca/en/articles-tools/money-finance/manage-finances/5-k ey-indicators-monitor

6 Best AI-Powered Business Plan Generators (December 2023) | Bizway Resources. (n.d.). https://www.bizway.io/blog/best-ai-business-plan-generators

7 Proven strategies to overcome fear of starting a business. (n.d.). https://www.candi cemontgomeryonline.com/blog/fear-of-starting-business

8 Incredibly inspiring examples of online brand communities | Disciple. (n.d.) . https://www.disciplemedia.com/engaging-your-community/8-brand-communit ies-examples/

11 great brand community examples for 2024 | Khoros. (n.d.). https://khoros.com /blog/brand-community-examples

13 Finance Experts Recommend Tech Tools For Managing Business And Personal Finances. (2023, February 27). Forbes. https://www.forbes.com/sites/forbesfinancecouncil/2023/02/27/13-finance-exper ts-recommend-tech-tools-for-managing-business-and-personal-finances/?sh=435f6 e1a746f

28 Free SEO tools to boost your search rankings in 2024. (n.d.). Buffer: All-you-need Social Media Toolkit for Small Businesses. https://buffer.com/library/free-seo-too ls/

Aastha. (2023, May 24). *Rising from the Ground Up 10 Inspiring Startup Success Stories*. Silicon Valley Innovation Center. https://siliconvalley.center/blog/rising-from-the-ground-up-10-inspiring-startup-success-stories

Admin. (2024, August 22). The role of artificial intelligence (AI) in cybersecurity: Enhancing threat detection and response - Atlantic Data Security. *Atlantic Data Security*. https://atlanticdatasecurity.com/blog/ai-cybersecurity-threat-detection/

Adobe Communications Team. (2022, September 2). *Email Marketing — a step-by-step guide to getting started*. Adobe Experience Cloud. https://business.adobe.com/blog/basics/guide-to-email-marketing

Advania UK. (2024, July 23). *How to choose the right technology for your business - Advania*. https://www.advania.co.uk/insights/blog/how-to-choose-the-right-technology-for-your-business/

Advertising & Signage. (n.d.). Stanton. https://www.stantonca.gov/departments/public_safety/code_enforcement/advertising___signage.php

Aghina, W., Handscomb, C., Salo, O., & Thaker, S. (2021, May 25). *The impact of agility: How to shape your organization to compete*. McKinsey & Company. https://www.mckinsey.com/capabilities/people-and-organizational-performance/our-insights/the-impact-of-agility-how-to-shape-your-organization-to-compete

Ahmed, A. (2024a, February 15). *Audience engagement: What it is and tips to improve it*. Sprout Social. https://sproutsocial.com/insights/audience-engagement/

Ahmed, A. (2024b, June 17). *20 of the best social media analytics tools for your brand in 2024*. Sprout Social. https://sproutsocial.com/insights/social-media-analytics-tools/

Ai, G. (2023, October 31). *The Role of AI in streamlining Business Processes and Increasing Efficiency*. https://www.linkedin.com/pulse/role-ai-streamlining-business-processes-increasing-efficiency-nxakf/

AI readiness checklist | Collibra. (n.d.). Collibra. https://www.collibra.com/us/en/resources/ai-readiness-checklist

AI ready. (n.d.-a). https://www.launchconsulting.com/airready-assessment

AI ready. (n.d.-b). https://www.launchconsulting.com/airready-assessment

AI Tax Software - Top AI tools. (n.d.). TopAI.tools. https://topai.tools/s/AI-tax-software

AI Your Marketing Analytics: 5 Innovative Ways to Leverage AI for Deeper data Insights. (n.d.). https://improvado.io/blog/ai-marketing-analytics

AI-Driven Market Analysis: Revolutionizing financial insights for AMEX:SPY by JS_TechTrading — TradingView. (2023, November 27). TradingView. https://www.tradingview.com/chart/SPY/V9OQ3yrL-AI-Driven-Market-Analysis-Revolutionizing-Financial-Insights/

Alagar. (2023, November 2). The intersection of AI and business analytics. *IABAC®.* https://iabac.org/blog/the-intersection-of-ai-and-business-analytics

Alblooshi, N. (2023, April 17). *How AI is Transforming the Financial Sector: Case Studies from UAE and around the World.* https://www.linkedin.com/pulse/how-ai-transforming-financial-sector-case-studies-from-alblooshi/

Alibaba.com. (2021, June 29). *Home-based business: 6 advantages and disadvantages.* Alibaba.com Seller Central. https://seller.alibaba.com/businessblogs/pxdod30u-home-based-business-6-advantages-and-disadvantages

AllBusiness Editors. (n.d.). *Top 10 Advantages of a Home-Based Business.* allBusiness: Your Small Business Advantage. https://www.allbusiness.com/top-10-advantages-of-a-home-based-business-11087-1.html

Amaresan, S. (2024, June 4). How to Make Money on Social Media [New Data + Case Studies]. *HubSpot.* https://blog.hubspot.com/marketing/social-media-shopping-case-studies

Ambrozi, A. (2023, October 24). *11 Challenges of Adopting AI in Business (And How to Address Them Head-On).* Forbes. https://www.forbes.com/sites/forbesbusinesscouncil/2023/10/24/11-challenges-of-adopting-ai-in-business-and-how-to-address-them-head-on/?sh=1d15d1934bfe

Anand, S. (2022, November 11). *7 common entrepreneurial fears and how to overcome them – Early Growth*. Early Growth. https://earlygrowthfinancialservices.com/blog/7-common-entrepreneurial-fears-and-how-to-overcome-them-early-growth/

Anthony, S. D. (2022, November 1). *The top 20 business transformations of the last decade*. Harvard Business Review. https://hbr.org/2019/09/the-top-20-business-transformations-of-the-last-decade

Api, & Api. (2024, May 7). *Tax Compliance Checklist | Process Street*. Process Street. https://www.process.st/templates/tax-compliance-checklist/

Artificial intelligence in fintech: Use cases and examples. (n.d.). https://www.itransition.com/ai/fintech

Arun, R. (2024, November 6). *What is Digital Marketing and How Does It Work?* Simplilearn.com. https://www.simplilearn.com/tutorials/digital-marketing-tutorial/what-is-digital-marketing

Athuraliya, A. (2023, January 5). *5 Gap analysis tools to identify and close the gaps in your business*. Creately Blog. https://creately.com/blog/strategy-and-planning/gap-analysis-tools/

Author_Name. (1970, January 1). *post_title*. U Of I Tax School. https://taxschool.illinois.edu/post/leveraging-the-power-of-chatgpt-and-other-ai-tools-in-your-tax-practice/

Autoness Media. (2024, January 23). *Top 10 AI tools for Business: 2024's Game-Changers*. https://www.linkedin.com/pulse/top-10-ai-tools-business-2024s-game-changers-autonessmedia-qfijf/?trk=article-ssr-frontend-pulse_more-articles_related-content-card

B, S. (2023, February 27). *5 Reasons Having an Online Presence is Essential in Today's Modern Business World*. https://www.linkedin.com/pulse/5-reasons-having-online-presence-essential-todays-modern-barnwell/

Bajpai, P. (2023, December 20). *Pros and cons of a Limited Liability Company (LLC)*. Investopedia. https://www.investopedia.com/articles/investing/091014/b asics-forming-limited-liability-company-llc.asp

Bakersfield.com. (2021, May 17). Key Components of Traditional Business Plans. https://www.bakersfield.com/kern-business-journal/key-components-of-tr aditional-business-plans/article_29b786f2-b1a7-11eb-be75-670fd587aadd.html

Banners / Wind Devices | Garland, TX. (n.d.). https://www.garlandtx.gov/2162/Banners-Wind-Devices#:~:text=Banner%20Per mits&text=Permitted%20temporary%20banners%20may%20have,area%20exceed% 2080%20square%20feet.

Bautista, M. (2023, March 1). *The Impact of Machine Learning on Business Processes - Digital CXO*. Digital CxO. https://digitalcxo.com/article/the-impact-of-machin e-learning-on-business-processes/

Beautiful business & accounting software. (n.d.). Xero. https://www.xero.com/us/

Berger, B. (2024, September 26). *The 6 elements of the content marketing process*. Search Engine Journal. https://www.searchenginejournal.com/content-marketing -process-elements/376908/

Best AI Financial Forecasting Tools - AI Tools Network. (2023, July 3). AI Tools Network. https://aitoolsnetwork.com/tools/financial-forecasting/

Blunt, W. (2018, March 8). 9 Key elements of an effective social media marketing strategy, and how to establish them. *Social Media Today*. https://www.socialmediatoday.com/news/9-key-elements-of-an-effective-soc ial-media-marketing-strategy-and-how-to/518639/

Brown, L. (2024, November 12). *Become a successful SMM in 10 steps*. Filmora. https://filmora.wondershare.com/more-tips/become-a-successful-smm.html

Build a scalable business model: Strategies and best practices | Mailchimp. (n.d.). Mailchimp. https://mailchimp.com/resources/scalable-business/

Business plan template for a startup business. (n.d.). SCORE. https://www.score.o rg/resource/template/business-plan-template-a-startup-business

Business Tax Basics for Beginners. (n.d.). The Hartford. https://www.thehartford.c om/business-insurance/strategy/business-taxes

Case Studies. (n.d.). Zinia. https://zinia.ai/casestudies/

Case Study – Enabling Operational Efficiency through process and Technology Transformation during Growth - SIKICH. (2024, April 3). Sikich. https://www.sikich.com/insight/case-study-enabling-operational-efficiency -through-process-and-technology-transformation-during-growth/

Catherine. (2024, April 29). 10 Best AI tax Software for Business in 2024 (Ditch the spreadsheet). *AI Mojo.* https://aimojo.pro/ai-tax-softwares/

Chacko, A. (2024, May 15). *5 overlooked B2B market research methods for understanding your customers.* Sprout Social. https://sproutsocial.com/insights/b2b-ma rket-research/

Chaffey, D. (2024, July 11). *Digital marketing strategy template - free planning tool. 2024 edition.* Smart Insights. https://www.smartinsights.com/digital-marketing-st rategy/digital-marketing-strategy-and-planning-template/

Charrington, D. (2024, November 21). Top 18 market research tools (Free & Paid): A buyer's guide. *Qualaroo Blog - User Research and Customer Feedback Trends.* https://qualaroo.com/blog/market-research-tools/

Chodipilli, K. (2023, July 13). *5 Reasons Why Agility is More Important Than Ever in the Enterprise.* Leadership Tribe US. https://leadershiptribe.com/blog/5-reason s-why-agility-is-more-important-than-ever-in-the-enterprise

Choosing the Right Technology Strategy For Your Business A Comprehensive Guide. (2024, June 14). Faster Capital. https://fastercapital.com/content/Choosing-the -Right-Technology-Strategy-For-Your-Business--A-Comprehensive-Guide.html

CMO's Guide to Email Marketing ROI. (2024, September 3). Litmus. https://ww w.litmus.com/resources/email-marketing-roi

Content Marketing — definition, types, and how to do it. (2023, May 23). *Adobe Experience Cloud Team*. https://business.adobe.com/blog/basics/content-marketing

Contributor, S. (2021, March 5). 5 ways to engage consumers on social media. *Forbes*. https://www.forbes.com/sites/square/2020/12/04/5-ways-to-engage-consumers-on-social-media/?sh=1ccd6273b3f4

Conway, S. (2023, June 21). *The role of AI in streamlining business operations*. https://www.linkedin.com/pulse/role-ai-streamlining-business-operations-sean-conway/

CoSchedule. (2024, October 30). *SMART Marketing Goal Examples for 2024*. CoSchedule Blog. https://coschedule.com/marketing-strategy/marketing-goals/smart-marketing-goal-examples

Craig, L. (2024, August 26). *10 top AI and machine learning trends for 2024*. Search Enterprise AI. https://www.techtarget.com/searchenterpriseai/tip/9-top-AI-and-machine-learning-trends

Creative and innovative ways to fund a business startup. (2024, June 26). Faster Capital. https://fastercapital.com/content/Creative-and-innovative-ways-to-fund-a-business-startup.html

Daley, S. (2024a, February 27). *13 blockchain companies paving the way for the future*. Built In. https://builtin.com/blockchain/blockchain-companies-roundup

Daley, S. (2024b, November 6). *76 Artificial intelligence examples shaking up business across industries*. Built In. https://builtin.com/artificial-intelligence/examples-ai-in-industry

Dallos, M. (2024, May 3). Business Modell Evolution - by BMC | M. Dallos. *Business Model Company*. https://businessmodel.company/business-model-evolution/

Das, S. (2022, December 12). *Business agility - why it's important and how to achieve it.* https://www.linkedin.com/pulse/business-agility-why-its-important-how-achieve-soumitri-das/

Davis, B. (2023, September 11). *Forbes*. AI in Accounting and Bookkeeping: Braving the New Digital Frontier. https://www.forbes.com/sites/forbestechcouncil/2023/09/11/ai-in-accounting-and-bookkeeping-braving-the-new-digital-frontier/?sh=4f318458350b

Davis, M. (2024a, September 27). *Identifying and managing business risks*. Investopedia. https://www.investopedia.com/articles/financial-theory/09/risk-management-business.asp

Davis, M. (2024b, October 17). *How to overcome the fear of financial risk when starting your own business*. Qonto - Blog. https://qonto.com/en/blog/creators/tools-tips/how-to-overcome-the-fear-of-financial-risk-when-starting-your-own-business

DeBellis, D. (2023, October 31). *Why Adaptability is the New Digital Transformation*. WGI. https://wginc.com/why-adaptability-is-the-new-digital-transformation/

Decker, A. (2024, August 21). Accounting 101: Accounting Basics for Beginners to Learn. *HubSpot*. https://blog.hubspot.com/sales/accounting-101

DeMarco, J., & Anthony, L. (2024, November 18). *Startup funding: What it is and how to get capital for a business*. NerdWallet. https://www.nerdwallet.com/article/small-business/startup-funding

Developer, W. (2024, November 22). *14 Financial Management Tools that Every Business Must Have*. Cflow. https://www.cflowapps.com/top-financial-management-tools/

Dialpad. (2024, June 6). *11 AI tools for small businesses (Low cost, big impact!)*. https://www.dialpad.com/blog/ai-tools-for-small-business/

Discover the Domo Data Experience Platform | DoMo. (n.d.). https://www.domo.com/

Doepping, A. (2024, July 31). *Your 2023 Financial Health Checklist: Set yourself up for success*. Lafayette Federal Credit Union. https://www.lfcu.org/news/managing-money-credit/your-2023-financial-health-checklist-set-yourself-up-for-success-this-year-with-our-financial-health-checklist/

Dua, M. (2024, October 29). *17 AI tools for small businesses to become more Productive*. Mailmodo. https://www.mailmodo.com/guides/ai-tools-for-small-businesses/

Due.com. (n.d.). 5 Ways Companies can pursue financial Sustainability. *Nasdaq*. https://www.nasdaq.com/articles/5-ways-companies-can-pursue-financial-sustainability

Edmond, R. (2024, July 11). Defining and achieving authentic engagement. *GaggleAMP*. https://blog.gaggleamp.com/what-is-authentic-engagement

Experts, D. (2023, August 10). *Revenue diversification*. DealHub. https://dealhub.io/glossary/revenue-diversification/

Farese, D. (2024, February 21). Market Research: A How-To Guide and Template. *HubSpot*. https://blog.hubspot.com/marketing/market-research-buyers-journey-guide#template

Feedspot. (2024, November 12). *Top 60 Tech Forums in 2024*. FeedSpot for Forum Lists and Online Message Boards. https://forums.feedspot.com/technology_forums/

Finance AI Tools. (n.d.). TopAI.tools. https://topai.tools/filter?t=finance

Flower, D. (2023, July 25). *The Power of Machine Learning: The Business Impact on Real-Time Data*. Forbes. https://www.forbes.com/sites/forbestechcouncil/2023/07/25/the-power-of-machine-learning-the-business-impact-on-real-time-data/?sh=7987302963b6

Forbes. (2023, September 11). The Future of Artificial Intelligence: Predictions and Trends. https://www.forbes.com/sites/forbesagencycouncil/2023/09/11/the-future-of-artificial-intelligence-predictions-and-trends/?sh=49ea95d12393

Fox, J. (2017, October 17). *Six factors to consider when choosing a business location | Virgin*. Virgin.com. https://www.virgin.com/about-virgin/latest/six-factors-consider-when-choosing-location-your-business

Fredrick, M. (2023, April 18). *10 Proven tactics to engage and attract your target audience online.* https://www.linkedin.com/pulse/10-proven-tactics-engage-attract-your-target-audience-marube-fredrick

FreshBooks. (2024, July 23). *12 Legal requirements for starting a small business.* https://www.freshbooks.com/hub/startup/starting-small-business-legal-requirements

Friedman, O. (2023, March 28). *Using technology in business for insights and strategy.* Forbes. https://www.forbes.com/sites/forbesbusinesscouncil/2023/03/28/using-technology-in-business-for-insights-and-strategy/?sh=52c819126284

Gadjev, B. (2023, May 9). *7 Strategies for improving operational efficiency in any small and medium-sized business.* https://www.linkedin.com/pulse/7-strategies-improving-operational-efficiency-any-small-bobby-gadjev/

GeeksforGeeks. (2024, July 23). *10 Best Budgeting Tools 2024 [Free].* GeeksforGeeks. https://www.geeksforgeeks.org/ai-tools-for-personal-finance-management-and-budgeting/

GoldenLink: Marketing Coaching & Training. (2023, April 26). *5 Essential Tips for Building Authentic Engagement with Your Audience.* https://www.linkedin.com/pulse/5-essential-tips-building-authentic-engagement-your-audience/

Gomez, R. (2024, June 6). *The importance of social media marketing: 7 stats that prove social's role in business success.* Sprout Social. https://sproutsocial.com/insights/importance-of-social-media-marketing-in-business/

Gonzalez, J. (n.d.). *Why is having an online presence important for a small business.* allBusiness: Your Small Business Advantage. https://www.allbusiness.com/why-is-online-presence-important-for-a-business

Graber, N. (n.d.). *Why are SMART Goals Necessary In Business? | MileIQ.* https://mileiq.com/blog-en-gb/smart-business-goals

Gravel, A., & Gravel, A. (2024, September 19). *17 examples of strong brand storytelling (updated 2024) - Toast Studio.* Toast Studio. https://www.toaststudio.com/en/articles/pg-volvo-and-other-examples-of-strong-brand-storytelling/

Great Learning. (2024, September 3). The fundamentals of digital marketing. *Great Learning Blog: Free Resources What Matters to Shape Your Career!* https://www.m ygreatlearning.com/blog/the-fundamentals-of-digital-marketing/

Griswold, D. (2024, March 22). *What is an LLC? Definition and steps on how to form an LLC.* https://www.wolterskluwer.com/en/expert-insights/how-to-form-a n-llc-what-is-an-llc-advantages-disadvantages-and-more

Haan, K. (2024, October 31). *How to start a business in 11 steps (2024 guide).* Forbes Advisor. https://www.forbes.com/advisor/business/how-to-start-a-business/

Haije, E. G. (2024, September 12). *Top 29 Best Customer Feedback Tools in 2024.* Mopinion. https://mopinion.com/customer-feedback-tools/

Han, S. (2024, August 23). *6 Market research benefits for your business.* Sago. https ://sago.com/en/resources/blog/what-are-the-business-benefits-of-market-research/

Harnish, B. (2021, April 30). *The 11 most important parts of SEO you need to get right.* Search Engine Journal. https://www.searchenginejournal.com/most-import ant-parts-of-seo/254225/

Harper, J. (2023, October 23). Machine Learning for Real-Time Data Analysis: Training models in production. *The New Stack.* https://thenewstack.io/machine -learning-for-real-time-data-analysis-training-models-in-production/

Harris, M. (2023, March 29). *Why adaptability is an essential business strat- egy.* https://www.linkedin.com/pulse/why-adaptability-essential-business-strategy -mikki-harris/

Hassan, A. U., CPA. (2023, May 7). *The importance of budgeting for business suc- cess.* https://www.linkedin.com/pulse/importance-budgeting-business-success-am mar-ul-hassan/

Heaslip, E. (2023, September 5). *How to use AI tools to write a business plan.* CO- by US Chamber of Commerce. https://www.uschamber.com/co/start/startup/ai-too ls-to-write-a-business-plan

Hegde, S. (2024, January 24). *Top 10 AI Marketing Tools that Can Increase Return-On-Ad-Spend.* https://www.linkedin.com/pulse/top-10-ai-marketing-tools-can-increase-shreeharsha-hegde/

Herzing University. (2020, May 18). A guide to setting up a dedicated workspace at home. *Herzing University.* https://www.herzing.edu/blog/guide-setting-dedicated-workspace-home

Hesseln, H. (2020, May 14). *4 Real-Life examples of successful change management in business.* https://www.linkedin.com/pulse/4-real-life-examples-successful-change-management-business-hesseln/

Higgins, M. (2021, May 19). *The Future Of Accounting: How Will Digital Transformation Impact Accountants?* Forbes. https://www.forbes.com/sites/forbestechcouncil/2021/05/19/the-future-of-accounting-how-will-digital-transformation-impact-accountants/?sh=5ec188e153fb

Hilson, S. (2023, September 15). *AI market Research: Tools, techniques, and trends.* Rock Content. https://rockcontent.com/blog/ai-market-research/

Home-Based business statistics to know going in 2023. (n.d.). Bizee. https://bizee.com/blog/post/shocking-us-home-based-business-statistics

Home-Based entrepreneur Stories. (2024). Home Business. https://homebusinessmag.com/categories/success-stories-lifestyles/

Hop. (2024, January 9). *Top 7 AI startups Revolutionizing data science and analytics.* https://www.linkedin.com/pulse/top-7-ai-startups-revolutionizing-data-science-analytics-hophr-xbnpe/

How AI can scale personalization and creativity in Marketing - SPONSOR CONTENT FROM INTUIT MAILCHIMP. (2023, August 17). Harvard Business Review. https://hbr.org/sponsored/2023/08/how-ai-can-scale-personalization-and-creativity-in-marketing

How can you create content that reflects your company's values and mission? (2023, September 27). https://www.linkedin.com/advice/0/how-can-you-create-content-reflects-your-companys

How can you ensure sustainable cost management strategies? (2023, September 18). https://www.linkedin.com/advice/0/how-can-you-ensure-sustainable-cost-m anagement-strategies

How can you use storytelling to maintain brand identity consistency? (2023, September 13). https://www.linkedin.com/advice/0/how-can-you-use-storytelling-maint ain-brand-identity

How To Create A Company Culture Of Continuous Learning And Development. (2023, April 24). Forbes. https://www.forbes.com/sites/forbeshumanresourcescouncil/2023/04/24/how-to -create-a-company-culture-of-continuous-learning-and-development/?sh=756c280 1387d

How to create a social media marketing strategy | Mailchimp. (n.d.). Mailchimp. https://mailchimp.com/resources/how-to-market-on-social-media/?ds_c=DEPT_ AOC_Google_Search_ROW_EN_NB_UpRet_Broad_50off_T5&ds_kids=p783 77605262&ds_a_lid=aud-1549074331369:dsa-1543646106214&ds_cid=7170000 0115522798&ds_agid=58700008586041932&gad_source=1&gclid=CjwKCAiA 3JCvBhA8EiwA4kujZlOqvYpS-Q5kobnF35IQHA25LthSTrinbx8JO8Sa9gAh9et Ss1YSwRoCU3sQAvD_BwE&gclsrc=aw.ds

How to register a business in the US | Stripe. (2023, April 6). https://stripe.com/res ources/more/how-to-register-a-business-in-the-us

How to Scale a business: 6 Tactics to Utilize | HBS Online. (2019, March 7). Business Insights Blog. https://online.hbs.edu/blog/post/how-to-scale-a-business

How to scale a business and proven techniques to do so. (n.d.). Tony Robbins. https://www.tonyrobbins.com/career-business/mindful-scaling/

How to stay Up-to-Date on tech trends and innovations | IronHack Blog. (n.d.). https://www.ironhack.com/us/blog/how-to-stay-up-to-date-on-tech-trends-and -innovations

How To Write a Business Plan: Seven Elements | Infographic. (2023, January 18). University of Arizona Global Campus. https://www.uagc.edu/blog/how-write-b usiness-plan-step-by-step

Howarth, J. (2024, November 21). 9 Best trend analysis software Tools (Detailed Overview). *Exploding Topics.* https://explodingtopics.com/blog/trend-analysis-so ftware

Huston, H. (2023, November 3). *Single-member LLC vs. sole proprietorship: Advantages & disadvantages.* https://www.wolterskluwer.com/en/expert-insights/single member-llc-vs-sole-proprietorship

Improving Operational Efficiencies: 4 Success stories in Digital transformation. (n.d .). https://www.techtarget.com/searchcio/MulticloudbyDesign/Improving-Oper ational-Efficiencies-4-Success-Stories-in-Digital-Transformation

Indeed Editorial Team. (2023, July 31). *7 Reasons Why Budgeting Is Vital for Successful Businesses.* Indeed. https://www.indeed.com/career-advice/career-developm ent/why-budget-is-important

Indeed Editorial Team. (2024a, February 12). *How To Stay Current With Technology Trends.* Indeed. https://www.indeed.com/career-advice/career-development/keepi ng-up-with-technology

Indeed Editorial Team. (2024b, August 15). *10 Methods of Market Research.* Indeed. https://www.indeed.com/career-advice/career-development/methods-of-ma rket-research

Indeed Editorial Team. (2024c, August 18). *10 Pros and Cons of Being in a Business Partnership.* Indeed. https://www.indeed.com/career-advice/career-development/ pros-cons-of-business-partnership

InfoDesk. (n.d.). Market Insights Strategy: Traditional Research vs. AI-Driven Analysis. *© 2024 InfoDesk. All Rights. Reserved.* https://www.infodesk.com/blog /market-insights-strategy-traditional-research-vs.-ai-driven-analysis

Infragist. (2023, October 26). *How AI and ML enhance cybersecurity in the business world*. https://www.linkedin.com/pulse/how-ai-ml-enhance-cybersecurity-busine ss-world-infragist-n5mre/

Ingov, P. (2024, October 13). *Data Storytelling Enhanced with AI: Tools and Courses*. ingoStudio. https://ingostudio.com/storytelling/data-storytelling/

Jagtap, A. (2024, September 13). *The Top 13 AI Business Plan Generators: A 2024 Guide*. Upmetrics. https://upmetrics.co/blog/ai-business-plan-generators

Jansons, K. (2024, September 8). *AI in Finance and Banking: Use Cases in 2024*. MindTitan. https://mindtitan.com/resources/industry-use-cases/ai-use-cases-in-fi nance-and-banking/

Jarboe, G. (2024, January 16). AI-enhanced YouTube marketing: Insights from 3 case studies. *Search Engine Land*. https://searchengineland.com/ai-youtube-mark eting-insights-case-studies-436536

Jegou, S. (2024, August 29). *How is IoT disrupting major industries– Benefits, Applications and Use-Cases*. Transatel. https://www.transatel.com/news-and-insights /blog/iot-disrupted-industries-applications/

Jhajharia, S. (2024, August 2). The importance of creating a scalable business model - Growth Idea Ltd. *Growth Idea Ltd*. https://growthidea.co.uk/blog/the-importa nce-of-creating-a-scalable-business-model

Jobanputra, K. (2023, April 18). You have to take risks to succeed. Here are 4 Risk-Taking benefits in entrepreneurship. *Entrepreneur*. https://www.entrepreneur.com/starting-a-business/want-success-you-have-t o-take-risks-4-benefits-of/449208

Johnson, J. (2024, October 30). *Would you make it on Shark Tank? The importance of scalable business models*. business.com. https://www.business.com/articles/the-i mportance-of-scalable-business-models/

Jones, S. (2024, February 2). *AI's Impact on Brand Storytelling: Crafting Compelling Narratives in 2024*. https://www.linkedin.com/pulse/ais-impact-brand-storytelling-crafting-compellin

g-narratives-jones-4pvwe/?trk=article-ssr-frontend-pulse_more-articles_related-co
ntent-card

Jordan, J. (2023, March 1). *The Power of Scaling: Why it's important for your business*. https://www.linkedin.com/pulse/power-scaling-why-its-important-your-bus
iness-jim-jordan/

Joy, K. (2023, May 17). *Optimizing Operational Efficiency with Generative AI: A
Case Study*. https://www.linkedin.com/pulse/optimizing-operational-efficiency-g
enerative-ai-case-study-kevin-joy-/

Kantrow, A. (2014, August 1). *The Strategy-Technology connection*. Harvard Business
Review. https://hbr.org/1980/07/the-strategy-technology-connection

Kart, R. (2023, July 12). *Crafting a Narrative: the crucial role of storytelling in an
AI-Driven future*. https://www.linkedin.com/pulse/crafting-narrative-crucial-role
-storytelling-ai-driven-randy-kart/

Kaur, F. P. (2024, October 23). *10 Creative AI in Marketing Examples and Use Cases*.
Mailmodo. https://www.mailmodo.com/guides/ai-in-marketing-examples/

Kelly,   R.   (2023,   June   1).   *Market   research:
an   important   investment   for   Long-Term   viability*.
Forbes. https://www.forbes.com/sites/forbestechcouncil/2023/06/01/market-res
earch-an-important-investment-for-long-term-viability/?sh=d910204551bc

Kenan, J., & Kenan, J. (2024, November 18). *Social media analytics: The complete
guide*. Sprout Social. https://sproutsocial.com/insights/social-media-analytics/

Kenton, W. (2024, June 22). *Organizational structure for companies with examples
and benefits*. Investopedia. https://www.investopedia.com/terms/o/organizationa
l-structure.asp

Kirk, R. S. (2022, January 6). *Commentary: American businesses need to invest in tech
education*. Fortune. https://fortune.com/2022/01/06/american-businesses-need-t
o-invest-in-tech-education-skills-gap-labor-shortage-verizon-csr-rose-stuckey-kirk/

Kirschenbaum, E. (2024, October 4). *How to Register a business in the USA in 7 easy steps [2023].* https://pay.com/blog/how-to-register-a-business-in-usa

Krissansen, J. (2023, July 12). *12 ways to find the perfect angel investor - Finmark.* Finmark. https://finmark.com/how-to-find-angel-investors/

Kumar, K. (2023, May 7). *Embracing change: The importance of adaptability in a Fast-Paced technological world.* https://www.linkedin.com/pulse/embracing-change-importance-adaptability-fast-paced-world-kumar/

Lake, R. (2024, June 3). *Your annual financial planning checklist.* Investopedia. https://www.investopedia.com/articles/personal-finance/your-annual-financial-planning-check-list.asp

LegalNature. (2024). Tax Obligations for Each Business Type. https://www.legalnature.com/guides/an-overview-of-tax-obligations-for-each-business-type

Lin, P. (2022, September 2). AI-Based Marketing Personalization: How Machines Analyze Your Audience. *Artificial Intelligence.* https://www.marketingaiinstitute.com/blog/ai-based-marketing-personalization

Livolsi, K. (2023, October 16). *Diversifying revenue streams - Strategies for business stability and growth.* https://www.linkedin.com/pulse/diversifying-revenue-streams-strategies-business-growth-livolsi/

Llc, B. A. (2023, April 25). *Fostering a more engaged and knowledgeable tech community.* https://www.linkedin.com/pulse/fostering-more-engaged-knowledgeable-tech-community/

Llp, I. I. (2023, August 24). *Digital Marketing Fundamentals: A Beginner's Guide for new businesses.* https://www.linkedin.com/pulse/digital-marketing-fundamentals-beginners-guide-new-businesses/

Loktionova, M. (2023a, January 26). *Brand Storytelling: The Definitive 2024 Guide (with Examples).* Semrush Blog. https://www.semrush.com/blog/definitive-guide-to-brand-storytelling/

Loktionova, M. (2023b, June 12). *Content marketing for small businesses: 9 essential tips*. Semrush Blog. https://www.semrush.com/blog/content-marketing-for-small-businesses/

Ltd, T. a. P. (2023, April 21). *10 ways to Foster a Culture of Continuous Learning in Your Company*. https://www.linkedin.com/pulse/10-ways-foster-culture-continuous-learning-your/

Lyons, A. (2023, July 6). *A Step-By-Step Process For Implementing AI In A Small Business.* Forbes. https://www.forbes.com/sites/forbesbusinessdevelopmentcouncil/2023/07/06/a-step-by-step-process-for-implementing-ai-in-a-small-business/?sh=240ed08d55d0

Machine Learning Market Size, Share, Growth | Trends [2030]. (n.d.). https://www.fortunebusinessinsights.com/machine-learning-market-102226

Machine Learning Startups funded by Y Combinator (YC) 2024 | Y Combinator. (n.d.). Y Combinator. https://www.ycombinator.com/companies/industry/machine-learning

March, L. (2024, September 3). *9 Highly successful market research examples*. Similarweb. https://www.similarweb.com/blog/research/market-research/market-research-examples/

Market Trends, & Market Trends. (2022, March 1). *AI-Powered Market Research: What are the benefits?* Analytics Insight. https://www.analyticsinsight.net/ai-powered-market-research-what-are-the-benefits/

Markets, R. A. (2022, September 28). Global digital advertising and marketing market to reach $786.2 billion by 2026 at a CAGR of 13.9%. *GlobeNewswire News Room.* https://www.globenewswire.com/news-release/2022/09/28/2524217/28124/en/Global-Digital-Advertising-and-Marketing-Market-to-Reach-786-2-Billion-by-2026-at-a-CAGR-of-13-9.html#:~:text=Amid%20the%20COVID%2D19%20crisis%2C%20the%20global%20market,Players:%20Acxiom%20Corporation.%20Alibaba%20Group%20Holding%20Limited.

Marr, B. (2021, July 13). *The 10 best examples of how companies use artificial intelligence in practice*. Bernard Marr. https://bernardmarr.com/the-10-best-examples-of-how-companies-use-artificial-intelligence-in-practice/

Martinuzzi, B. (2023, June 23). *The advantages and disadvantages of a business partnership*. Business Class: Trends and Insights | American Express. https://www.americanexpress.com/en-us/business/trends-and-insights/articles/what-are-the-advantages-and-disadvantages-of-a-partnership/

Maslan, A. (2024, January 24). *What are the Most Common Business Expansion Strategy Mistakes?* Pinnacle Global Network. https://pinnacleglobalnetwork.com/what-are-the-most-common-business-expansion-strategy-mistakes/

McCue, I. (2020, October 21). *15 Key Financial Metrics & KPIs for Small Businesses*. Oracle NetSuite. https://www.netsuite.com/portal/resource/articles/financial-management/small-business-financial-metrics.shtml

Michaelis, C. (2023, July 12). *Fearless entrepreneurship: tackling your fears and unlocking your potential*. https://www.linkedin.com/pulse/fearless-entrepreneurship-tackling-your-fears-christine/

Minasyan, A. (2024, November 11). AI Business Plan Generator Examples: demos, insights, and tips. *10Web - Build & Host Your WordPress Website*. https://10web.io/blog/ai-business-plan-generators/

Mohan, P. R. (2023, September 10). *5 AI tools for planning your Budget*. https://www.linkedin.com/pulse/5-ai-tools-planning-your-budget-priya-ranjani-mohan/

monday.com. (n.d.). *Customizable Marketing Templates | Monday.com*. https://monday.com/lp/templates/marketing?cq_src=google_ads&cq_cmp=2095 2043111&cq_term=digital%20marketing%20strategy%20template&cq_plac=&cq _net=g&cq_plt=gp&utm_medium=cpc&utm_source=adwordssearch&utm_cam paign=ww2-en-prm-workos-marketer-marketing_templates-h-search-desktop-core -aw&utm_keyword=digital%20marketing%20strategy%20template&utm_match_ type=e&cluster=marketing&subcluster=marketing_plan&ati=&utm_adgroup=m arketing%20strategy%20template&utm_banner=687842504811&gad_source=1&

gclid=CjwKCAiA3JCvBhA8EiwA4kujZo4V-dvWPIe2bAV9oWnxiLtL1CjwoBU
vz-eWAxVnEFqloOR3VhqPlxoCFugQAvD_BwE

Monster.com. (2021, November 10). *7 Small business hiring Strategies | Monster.co m.* https://hiring.monster.com/resources/small-business-hiring/hiring-process/hiring-strategies/

Morley, K., & Morley, K. (2024, August 14). *10 Best AI personalization tools for websites, apps, email, and more.* Insider. https://useinsider.com/ai-personalization-tools/

Mullinix, B. (2023, June 2). *How AI makes Forecasting Better for your startup.* https://www.zeni.ai/blog/how-ai-makes-forecasting-better

Mutua, M. (2024, September 16). *11 Companies That Are Killing It with Their Digital Marketing Campaigns.* Convince & Convert. https://www.convinceandconvert.com/digital-marketing/killing-it-with-digital-marketing-campaigns/

Narain, A. (2023, November 7). *How Generative AI transforms fundraising.* Spiceworks Inc. https://www.spiceworks.com/tech/artificial-intelligence/guest-article/generative-ai-in-fundraising/amp/

Newberry, C. (2024, November 12). *What is social media analytics? The 2024 guide for marketers.* Social Media Marketing & Management Dashboard. https://blog.hootsuite.com/what-is-social-media-analytics/

NI Business Info. (n.d.). *Advantages and disadvantages of starting a business from home | nibusinessinfo.co.uk.* https://www.nibusinessinfo.co.uk/content/advantages-and-disadvantages-starting-business-home

Ocasio, N. (2024, February 26). *AI tools for Business: 15 of the best.* Small Business Trends. https://smallbiztrends.com/2024/02/ai-tools-for-business.html

Oetting, J. (2024, April 30). *28 Tools & Resources for Conducting Market Research. HubSpot.* https://blog.hubspot.com/marketing/market-research-tools-resources

Oluwatoni, O., & Oluwatoni, O. (2024, October 2). *14 Best AI Business Plan Generators (Free and Paid) in 2024.* Visme Blog. https://visme.co/blog/ai-business-plan/

Online marketing strategies for increasing sales revenues of small retail businesses. (2018). Walden University ScholarWorks. https://scholarworks.waldenu.edu/cgi/viewcontent.cgi?article=7175&context=dissertations

Orion Innovation. (2024, September 19). *Tax transformation for a Gobal enterprise.* https://www.orioninc.com/case-studies/tax-transformation/

Osman, M. (2024, July 22). Overcoming Your Fear of Failure as an Entrepreneur. *HubSpot.* https://blog.hubspot.com/the-hustle/fear-of-failure

P, P. (2024, April 9). *How to create an SEO-Friendly Website: 14 tips for Long-Term Organic Growth.* Hostinger Tutorials. https://www.hostinger.ph/tutorials/seo-friendly-website

Panel, E. (2023, March 16). 15 Ways Businesses can Keep up with Trends in the tech world. *Newsweek.* https://www.newsweek.com/15-ways-businesses-can-keep-trends-tech-world-1787815

Pec, T. (2022, September 6). *Why Businesses And Brands Need To Be Taking Advantage Of Social Media.* Forbes. https://www.forbes.com/sites/forbesagencycouncil/2022/09/06/why-businesses-and-brands-need-to-be-taking-advantage-of-social-media/?sh=26809f27216c

Peckover, T. (2024, October 2). *The 8 Best Brand Communities and Why They're Successful.* Loyalty & Reward Program Insights From Smile.io. https://blog.smile.io/8-best-brand-communities/

Perell, K. (2020, July 16). *5 Fears all entrepreneurs face (and how to conquer them).* Entrepreneur. https://www.entrepreneur.com/leadership/5-fears-all-entrepreneurs-face-and-how-to-conquer-them/353219

Petrat, P. (2024, October 22). *Why market research is important.* Cint^{TM} | the World's Largest Research Marketplace. https://www.cint.com/blog/why-market-research-is-important

Pgadmin. (2022, October 26). *PlanGuru | Business Budgeting Software, Business Planning Software.* PlanGuru. https://www.planguru.com/

Pratt, M. K. (2024a, June 11). *Top 12 machine learning use cases and business applications*. Search Enterprise AI. https://www.techtarget.com/searchenterpriseai/feature/10-common-uses-for-machine-learning-applications-in-business

Pratt, M. K. (2024b, August 6). *12 key benefits of AI for business*. Search Enterprise AI. https://www.techtarget.com/searchenterpriseai/feature/6-key-benefits-of-AI-for-business

PricewaterhouseCoopers. (n.d.). *Generative AI in tax: 5 essential insights for leaders*. PwC. https://www.pwc.com/us/en/tech-effect/ai-analytics/generative-ai-insights-for-tax-leaders.html

Pros and Cons of a Home-Based Business vs. Brick and Mortar Business. (2021, May 26). Accion Opportunity Fund. https://aofund.org/resource/pros-and-cons-home-based-business-vs-brick-and-mortar-business/

Quantilope. (2024, November 22). 10 AI Market Research Tools & How To Use Them. *Quantilope*. https://www.quantilope.com/resources/best-ai-market-research-tools

Quora. (2019, October 31). Why is scaling so important in business? *Forbes*. https://www.forbes.com/sites/quora/2019/10/31/why-is-scaling-so-important-in-business/

Rajagopalan, R. (2024, November 20). *10 Examples of artificial intelligence in business*. University of San Diego Online Degrees. https://onlinedegrees.sandiego.edu/artificial-intelligence-business/

Renuka. (2021, March 1). *My guide to Champaner – the ancient city of Gujarat - Voyager for life*. Voyager for Life. https://www.renuka-voyagerforlife.com/2019/09/my-guide-to-champaner-the-ancient-city-of-gujarat.html

Reporter, G. S. (2022, September 30). Glossary of business terms - A to Z. *The Guardian*. https://www.theguardian.com/business/glossary-business-terms-a-z-jargon

Resilience and adaptability are key to navigating today's world. Here's why. (2024, September 10). World Economic Forum. https://www.weforum.org/agenda/2024/01/resilience-adaptability-key-navigating/

Revnuu. (2023, August 9). *The Role of Artificial Intelligence in Marketing: Enhancing Decision-making with AI-Driven Insights.* https://www.linkedin.com/pulse/role-artificial-intelligence-marketing-enhancing-decision-making/

Riddall, J. (2024, April 4). *35 Content marketing Statistics You should know.* Search Engine Journal. https://www.searchenginejournal.com/content-marketing-statistics-you-should-know/507173/

Risk assessment: process, tools, & techniques | SafetyCulture. (2024, September 12). SafetyCulture. https://safetyculture.com/topics/risk-assessment/

Robinson, B. (2024, April 4). *9 Bookkeeping basics Every bookkeeper needs.* Bookkeepers.com. https://bookkeepers.com/bookkeeping-basics/

rob.llewellyn@cxotransform.com. (2024, May 7). AI for Business - 30 case studies that led to competitive advantage. *Digital Transformation Skills.* https://digitaltransformationskills.com/ai-for-business/

Roman, M. (2024, June 10). *The 8 best AI tools for small Business.* Timeular. https://timeular.com/blog/best-ai-tools-small-business/

Sachdeva, A. (2023, February 7). *5 market research tools to help you research faster.* GapScout. https://gapscout.com/blog/market-research-tools/

Sajid, H. (2024, April 23). *The Intersection of AI across 6 major industries: Exploring latest AI applications from business perspective.* Unite.AI. https://www.unite.ai/the-intersection-of-ai-across-6-major-industries-exploring-latest-ai-applications-from-business-perspective/

Salah, H. (2023, May 7). *Blockchain Technology: a transformative force for all industries!* https://www.linkedin.com/pulse/blockchain-technology-transformative-force-all-industries-salah/

Santa Clara University. (n.d.). *Business Terms Glossary - My own Business Institute - Learn how to start a business.* https://www.scu.edu/mobi/resources--tools/business-terms-glossary/

Schooley, S. (2024, October 3). *Pros and cons of forming a corporation.* Business News Daily. https://www.businessnewsdaily.com/15805-corporation-advantages-and-disadvantages.html

Schramade, W. & Erasmus Platform for Sustainable Value Creation. (2019). Mc-Donald's: a sustainable finance case study. In *Erasmus Platform for Sustainable Value Creation* [Journal-article]. https://www.rsm.nl/fileadmin/Faculty-Research/Centres/EPSVC/Case_study_sustainable_finance_McDonalds.pdf

Schramm, B. (2023, July 12). *20 Financial metrics Every business should track - Finmark.* Finmark. https://finmark.com/financial-metrics/

Scott-Briggs, A. (2020, October 6). *10 popular online technology forums for tech discussions.* TechBullion. https://techbullion.com/10-popular-online-technology-forums-for-tech-discussions/

Scout, H. (n.d.). *AI Customer Support Software: The 10 Best Tools for 2025 - Help Scout.* Help Scout. https://www.helpscout.com/blog/ai-customer-support-software/

SentiOne. (2023, September 20). *Revolutionizing marketing: Inspiring AI Success Stories.* https://www.linkedin.com/pulse/revolutionizing-marketing-inspiring-ai-success-stories-sentione/

Set goals for your business. (2024, July 11). Australian Government Business. https://business.gov.au/planning/business-plans/set-goals-for-your-business

Shabalin, D. (2024, November 7). *Business Startup Checklist | MyCompanyWorks.* MyCompanyWorks. https://www.mycompanyworks.com/checklist.htm

Shad, A. A. (2024, September 15). *Feedback Analysis: analyzing quantitative and qualitative data.* Thoughts About Product Adoption, User Onboarding and Good UX | Userpilot Blog. https://userpilot.com/blog/feedback-analysis/

Shah, H. (2024, June 3). *Advantages of Artificial Intelligence (AI) for Your Business (2024 Updated)*. Prismetric. https://www.prismetric.com/benefits-of-ai-for-busin ess/

Singh, S. (2024, October 30). Improving Operational Efficiency for your business: A playbook for 2024. *Scribe*. https://scribehow.com/library/operational-efficiency

Siu, E. (2024, April 5). *How to implement AI in your business: A Step-by-Step guide*. Single Grain. https://www.singlegrain.com/blog/how-to-implement-ai-in-my-bus iness/

Skillabilly. (2024, January 28). *Building resilience: Strategies for adapting to techno-logical changes*. https://www.skillabilly.com/building-resilience-strategies-for-adap ting-to-technological-changes/

Small business compliance checklist. (n.d.). Always Designing for People (ADP). https://www.adp.com/-/media/adp/resourcehub/pdf/sbs-fy20-complian ce-checklist.pdf?rev=707e97e0c8b1430f81b900f011a30120

Small business website design: 8 tips for creating a website | Mailchimp. (n.d.) . Mailchimp. https://mailchimp.com/resources/small-business-website-design-tips

Solutions, V. (n.d.). *Vena Insights - Get secure, powerful & strategic insights | Vena Solutions*. https://www.venasolutions.com/platform/microsoft/insights

Solutions, V. (2024, June 17). The 9 Best AI Tools for Finance & FP&A (2024) - Vena. *Vena Solutions*. https://www.venasolutions.com/blog/best-ai-tools

SPD Technology. (n.d.). *AI-Powered Customer Behavior Prediction for eCommerce | SPD Technology*. https://spd.tech/artificial-intelligence/ai-for-customer-behavior -analysis/

Srmcp, T. R. M. C. F. (2023, March 11). *The top 10 tips for risk managers: Risk management*. https://www.linkedin.com/pulse/top-10-tips-risk-managers-manag ement-tony-ridley-msc-csyp-msyi

Startup financing. (n.d.). The Hartford. https://www.thehartford.com/business-i nsurance/strategy/startup/money

Statista. (2024, November 5). *Worldwide digital population 2024.* https://www.statista.com/statistics/617136/digital-population-worldwide/#:~:text =Worldwide%20digital%20population%202024&text=As%20of%20July%202024 %2C%20there,population%2C%20were%20social%20media%20users.

Stay legally compliant. (n.d.). U.S. Small Business Administration. https://www.s ba.gov/business-guide/manage-your-business/stay-legally-compliant

St-Jean, E. (2023, October 23). *12 ways to create a continuous learning culture.* Search HR Software. https://www.techtarget.com/searchhrsoftware/feature/4-ways-to-c reate-a-continuous-learning-culture

Sustainable Cost Management: Balancing Sustainability and Cost Management Strategies. (2024, June 4). Faster Capi- tal. https://fastercapital.com/content/Sustainable-Cost-Management--Balancing -Sustainability-and-Cost-Management-Strategies.html

Sydle. (2024, January 11). *Business agility: What is it and how can it help you?* Blog SYDLE. https://www.sydle.com/blog/business-agility-what-is-it-63359b511770c 5640cf3b03b

Talent, A. (2023, September 28). *Unlocking Success: The importance of a Well-DEsigned Website for Artists, Brands, and businesses.* AMP Tal- ent. https://amptalent.com/learning_centers/unlocking-success-the-importance -of-a-well-designed-website-for-artists-brands-and-businesses/

Tax transformation with cloud ERP. (n.d.). Deloitte United States. https://www2.deloitte.com/us/en/blog/deloitte-on-cloud-blog/2023/tax-t ransformation-with-cloud-ERP.html

Taxology. (2023, March 8). *Digital transformation in accounting Firms: Benefits and challenges.* https://www.linkedin.com/pulse/digital-transformation-accounti ng-firms-benefits-challenges/

Taylor, C. (2023, October 5). How artificial intelligence is helping today's small businesses. *Forbes.* https://www.forbes.com/sites/charlesrtaylor/2023/08/09/how -artificial-intelligence-is-helping-todays-small-businesses/?sh=2aca2db71a48

Team, A., & Team, A. (2023a, May 30). *Predicting Customer Behavior with the Power of AI Marketing Tools*. AIContentfy. https://aicontentfy.com/en/blog/predicting -customer-behavior-with-power-of-ai-marketing-tools

Team, A., & Team, A. (2023b, June 30). *How to overcome fear and start your own business*. AIContentfy. https://aicontentfy.com/en/blog/how-to-overcome-fear-a nd-start-own-business

Team, A., & Team, A. (2023c, July 5). *The Beginner's Guide to understanding SEO Tools*. AIContentfy. https://aicontentfy.com/en/blog/beginners-guide-to-underst anding-seo-tools

Team, A., & Team, A. (2023d, November 6). *From Dreamers to Achievers: Stories of Entrepreneurship success*. AIContentfy. https://aicontentfy.com/en/blog/from-dre amers-to-achievers-stories-of-entrepreneurship-success

Team, C. S. (2018, June 26). Top 10 Federal Tax Compliance Issues for Businesses: Serving clients since 202. *CFO Selections*. https://www.cfoselections.com/perspect ive/top-10-federal-tax-compliance-issues-for-businesses

Team, S. (2024, November 11). Digital Marketing Case studies for small business- es. *SocialSellinator*. https://www.socialsellinator.com/social-selling-blog/digital-m arketing-case-studies-for-small-businesses

Team, W. (n.d.). *Why is web design important?* WebFX. https://www.webfx.com/ web-design/learn/why-is-web-design-important/

Team, W. (2023, October 5). *Scaling for Growth: Strategies for Successful Expansion*. Blog Wrike. https://www.wrike.com/blog/scaling-for-successful-growth/

TechAhead. (2024, August 16). *Top 25 Fintech AI use cases | TechAhead*. https://w ww.techaheadcorp.com/blog/top-25-fintech-ai-use-cases/

Technologies, B. (2024, November 14). *5 Benefits of AI in Inventory Management: Key Insights*. Binmile - Software Development Company. https://binmile.com/bl og/ai-inventory-management/

Technology, P. (2023, June 14). *AI: The Game-Changer for Small Businesses.* https ://www.linkedin.com/pulse/ai-game-changer-small-businesses-pulse-tech/

The How of Business Podcast. (2024, November 18). *Overcoming Fear to Grow Your Small Business with Ruth Soukup.* The How of Business Podcast & Resources. https://www.thehowofbusiness.com/episode-255-ruth-soukup/

The power of AI: What accounting and tax professionals need to know. (2024, July 2). Wolters Kluwer. https://www.wolterskluwer.com/en/expert-insights/the-power-o f-ai

The rise of Sustainable Finance: green investing, ESG and impact on finance careers. (2001, April 21). *William & Mary.* https://online.mason.wm.edu/blog/the-rise -of-sustainable-finance

The role of artificial intelligence in personalized marketing. (n.d.). https://abmatic. ai/blog/role-of-artificial-intelligence-in-personalized-marketing

The Top 5 Benefits of Adopting an AI-first Mindset in Business (and how to get employ-ees on board). (n.d.). https://www.launchconsulting.com/posts/the-top-5-benefits -of-adopting-an-ai-first-mindset-in-business-and-how-to-get-employees-on-board

The Unquestionable Benefits of AI in Accounting & Finance for 2024. (2023, Decem-ber 14). Quantic School of Business and Technology. https://quantic.edu/blog/2 023/03/20/artificial-intelligence-in-accounting-and-finance/

The Upwork Team. (2024, August 23). *Top 9 AI Tools for Finance Professionals: Discover 9 AI tools for finance professionals and how AI enhances financial services, from fraud detection to automated investing and tax help.* Upwork. https://www.u pwork.com/resources/ai-finance-tools

Thiemann, M. (2021, February 4). *Why is agility so important to the success of companies?* Forbes. https://www.forbes.com/sites/forbescoachescouncil/2021/02 /04/why-is-agility-so-important-to-the-success-of-companies/?sh=13c02f486f29

Thirteen essential tips for pitching to venture capitalists | Stripe. (2022, October 6). https://stripe.com/resources/more/pitching-venture-capitalists

Thompson, C. (2024, February 14). The role of artificial intelligence in cybersecurity. *Meriplex.* https://meriplex.com/the-role-of-artificial-intelligence-in-cybersecurity

Thompson, J. (2024, August 22). *Starting a business from home: The Ultimate checklist.* business.com. https://www.business.com/articles/starting-a-business-from-home-the-ultimate-checklist/

Todoros, O., & Todoros, O. (2024, September 3). *Why Digital Transformation is Essential for Accountants and CPA.* Spike. https://www.spikenow.com/blog/productivity/why-digital-transformation-is-essential-for-accountants-and-cpas-in-2023/

Top 10 Tax Compliance Pitfalls to avoid in 2024. (2023, December 19). Fonoa. https://www.fonoa.com/blog/top-10-tax-compliance-pitfalls-to-avoid-in-2024

TopAI.tools. (n.d.). AI Tax Calculator - Top AI Tools. https://topai.tools/s/AI-tax-calculator

Transforming Financial Planning in Food and Beverage: A Growth Case Study - 8020 consulting posts. (n.d.). https://8020consulting.com/food-beverage-financial-transformation-case-study/

Turnbull, A. (2020, February 6). *How I overcame one of my deepest fears as an entrepreneur | Groove Blog.* Groove Blog. https://www.groovehq.com/blog/overcoming-fear-as-an-entrepreneur

Twin, A. (2024, June 18). *What is a sole proprietorship?* Investopedia. https://www.investopedia.com/terms/s/soleproprietorship.asp

Ueland, S. (2023, February 23). 11 Outstanding Digital Media Campaigns from 2021. *Practical Ecommerce.* https://www.practicalecommerce.com/11-outstanding-digital-media-campaigns-from-2021

Uzialko, A. (2024, August 27). *How artificial intelligence will transform businesses.* Business News Daily. https://www.businessnewsdaily.com/9402-artificial-intelligence-business-trends.html

Vasilchenko, A. (2024a, November 1). *TOP 12 Machine Learning Technology Trends to Impact Business in 2024*. MobiDev. https://mobidev.biz/blog/future-machine-l earning-trends-impact-business

Vasilchenko, A. (2024b, November 6). *TOP 10 artificial intelligence trends that will make a big difference in business in 2024*. MobiDev. https://mobidev.biz/blog/fut ure-artificial-intelligence-technology-ai-trends

Vinton, P. (2024, July 29). *Navigating the data Landscape in 2024: 2 Key Trends to Watch*. Analytics8. https://www.analytics8.com/blog/top-trends-in-data-and-ana lytics/

Virtualinfocom. (2023, July 28). *Crafting a compelling pitch deck for your AI startup to secure funding*. https://www.linkedin.com/pulse/crafting-compelling-pitch-dec k-your-ai-startup-secure-funding/

Volopay. (2024, November 7). 7 reasons Why business budgets Fail | Volopay. *Volopay*. https://www.volopay.com/blog/why-do-business-budgets-fail/

Vzhuk. (2023, December 19). *The 4 Steps to Building an Effective AI Strategy | Stanford Online*. Stanford Online. https://online.stanford.edu/4-steps-building-ef fective-ai-strategy

Wavelaunch, & Wavelaunch. (2023, May 8). *7 Innovative ways to fund your startup*. Wavelaunch VC. https://wavelaunch.org/7-innovative-ways-to-fund-your-startup/

Weller, J. (2024, September 9). Simple business plan templates. *Smartsheet*. https: //www.smartsheet.com/content/simple-business-plan-templates

Westwater, S. (2023a, November 20). AI Marketing Case Study: Discover Success Stories and Cutting-Edge Strategies. *Pragmatic*. https://www.pragmatic.digital/bl og/ai-marketing-case-study-successful-campaigns

Westwater, S. (2023b, November 27). *AI Marketing Case Studies – Discover success Stories and Cutting-Edge Strategies*. https://www.linkedin.com/pulse/ai-marketin g-case-studies-discover-success-stories-scot-westwater-ag4ic

358   RUSSEL GRANT

What are the financial metrics that a startup must track. (n.d.). InetSoft. https://www.inetsoft.com/business/bi/financial-metrics-startups-must-track/

What are the fundamentals of digital marketing? (2024, November 7). SNHU. https://www.snhu.edu/about-us/newsroom/business/what-are-the-fundamentals-of-digital-marketing

What is crowdfunding? Here are four types to know | Stripe. (2024, May 7). https://stripe.com/resources/more/four-types-of-crowdfunding-for-startups-and-how-to-choose-one

Whelan, T. (2017, June 1). *The Comprehensive Business Case for Sustainability.* Harvard Business Review. https://hbr.org/2016/10/the-comprehensive-business-case-for-sustainability

Why is budgeting important in business? 5 reasons. (2022, July 6). Business Insights Blog. https://online.hbs.edu/blog/post/importance-of-budgeting-in-business

Williams, M. (2023, June 14). *ENGAGING YOUR AUDIENCE THROUGH AUTHENTIC SOCIAL MEDIA COMMUNICATION.* https://www.linkedin.com/pulse/engaging-your-audience-through-authentic-social-media-mandy-williams/

wiseAdvizor. (2023, December 5). *Real-life Examples: Successful Startups that Secured Funding.* https://www.linkedin.com/pulse/real-life-examples-successful-startups-secured-funding-wiseadvizor-pe39f/

Wood, M. (n.d.). *10 Financial Tools Your Small Business Can't Live Without.* allBusiness: Your Small Business Advantage.

WordStream. (2023, November 13). *What is PPC? Learn the basics of Pay-Per-Click marketing.* https://www.wordstream.com/ppc

Workspace. (2011, September 5). *Glossary of business terminology.* Workspace ®. https://www.workspace.co.uk/content-hub/business-insight/glossary-of-business-terminology

Yoon, D. (n.d.). *11 Examples of continuous improvement companies | KaiNexus.* https://blog.kainexus.com/continuous-improvement-companies

York, A. (2024a, July 10). *10 best AI tools for customer Service to elevate your support.* ClickUp. https://clickup.com/blog/ai-tools-for-customer-service/

York, A. (2024b, August 23). *10 Best AI Tools for Accounting & Finance in 2024.* ClickUp. https://clickup.com/blog/ai-tools-for-accounting/

Your business needs to predict future trends. How can you get the most accurate results? (2024, January 26). https://www.linkedin.com/advice/0/your-business-needs-predict-future-trends-w3zef

Yuen, M. (2024, April 11). *Consumers worldwide prefer searching online over in-store for electronics, clothes, and other select categories.* EMARKETER. https://www.emarketer.com/content/consumers-search-products-online-over-in-store

Zenger News. (2024, June 3). Small businesses and their CEOS are starting to find success with AI. *Forbes.* https://www.forbes.com/sites/zengernews/2023/08/26/small-businesses-and-their-ceos-are-starting-to-find-success-with-ai/?sh=58d0209f15d6

Zeni. (n.d.). *Zeni: The #1 AI Bookkeeping Software | Automated Accounting.* https://www.zeni.ai/blog/ai-bookkeeping

Zerkalenkov, Z. (2024, January 8). *Brand Identity: What it is and how to create a strong one.* Semrush Blog. https://www.semrush.com/blog/build-brand-identity/

Zharovskikh, A. (2023, December 12). *Today in focus: ad spend optimization with artificial intelligence.* InData Labs. https://indatalabs.com/blog/ad-spend-optimization-with-ai

www.ingramcontent.com/pod-product-compliance
Lightning Source LLC
Chambersburg PA
CBHW071539210326
41597CB00019B/3051